Chicken Soup
for the Soul®

Married
Life!

Chicken Soup for the Soul: Married Life!
101 Inspirational Stories about Fun, Family, and Wedded Bliss
Jack Canfield, Mark Victor Hansen, and Amy Newmark

Published by Chicken Soup for the Soul Publishing, LLC   www.chickensoup.com

The publisher gratefully acknowledges the many publishers and individuals who granted Chicken Soup for the Soul permission to reprint the cited material.

Front cover photo courtesy of iStockphoto.com/Yuri_Arcursview (© Jacob Wackerhause). Back cover and interior photo courtesy Photos.com.

Cover and Interior Design & Layout by Pneuma Books, LLC
For more info on Pneuma Books, visit www.pneumabooks.com

Distributed to the booktrade by Simon & Schuster. SAN: 200-2442

Publisher's Cataloging-in-Publication Data
(Prepared by The Donohue Group)

Chicken soup for the soul : married life! : 101 inspirational stories about fun, family, and wedded bliss / [compiled by] Jack Canfield, Mark Victor Hansen, [and] Amy Newmark.

  p. : ill. ; cm.

  Summary: A collection of 101 true personal stories, mostly humorous, about married life, written by wives and husbands of all ages.
  ISBN: 978-1-935096-85-6

  1. Marriage--Literary collections. 2. Man-woman relationships--Literary collections. 3. Marriage--Anecdotes. 4. Man-woman relationships--Anecdotes. I. Canfield, Jack, 1944- II. Hansen, Mark Victor. III. Newmark, Amy. IV. Title: Married life
  PN6071.M2 C45 2012
  810.2/02/354/3   2012930595

PRINTED IN THE UNITED STATES OF AMERICA
on acid∞free paper
21 20 19 18 17 16 15 14 13 12   01 02 03 04 05 06 07 08 09 10

Chicken Soup for the Soul

Married Life!

101 Inspirational Stories about Fun, Family, and Wedded Bliss

Jack Canfield
Mark Victor Hansen
Amy Newmark

Chicken Soup for the Soul Publishing, LLC
Cos Cob, CT

www.chickensoup.com

Contents

❶

~How Sweet It Is to Be Loved by You~

❷

~Have I Told You Lately that I Love You~

❸
~Because You Loved Me~

❹
~Why Do Fools Fall in Love~

❺
~What's Love Got to Do with It~

❻
~Love Will Keep Us Together~

❼
~Crazy Love~

❽
~Will You Still Love Me Tomorrow~

❾
~I Will Always Love You~

❿
~Circle of Love~

Married Life!

Chapter 1

How Sweet It Is
to Be Loved by You

The first love letters are written with the eyes.

~French Proverb

Thanks for the Flowers

Attitude is a little thing that makes a big difference.
~Winston Churchill

he strains of Barbra Streisand and Neil Diamond singing, "You don't bring me flowers anymore.... You don't sing me love songs…" drifted into my room via the radio.

The lyrics, designed to rip one's heart out, matched my mood that cold, dreary January morning. I wrapped the poignant words around my heart as I dressed for an early morning speaking engagement. How true, I thought—the last time David brought me flowers was twenty-five years ago, when our youngest son Bob was born.

This morning David had already left for work in our more reliable car. I bundled up against the cold and headed out for the dreaded task of starting the old Chrysler. The beast normally took great offense at the cold and refused to start without coaxing. To start it, one had to find the lever inside the grill to release the hood, lift it, and then find the stick to prop it open. Next, one had to remove the wing nut from the big round thing, take it off, push the little copper thing, get back inside the car and start it. If it went "Pfft," one had to go back outside and push the copper thing again. If it started coughing and then actually turned over, one had to get out, put the big round thing back on, screw the wing nut tightly, hold up the hood while putting the holder stick back, and then shut the hood. By this time one's hands were usually pretty dirty.

I decided to try to start the car first, to see how bad it really was. I slid behind the steering wheel and turned the key. Varoom!

In spite of the cold it started right up! My goodness, listen to that, I thought. David must have warmed the car for me before he left for work. How nice of him. I was ready to back out, when I heard an inner voice say, "Go back and thank him for the flowers."

"What? Thank him for the flowers?"

"Yes."

This was before cell phones so I went back inside the house, called him at work and said, "David I just now found some petunias in the car. Thank you for the flowers! What a nice thing to do."

Later on that week, I decided to try to shove one more can in the trash compactor. The last time I'd looked, there wasn't much room for anything but an envelope! I opened the compactor drawer and there it was, clean, empty and relined and it wasn't even trash day.

I heard the quiet inner voice again, "Thank him for the flowers."

I called him at work again. "David, I just found daffodils in the trash compactor. You are so thoughtful, thank you for the flowers."

I'm sure David smiled as he hung up the phone.

Another day I was feeling ill, and David urged me to go to the doctor.

"I don't want to go to the doctor." I said.

"Why not?" he asked.

"Because even if all I have is a hangnail he'll tell me to lose weight."

David sighed. "Then I'll go with you."

"I don't want you to hear him tell me to lose weight."

David tilted his head. "What's the difference if you weigh one pound per cubic inch, or three pounds per cubic inch? I'm absolutely crazy about you!"

"Oh David!" I said. "Three dozen, long stemmed, American Beauty Roses!"

A while later, on Valentine's Day, my hairdresser asked, "Did you get anything special today?"

I smiled and said, "Oh, I have three dozen roses that are still fresh and fragrant."

Another time I was speaking at a women's weekend retreat. The conference center was an hour's drive from our home. I was housed in a nice cabin where David and I had previously stayed for a couples' retreat.

That night had been a particularly difficult first session. I couldn't seem to get through to the women. Then I remembered this was one of my "Mount Rushmore" church groups, where the faces were set in stone, chiseled into the mountain, and refusing to move. I'd previously made a mental note not to return, but must have forgotten. I called David, even though it was after midnight. I heard a sleepy "Hello."

"Honey, I hate to bother you at this time of the night."

"You're allowed," he said patiently.

"It's just that I'm having a really hard time with this group. Would you please pray for me?"

He prayed a nice, although sleepy, prayer. I thanked him and went to bed. About an hour later, as I was drifting off to sleep, I heard a tapping at my door. I got up and opened the door, and there, standing in the rain, was David. "I thought you needed a buddy," he said.

He stayed the night and left before breakfast. That beautiful spring bouquet has never left my heart.

One weekend David and I were speaking at a small town in Oregon. At the Sunday morning service, several people were visiting because of a local family reunion. After the service a man from Libby, Montana came up to me. He asked, "Did you do a women's retreat in Sandpoint, Idaho?"

"Yes," I said.

"I thought it was someone with an unusual first name. I have you to thank for a whole new marriage."

"Really?" I said.

"Yes, my wife came home from the retreat and began thanking me for flowers. Now I lie awake nights, thinking about what I can do for her, and wondering what flower she's going to call it."

~Zoanne Wilkie

The Gold Ring Club

Two souls, one heart.
~French saying used on poesy rings

Lately, I've been showing off my wedding ring. No, it isn't new and not particularly clean—I gave up trying to keep lotion and meatloaf out of the diamonds sometime after the rigors of motherhood had snuffed most of the youth out of me. Sort of without warning though, my gold wedding set has become a national treasure. It's like a fossil found unexpectedly during an annual fishing trip, brought home and displayed for neighbors, who stand around marveling, "Well, would you look at THAT!" as they inspect something so primeval and antique.

People ask to see my fossil.

My children are getting to the age now where they are attending weddings with interest and they know people who are engaged to be married. Each bride's flashy platinum wedding set must instantly invoke images for my kids of their mom's ancient gold ring—the ring they have seen most often because it is connected to the hand that wipes the counter, their noses, and tears from their face. When my children ask to see the ring, it is no passing glance; they examine it closely and with the fascination of seeing a trinket that has washed ashore from the Titanic.

"So, this is the ring Dad bought you?" said my son, fully grown now and having thoughts of a future with his girlfriend.

"Yes, this is it," I answered as we stared at the ring. It's a good size with plenty of diamonds—I liked it then and I like it now.

"Gold, huh?"

There it was. He was smiling and looking at me with amusement in the way I must have looked at my grandma when we discussed her platinum wedding band. When I was a little girl, only old people had silver on their fingers. Naturally, when I got married, the only option for me was the very hip and contemporary gold wedding set of the 1980s.

I'm not sure when having a gold wedding ring went out of style, mostly because I was busy starting a marriage and having babies and was more worried about finding the elusive green Power Ranger toy than I was ensuring that my original wedding ring was still fashionable.

But, it happened. At some point, gold wedding rings became as dated as avocado colored appliances and leisure suits. I am now wearing the equivalent of a Studebaker on my finger.

I'm old because I wear a gold wedding ring, but more to the point—I have an old marriage. I want to start a club where the only requirement is that you must be wearing a gold wedding ring to join. I know a few people in my generation of friends and family who are already in the club, and we have a lot in common.

We have been married over twenty years. We've climbed the thorny hills and fallen into the barren valleys associated with a long-term marriage. We've loved, hated, became apathetic, and then loved again in regular intervals. We've felt like giving up, giving in, and not just throwing in the towel—but burning the towel and everything else with it, too. We've stayed together. We've lost jobs, vision, hair, or athletic prowess, but we've gained patience, understanding, respect, and the ability to communicate without words. When couples we knew were breaking up, in search of the more improved platinum version of marriage, we barricaded ourselves with stubborn commitment, grudgingly finding a way through the sludge to make our gold-banded marriages work, sure that there had to be something better if we could survive another battle.

A gold wedding ring means that the wearer's relationship stood a twenty-year test of time, children, and inevitable problems. It isn't a sign of romance or perfection, because you can't get this far sharing life with another person without making an occasional mess. It means that we've collaborated with our partners for a cause greater than "self." If we removed that gold ring, for example, we would be performing minor surgery on our children, too—lacerating their childhoods and creating deep craters where pleasant memories should have been. At some point, we all decided that our kids were more important than leaving and starting anew. Our children may have been the occasional impetus for staying married, but ultimately, they were the steel spike strips that simply prevented us from going the wrong direction in the first place.

The nice thing about wearing my original wedding set is that, unlike any other precious metal, the gold wedding ring is a symbol of triumph, a trophy—if you will—for someone who has tamed the wild beast of a long marriage within a generation where most marriages have dissolved. Right now, gold is the only color of wedding band that says, "I got this ring before cell phones."

For me, I'll stick to the gold wedding band and cherish its symbol of triumph over adversity, good decisions over bad, and for love conquering all. And to the man and my lifelong partner who gave it to me twenty-two years ago, thank you for a constant reminder of what we have accomplished. I am a proud member of the Gold Ring Club.

~Dana Martin

A Different Story

There is no more lovely, friendly and charming relationship,
communion or company than a good marriage.
~Martin Luther

"I just want what you and John have," my beautiful forty-something single friend tells me. Immediately humbled, I realize that I heard the same thing from a single, searching, female cousin just recently. My husband John and I have not even been together for that long.

I am overcome by humility, pleasure, and almost wistfulness because I "want what we have" as well. I wanted it long before I met John and my life has been a whirlwind ever since, and here I am living out my own dreams.

We met when we were thirty-four years old. In a short time we realized that we loved each other and desired the same things: marriage and a family. By my thirty-fifth birthday we were in the middle of planning a wedding and enjoying every date we spent together. When I turned thirty-six, we'd been married almost six months, had our own home and found ourselves settling into our lives together. We had occasional fights that make me laugh now. Mostly we worried about the other invading our space and freedom; we'd been single for so long we had to relearn the concept of sharing.

By my thirty-seventh birthday, I'd spent much of the previous year pregnant. We had painted a baby's room together and prepared for his arrival as we learned to start thinking outside of ourselves.

Our first child, Martin, came home on my thirty-seventh birthday. His father brought him into the house first and then walked back to the car to help me—escorting me in. I found my new son in his carrier on the kitchen counter, a balloon saying "Happy Birthday Mom" floating just above him.

"Loving and thoughtful." I smiled.

"I wondered if you'd notice," John replied.

Life changed drastically as two salaries became one and we never left the house together without Baby Martin or having made arrangements for a babysitter. The new guy brought great joy to our lives, of course, along with all the normal new baby stresses. I do remember that feeling of relief on certain nights, when John walked in the door and I could just hand him that baby! We realized a different degree of love for each other than we had ever known, as well as a whole new definition for our own space and freedom.

When I turned thirty-eight we had a one-year-old, a busy life with our combined family and friends, and a desire to add to the brood we'd begun. "I have news," I told John one Saturday morning the next September, causing him to rush to the bathroom sink on a hunch, where he found a positive pregnancy test.

"Awesome, honey." With that I got kissed.

As my thirty-ninth birthday approached, Joe, the most beautiful of completely bald colicky babies who ever existed, joined our home. Our sense of individual space and freedom were again redefined; sleep and quiet became rare commodities as well.

Joe grew… Martin grew. We were raising fun little people and had no real complaints about anything. "I wake up tired," John sometimes grumbled, and still does, but mostly we were living the lives we'd chosen. Space and freedom almost forgotten, except when one or the other of us really needed some of it; communication and humor became our greatest tools in surviving the day-to-day of family life with two young children and the regular stresses of job and owning/running a home.

Somewhere close to forty, on a week-long family vacation we decided to "roll the dice" and see if God had any more plans to give us children. John made me promise "not to try for a girl." I knew I'd never be disappointed anyway, and on my forty-first birthday, our third son, Tim, celebrated his first outing as our new family of five picnicked on submarine sandwiches at our favorite neighborhood park. My thirty-fifth birthday had been spent in a fancy restaurant in downtown Chicago and was followed by attending a musical with my new fiancé. Six years later, our identities rewritten several times, I couldn't imagine a better way to spend the day.

"Do you love me as much now as when you married me?" I had asked John in post-partum haze.

"Way more…."

This year we'll celebrate my forty-third birthday the same week my oldest turns six and my youngest hits two. Certainly, space and freedom continue to come only with compromise as we figure out how to balance family life and get to know the people we have become. Our first priority now is always parenthood; we've learned that our lives are no longer our own. We still love each other, probably "way more" than we once did, because it feels good, but also because we're invested in the family we've been given. And as John likes to say, "It's their world now, not ours!"

The vast majority of my days, I work to entertain and meet the needs of the three little boys who have become the greatest focus of our lives. I maintain that tremendous feeling of relief on many evenings when John walks in the house. No matter how stressful the day, his presence makes it doable. We are partners working through it together for the long haul!

Keeping all this in mind, I look at my friend and into her heart as much as I can. "You know," I confess, "I haven't had five minutes to myself today, not even to go to the bathroom."

She laughs. Freedom, space and independence are the rewards of single life, but loneliness and uncertainty about the future offset those. Would I change what I have in order to go on even one more blind date or out to a bar for a girls' night at whim, without arrangement? Never! Would I give up my chaotic household for the almost always straightened and never sticky townhouse I owned just nine years ago? No!

Life brings its compromises. Marriage and parenthood are a lot of work, but well worth it. I wish my friend and my cousin each receive the fairy tale ending they wish for themselves. As an insider, I know that the perks to marriage and a house full of kids, when combined with love and compromise, far outweigh any sacrifices.

~Gina Farella Howley

The Day I Ran Away from Home

*Having someone wonder where you are when you don't come home at night
is a very old human need.*
~Margaret Mead

I stood at the front door, looking out over the cold wet lawn. It had been a soggy couple of weeks. Overhead, the sky hung low and gray. The big oak, stripped barren, pointed crooked fingers toward the heavens as if pleading for the sun's warmth. I echoed that sentiment. Would the sun ever shine again?

I don't know what came over me, but in that moment, I longed to run away from home, to an exotic place filled with sunshine and sea, where no one knew my name, where the wind blew through my hair, and umbrellas were used only for shade.

Have you ever wished, even for a split second, to drive off to places unknown, alone? To a place where you don't have to deal with the same old issues that keep turning up through the years, seemingly never to be resolved?

There was that time I actually did run away, sort of. The details went something like this.

It was late one evening. I don't recall what it was about, but The Man and I had a very big and ugly argument. We both said things we didn't mean and, in the end, I said, "I'm leaving," and he said, "Good. The sooner, the better."

I threw a few things in a small suitcase and slammed the door behind me, not having a clue where I was going. After driving in circles for several minutes, I stopped at my local grocery to pick up some personal items I'd forgotten to pack in my heated rush to get out of the house.

But before I got down the first aisle, my cell phone rang. It was my grown daughter calling. I answered the phone and she said, "Hey, Mom. Where are you?"

Instantly, I knew she knew. Something in her voice gave it away.

"Hey, sweetie. I'm out for a bit. What's up?"

"Well, where are you?" Persistence is her middle name.

"Just out. Why?"

"Mom, Dad is worried about you."

"How can he be worried about me? I've been gone a total of twenty minutes. Did he call you?" I was perturbed.

"No, he didn't call me. I called and asked to talk to you and yes, he is really worried about you."

"Well, he should have thought of that sooner," I said, my anger returning, remembering all of the hateful things he'd spouted. "Listen, sweetie. I really need to get off the phone. You can tell your dad that I'm fine. I'm just fine. I love you, and I'll call you tomorrow."

I hung up and lingered in the store, trying to get my thoughts together. I had money, so I decided I'd go to a nearby hotel and attempt to get some sleep. Lord knew I needed it.

By the time I paid for my purchases, it was much later than I liked to be out alone. I'd parked a good distance from the store and practically ran to my car. Once inside, I locked the doors, cranked the engine, and started to drive off. But I couldn't see out. A large square of white paper was stuck under my windshield wiper. What on earth?

As my eyes adjusted to the dark, it became clear. There, on a white piece of copy paper, drawn with a black marker, was a big heart encircling these words: "Please come home!! I miss you! I love you!"

Before I could process it all, a truck pulled up alongside me. Hanging out the window was none other than my husband. Apparently, he'd called out the search party. Beside him, grinning from ear-to-ear, sat my daughter.

And that's when I started laughing. I laughed so hard I cried. Despite my best efforts to run away from home, the wild and zany man who loved me had managed to track me down. I couldn't very well leave now, not with him sitting there with puppy-dog eyes.

As I followed him out of the parking lot, I realized how foolish we'd been, arguing over insignificant things, and how blessed I was that the man I loved most in the world loved me back and had come looking for me and found me, and was leading me home again.

~Dayle Allen Shockley

*"All I said is I'd like a little more attention.
I don't need the shenanigans."*

Oops

Never say, "oops." Always say, "Ah, interesting."
~Author Unknown

My husband, Darryl, and I have four kids, spread out over a fourteen-year period. For several years we had a preschooler, elementary schooler, middle schooler and high schooler all at the same time. With four kids at completely different stages and on entirely different schedules, finding quality "private" time for just the two of us was a challenge.

Since we rarely had the house to ourselves, we made it a point to schedule time away from work during the few brief hours one day each week when our youngest was at Mother's-Day-Out at the same time the older kids were at their various schools—time we could meet at home for some unhurried, uninterrupted romance.

When Darryl got back to the office after one such encounter, he sent me a sweet and sexy e-mail referring to the pleasures of our intimate time together. When I hadn't responded after a couple of days he mentioned it. I'd never received his e-mail. But since it hadn't come back as "undeliverable" we knew someone had.

My e-mail address consisted of my given name, last initial and dot-com address. Darryl had forgotten to include my last initial. When he realized his mistake he had a sudden vision of his name in our local newspaper, in bold print, under the headline "Local Businessmen Arrested for E-mail Harassment." He quickly sent off an apology to the mistaken address, explaining the mix-up. Within minutes he received a reply!

"No apology necessary. Although I'm getting up in years and it's been a long time since I've had the experience you described, I very much enjoyed the reminder. Best wishes for you and your wife to enjoy many more such afternoons."

~Lynn Worley Kuntz

He Listened

The most precious gift we can offer anyone is our attention.
~Thich Nhat Hanh

Christmas was three weeks away and my husband was fishing for ideas for my present. I smiled because he is always so thoughtful when it comes to buying Christmas gifts and I have never been disappointed by his choices.

"Actually," he announced, "I'd like to buy you some bras."

That got my attention and I listened intently as he explained that, while he was relatively familiar with the broader world of lingerie, he wasn't quite sure what size or kind of bra I would wear. He wanted some direction.

I paused. He waited. We sat together on the couch looking at each other with a funny smirk on our faces until I finally broke the silence.

"I would love for you to buy me a bra, but what I really need are practical bras. I don't need fancy, frilly, romantic, lacy bras for our intimate rendezvous in the bedroom. I already have a wide variety of items for that, many of which you bought for me. What I really need are practical bras to wear during the day and your timing is great... mine are almost shot."

Disappointment spread across his face as I explained what I meant by practical bras. I needed at least three, all in neutral colors: one black, one white, and one ivory. I needed bras that were comfortable enough to wear all day long, and for me that meant bras with support but no underwire. I needed bras with a little padding so that I could avoid embarrassment while wearing a lightweight and formfitting blouse to the office during the summer months when the AC kicks into high gear. I needed bras that were solid color and sparing in lace and design because the additional detail, while pretty and feminine, might show through some of my more delicate, yet professional sweaters.

My husband paid close attention, but I could tell that practical wasn't what he had in mind. Regardless, I was delighted Christmas morning when I opened one of my many presents and found three practical bras: one white, one ivory, and one black! He had done it. My husband had listened carefully to my wishes and delivered on every aspect. I was so pleased I giggled with joy, and then he handed me my next present. Gently, I unwrapped three beautiful and sexy dresses, each one designed with lots of color, lace and fabulous detail.

"One to wear over each new bra," he said, and we both laughed out loud.

Those three bras turned out to be my favorite Christmas present and a fond memory. They were not overly expensive. They were not elegant or lavish. They were not even anything I'd want to brag about to our friends and family members. But, they were everything I asked for. They were also symbolic of my husband's effort to keep his wedding vows. On our wedding day, before God and many witnesses, we promised to be loving and faithful: in plenty and in want, in joy and in sorrow, in sickness and in health, as long we both shall live. Little did he know that "plenty and want" might someday include practical bras.

~Kristen Clark

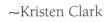

Happy Anniversary

Now the thing about having a baby —
and I can't be the first person to have noticed this — is that
thereafter you have it.
~Jean Kerr

Seven years ago, at this very hour, my new husband, Craig, and I were dancing at our wedding reception. We danced and visited with our guests until it was time to climb in our limousine and ride to the hotel.

We spent the night at a Holiday Inn and the next morning, we flew to Montego Bay, Jamaica to stay at a beautiful, all-inclusive resort. Our honeymoon was fantastic. The weather was perfect, the resort was gorgeous, and the locals were friendly and accommodating. We could not have asked for a better week. We were sad to leave and on our departing flight, we vowed to return one day.

Over the past seven years, we have made it a point to do something special on our anniversary. One year we traveled to Vermont; another year we went to Nassau, Bahamas; and three years ago, we spent our special day in Flagstaff, Arizona as part of a whirlwind trip to the Grand Canyon.

We enjoy travel, we love adventure, and we cherish our time together. But we are also realistic and we know that we cannot afford a big vacation for every anniversary, especially in a year in which we gained a new family member.

This year, we were blessed with our beautiful baby boy, Evan. He is the joy of our lives and also a major expense. So, needless to say, we weren't planning an elaborate anniversary trip to the Caribbean or a trek across the United States. We did, however, hope to celebrate with a nice dinner and a glass of wine.

If there is one lesson we have learned in seven years of marriage, it's that things rarely go as planned. We have missed weddings because of illnesses. We have canceled a camping trip because of a death in the family. Our cars and major appliances have all conspired to break down at the most inopportune times. On Evan's first Christmas, we sat shivering in our snow-covered home while the repairman worked to restore our heat. Craig and I are not strangers to inconvenience.

So, it is only fitting that on our seventh anniversary, instead of dining on a juicy filet or a succulent lobster tail, we are wrestling our eight-month-old in an effort to get the antibiotic down his gullet. Right now, Evan is winning and the medicine is all over the carpet.

Our baby became sick two days before our anniversary. After one misdiagnosis and two visits to the doctor, we know that Evan has an ear infection and we have started treatment. He should be well in a few days, but our anniversary night is not as we envisioned.

We are regularly checking Evan's temperature, administering Tylenol, and giving him cool baths to keep him comfortable. He finally starts to yawn while I rock him and sing him soft, familiar lullabies. I take him to his room and place him in the crib.

When I return, Craig has poured wine into the glasses we drank from on our wedding night. We toast to our seven, wonderful years together as we look through our wedding albums and remember our special day.

Craig and I talk late into the night about how special this anniversary is. It is our first one as parents. We are a family and we are figuring things out. We have learned that air conditioners freeze up on the hottest day of the year, heaters fizzle out on the coldest, and cars break down right before vacations. We know that children are not born with calendars or clocks, and they cry when you're tired, they scream in the middle of restaurants, and they even get sick on your anniversary.

Because I married the perfect man for me, most of these circumstances are laughable, at least in retrospect. We kiss and say goodnight and Craig gets up to turn off the television. At that moment, an ad plays for a luxury resort in the Caribbean. We smile and head upstairs. I go to bed happy and grateful. My daily life may not always go as planned, but my marriage is exactly what I wanted.

~Melissa Face

Diamond in the Rough

As I grow older I pay less attention to what men say.
I just watch what they do.
~Andrew Carnegie

When my husband and I were married, I accepted the fact that he wasn't the kind who would shower me with fancy words and expensive diamonds. I appreciated his gentle, honest love and found great pleasure in all of the beautiful cards he gave me, reading them often, and then putting them safely away. "I'm not good with words," he'd say, as he hugged me close, "but this card says everything that's in my heart."

I loved him deeply, yet part of me longed for the flowers and diamond rings my girlfriends' husbands gave them. What was wrong with me? Why did I have this need for flamboyant demonstrations of love? Why couldn't I just accept him as he was?

As time passed, we became parents of two little girls. With the extra expenses, my husband decided to go back to school and train as a mechanic. He would go to the city for the week and return home on the weekends. We had never been apart, and I, ever the romantic, cut off a lock of my hair. "Take this," I told him. "And whenever you're lonely, just run your fingers over it, and I'll be there with you." He grinned, placed the hair in a small plastic bag, and tucked it into his wallet.

The following years were a mixture of good and bad. We struggled financially. I went to work as a bookkeeper. The girls went to school and to a babysitter's. There was little time to worry about the lack of romance in our marriage. There certainly wasn't money for extravagant gift giving.

But as times improved and our girls became quite self-sufficient, I again fought the feelings of disappointment, when I only received a card for a birthday or anniversary. Perhaps, I told myself as I cried silent tears into my pillow at night, he didn't feel I was worth anything but a card. Or did wooing die once the wedding rings were slipped on?

"Don't be a fool," my best friend said one day, as I told her of my longing. "Can't you see how much that man loves you?"

I sighed and nodded. I was being foolish. I decided it was time to put the nonsense behind me. I would not think of it again, I told myself.

Then one day many years later, as we sat at the kitchen table, Ivan dumped out his wallet in search of an elusive receipt. There among bits of paper was a familiar looking small plastic bag.

But it couldn't be.

Reaching across the table, my hand trembling with emotion, I picked up the bag. My eyes grew misty as I looked upon the brown lock of hair I had given Ivan fifteen years earlier. My heart swelled with love for him.

"I can't believe you saved this all of these years," I said.

He squeezed my hand; then shrugged. "I'll always keep it," he said gently. "I love you."

This past year, my darling and I were married forty-four years. He still is the quiet type and my once brown hair, has turned grey. But the lock of hair that remains tucked lovingly away in his wallet, speaks volumes. I may not have diamonds to sparkle on my fingers, but I have a diamond in the rough and his steady love is worth more than gold or silver. He's what lasting dreams are made of.

~Christine Mikalson

My Husband's Hands

I love thee to the depth and breadth and height my soul can reach.
~Elizabeth Barrett Browning

This is a story of my husband's hands. They are not delicate hands by any means. They are the hands of a man who has worked hard all his life. They are capable and clumsy at the same time, earning him both a good reputation with tools and the family nickname of "dill pickle fingers." They are calloused and kind.

The same hands that placed a wedding band on my finger thirty-five years ago are the same hands that held mine when we sat together, disbelievingly, to receive my cancer diagnosis a few months ago. Primary source breast cancer, spread to my spine. The same hands that caressed me in passion now gently wash and towel-dry my broken back, still caressing and still with love. Our intimacy now consists of my bedpan being emptied, and thanks to his willing hands, it doesn't make me feel any less cherished.

Those hands that remember the soft skin of our babies now hold my wheelchair firmly for me, so I can safely sit. They proudly carry a little bowl of carefully washed green grapes to have with my lunch: a heavenly offering. They smooth my covers and pick up my pills at the pharmacy.

This past spring, the strong fingers that held the pen to sign our marriage certificate held a different pen to sign a contract for a burial plot at our local cemetery, thus ensuring our eternal resting place. Those hands are not afraid to do the needful.

Sometimes, in trying to please me, his hands shake subtly with good intentions. Right now, as I am writing this, they are scrubbing the bathroom with great zeal.

They are magic hands. Upon my touching them, they talk to me of the things they have seen and done over the years. They can describe the smells of freshly cut lumber, and of savoury hamburgers grilling on the barbecue.

Tales are told about the long ago glories of a young man who carried the football across the field, and held tightly to ski poles on the way down a frozen mountain. They recall playing with his beloved dog, followed by the sad story of how they held his faithful old friend when the time came to say goodbye.

They speak out loud the things my husband has trouble saying, out of shyness or just not knowing how. They say that no matter what the joys and struggles of our life together have been, he loves me even now.

They are the hands that I know as well as my own. My husband's hands.

~Diane Wilson

Are You Happy?

If you want to be happy, be.
~Leo Tolstoy

I never meant to be married three times. My one and only marriage was going to be a delight of witty banter and happily ever after. I'd been studying for this since I picked up my first Georgette Heyer romance, so I knew exactly what to expect. After the second divorce, I went on a crying jag, threw out all of my romance novels and went to therapy.

I started understanding me.

I treasured those teenage years of curling up with a romance novel. That's when I fell in love with the paper hero. He was strong, dark and handsome, carelessly bestowing a kiss or promising glance that filled the heroine's dreams. A paper hero is told what to say, how to act, in fact, how to be the perfect man. But, he only exists on the pages of a book.

Let me translate those qualities into down-to-earth terms. He's the sexy bad boy every woman wants. Bad boys like having lots of women. They love the attention. They are experts at giving out crumbs of attention—just enough to give us hope that he'll be the one.

Bad boys are sexy, flirtatious and intelligent. The ones I loved were not bad men, but none of them was the right man for me.

Once I realized this, I got out of my own way and decided that I wanted more than a paper hero. Once I did that, I met Larry. We got married a year and a half later.

My ever-so-wise daughters said it best. "The first time was to make us. The second was to raise us. The third time is for you, Mom."

My husband and I were scared to death, like most newlyweds! After all, I was a two-time loser. He'd never been married. Mixed in with the good wishes from family and friends, there were a few snide comments: "Are you crazy? You fall in and out of love like a teenager." "Why would you give up your freedom?" And my personal favorite was "Look at your track record. Maybe you're not marriage material."

So, I did a new dance. I ignored them and started listening to my husband. He kept saying something that I'd never heard before.

Are you happy?

"What?" I asked, scared that I was completely screwing up. Again.

He smiled. "I'm happy if you're happy."

Later on, I thumbed through several romances to reference his comment. Aha! Just as I thought!

After much struggle and turmoil, the paper hero and heroine kiss passionately and ride off in his Ferrari or sail off on his yacht. But it ends there.

The ordinary everyday hero who wants his wife to be happy is ignored.

My husband, who also happens to be sexy, handsome and intelligent, is the real deal! None of those paper heroes ever cared about a woman's happiness... just theirs.

Larry has had to nudge me a bit. I'm accustomed to making everyone else happy, not myself.

"Does your job make you unhappy? Find a new one," he said, looking up from his computer with a frown as I tried to hide my tears.

I did. I quit my stressful job as a federal officer that involved a daily three-hour commute and became a nursery school teacher. It takes me eight minutes to get to work.

"You miss swimming? Find a pool and make the time to go." He sighed while I collapsed after doing a pathetic number of sit-ups.

I started swimming at the local high school.

"Where are your pretty clothes? Pretty women need to wear pretty outfits. Go shopping." He patted my back as I stared at the clutter of old clothes in my closet.

Well, he still has to drag me shopping, but at least I'm getting the hang of it again.

I try to make him happy. I'm not such a junk monkey and I'll watch his shows. *Star Trek* has tons of generations and explores strange new worlds so it's actually pretty entertaining!

I've never been married like this, but I've become the woman I've always wanted to be. I've kicked those negative comments to the curb and hung up a "Do Not Disturb My Happiness" sign.

A year later, when Larry asks "Are you happy," I kiss him and answer "Yes."

Thanks for asking, sweetie.

~Karla Brown

Married Life!

Have I Told You Lately that I Love You

*Married couples who love each other
tell each other a thousand things without talking.*

~Portuguese Proverb

My Hero

All men are created equal, then a few become firemen.
~Author Unknown

Often firefighters are referred to as heroes because they are willing to put their lives on the line and face danger to help or save others. A firefighter doesn't think twice about entering a burning building to rescue someone in need or about climbing onto a blazing roof to put out a fire.

My husband is a firefighter. He has been in dangerous situations and has had to put his life on the line many times over the years. After being married to him for almost twenty years it is probably odd that I don't often worry about the risks my husband takes in his job. That's just what he does. What makes him a hero to me are all the things that he gives up in his personal life while being a firefighter in his professional life.

We've had friends comment on how lucky he is to have a work schedule that allows him to be home in the middle of the week. But what is often overlooked is the time that he is away. My husband's job requires that he leave his family and sleep away from home half the month as firefighters work twenty-four-hour shifts. He has to trust that while he is taking care of others, his own family is safe. And what is also overlooked is how much I have to be on my own. But it works for us and our marriage is stronger for it.

In our marriage, my husband George and I have had to sacrifice many important family events, such as our anniversary, our son's soccer games, first dances, and many holidays for the sake of his job. In our marriage we have had to make adjustments because of his absence. Some years we celebrate Christmas on the 26th because he is working on the 25th. Thanksgiving or a birthday celebration may take place the day before or after to accommodate his schedule. He cannot come home for a broken pipe or to help with a chore just because I am feeling overwhelmed, and I have never thought of asking him to do that. When he does come home on his days off he doesn't mention his lack of sleep from the night before and he can be found immediately at the kitchen table helping our son with a school project or running some household errands for me as I work on a deadline.

Although George knows that I am a very capable adult who has handled this type of lifestyle for almost twenty years there are a few things that I know put his mind at ease. His calls throughout the day show his love and are his lifeline to his family. He calls in the afternoon to see how my day is going. He calls when our son comes home from school to check on him and to see how his day went. I receive a call at nine o'clock each night he is away to make sure we are safely home from whatever practice or event we were attending. I have been teased about my "curfew" by well-meaning friends but what they don't seem to understand is that George cannot rest for the night without word that his family is safe and okay. I am not bound to the nine o'clock curfew if I am not going to be home by then I let him know.

I can only imagine how hard it is to receive a call from a frantic wife when the car won't start due to a dead battery or the water heater is leaking. I try not to bother him with those types of things because there is not a thing he can do about them. My calls to him are more to vent than anything else, and he is always willing to listen. Writing this reminds me of how hard it must be for him to be away from us as much as he is.

This type of marriage might not work for everyone but George and I are willing to do what it takes to make it work. And it does work for us. When George comes home, we have all of his attention.

He leaves his helmet behind at work and puts on his husband, father, gardener, or pool man hat. When I picture in my mind, my firefighter—the hero—I see the amazing personal sacrifices my husband makes to make sure others are safe while always trusting that we are too. He is my hero.

~D'ette Corona

The Wedding Band

For every minute you are angry, you lose sixty seconds of happiness.
~Author Unknown

I sat with my lips in a tight line, a dark feeling enveloping me. It was better to say nothing than to continue more negativity in the car. It was going to be a long trip.

As we started our trip to Las Vegas to attend my husband's brother's wedding, it seemed like everything went wrong. My husband Bob was supposed to pick me up early from work, after I had made arrangements for my replacement for the day, but he did not come. When we met up, the car wasn't ready and gassed, causing more delays and worries about the distance we needed to make that night. Additional irritations made us both tense. Snippy words were tossed to and fro. I hunched miserable in my seat.

Usually when we traveled together the trips were made short by our companionable chatting, discussing our children and our dreams, making plans, telling stories, and laughing. This time I felt totally out of sorts. Neither of us felt like talking. It was going to be a late night. We just drove in silent determination to get to our stopping point. The air conditioning put an additional chill in the car, but neither of us turned it off.

After several hours, Bob asked me to take a turn driving, and we pulled off the freeway onto a deserted off-ramp under a cold, moonless sky, in the middle of nowhere, to change drivers. It felt literally as dark as pitch as I walked slowly around to the back of the car, letting the cold air seep through me to refresh and wake me. To make sure I was completely alert and ready to drive, I starting vigorously shaking my hands and arms. That was a terrible mistake! Immediately, I felt my wedding band fly off my finger, disappearing into the blackness. A split second later, I could hear it rolling somewhere along the asphalt.

"My ring!" I shouted. "Bob, I lost my ring!" He hurried to where I stood panicking in the darkness. "How could this happen?" I wailed. "It has never been loose. It must be because I was cold from the air conditioning. We have to find it!"

How could we find it in that impenetrable darkness? It seemed impossible. Bob had a small penlight he always carries with him, and I started crisscrossing the road with it, straining my eyes in the darkness and the small beam of light. The light picked up occasional glints in the asphalt, but no ring. I started to despair. How far had the ring rolled?

I concentrated on my memory of the sound of the rolling ring, and tried to follow the direction I thought it traveled. In my mind, each roll of the ring brought back a memory: our last trip together, laughing and talking animatedly; picnics and hikes in the mountains with our children; happily riding our bikes; walking the dogs together; Saturday morning breakfasts, lounging in our pajamas, etc. The thought of another roll of the ring brought memories of hard times: my cancer diagnosis and surgery; his heart attack and recovery—the way we always knew the other would be there—no matter what. That ring was more than gold and diamonds. It was a memory of our lifetime together—over thirty years—a forever commitment! It had to be found!

By now, though, the search began to seem more and more futile. I had a thought. "Bob, turn the car around so the lights are shining across the road more," I suggested. With this greater light both of us continued searching. This off-ramp road seemed to have grown immense in the darkness. There was so much area where a small ring could have finally stopped rolling.

I wondered if we would have to leave, never to find my ring.

Would it be lost forever? I couldn't picture anyone ever being in such a deserted area to happen upon it. If only it were daylight, we might have a chance, but we were enveloped in darkness.

As I was about to give up hope, Bob, without the flashlight, but standing behind me in the glow of the car's headlights shouted, "I found it! It was almost in the weeds on the other side of the road!" I ran to him and buried my face against his strong shoulder, and cried, "Oh Bob!" as he slipped the ring on my finger. Great sobs tumbled out of me. We stood there embracing, in the blackest of nights while I cried—not just in relief for finding the ring but with regret for the tense hours previously, and in gratitude for having another chance to remember all that wedding band represented. As we got back in the car, I smiled. It was going to be a great trip after all.

~Barbra Yardley

There's Always Pie

13

Home cooking:
where many a man thinks his wife is.
~Author Unknown

I married a man whose mother loved to bake. Naturally, he assumed I would be just like her. I wasn't. My mother served Jell-O, store-bought pies, or fruit for dessert. I took after her in the extreme. When it was time for dessert, I would get a can of fruit cocktail out of the fridge and say, "Have at it!" For some reason, that didn't go over too well with my new husband.

After our honeymoon, we settled in a nice apartment with everything any housewife would need. Unopened gifts were our first order of business and they filled me with trepidation. Pots, pans, dishes and cookbooks reminded me of one thing I had failed to mention to my dear husband. I didn't know how to cook.

Unfortunately, that did not stop me from trying.

One day, while making spaghetti, Jim walked into the kitchen and caught me throwing wet noodles at the wall.

"What are you doing?" he asked as I peeled the noodles away from the wall.

"I'm checking to see if they're done."

Something akin to revulsion played itself over Jim's face. "Do you do that with all the food?"

"Of course not! Everyone knows you throw spaghetti at the wall to see if it's done."

That night, Jim decided to teach me how to cook.

While I soon mastered "meals," my true test would come when I made his favorite—lemon meringue pie. I followed the recipe diligently. Egg whites were separated with the skill of a professional. My meringue whipped into a perfect foamy froth and before I knew it, I had created my first dessert. The oven was ready. I slipped the pie inside and waited to present my husband with something I knew would be just as good as his mother's.

My anticipation grew as delicious smells emanated from the kitchen. The timer on the oven sounded and with oven mitts at the ready, I carefully reached in and drew out my perfect pie.

Only to have both sides of the foil plate I had used, fold in half, dribbling my beautiful pie all over my oven door!

My husband came running at my cries and stared at the oven door, then at me. He didn't say anything. He turned the oven off, retrieved two forks from the kitchen drawer, sat down in front of the oven door and proceeded to eat his pie.

Instead of tears, there was laughter. Instead of anger there were giggles. I joined him on the floor and we ate the entire pie off the oven door, knowing that in years to come this would be a story to share with our children.

Today, I make a mean lemon meringue pie, with a proper glass pie plate. I've learned a valuable lesson that has kept my marriage strong for twenty-eight years. Compromise is always a good alternative to anger and there are no troubles in life that can't be solved with a piece of pie!

~Laura J. Davis

14

The Nine O'clock Rule

Love is, above all, the gift of oneself.
~Jean Anouilh

The toughest part about being married was finding time to be married. "Lonny," I said. "We haven't had a date in one hundred years."

"I know," my husband said, even though we'd been married for only twenty. "We're way overdue."

Lonny and I were in love. Deeply. Completely. Our marriage was time-tested. We'd walked through the fire and had emerged refined. But even the healthy need nourishment, and our marriage was getting the short end of the stick.

"Let's go out Friday night," he said.

"Basketball game at the junior high," I said.

"Saturday?"

"Cub Scout dinner."

Such was life. We were blessed with five amazing sons. Lonny and I tried, nonetheless, to keep our marriage on the forefront. Marriage first. Kiddos next. It sounded good in theory. Just didn't pan out that way in time.

"Well why don't we reserve a table, for two, in the year 2020?" I said, with a laugh.

"Sold," he said. But the smile on his face made me not want to wait.

Lonny must've felt the same. He approached me a few days later, while I piled never-ending clothes into the never-resting washing machine.

"Hey," he said. "We do, totally, need to work on a date night. But what if we claim some time alone, in our home, on a regular basis?"

"Show me how."

"We'll call it the Nine O'clock Rule. Each night, at nine o'clock, we'll be in our bedroom. Alone."

"Easier said than done," I said.

"Well, the three smaller boys go to bed at eight. The two older ones can understand the need to give us time together."

True. They were teenagers. But still?

"Let's give it a try. What have we got to lose?"

I shut the lid on the washer and turned the dial. "See you at nine."

Lonny winked.

At eight o'clock, three little boys stood at the bathroom sink with foaming mouths.

"Okay, guys, brush well! Then meet me in your room for tuck-in and prayers," Lonny said. I trailed after him, to help get the boys settled and still. Our older two sons were hunkered over homework. It appeared that the first Nine O'clock Rule night was going to work.

Lonny and I snuggled our little sons in for the night. Then my husband gave me the thumbs-up as he headed into the bathroom for his shower. I glanced at the tall, dark grandfather clock in the corner. Eight forty-five. I grabbed my own pajamas and bolted upstairs to the boys' bathroom for my own nighttime shower.

"We did it!" I exclaimed, fifteen minutes later, back pressed against our closed bedroom door. Lonny was sitting on our bed already. He patted the empty spot beside him.

"Grab a seat," he said. "Let's talk."

I'd no sooner snuggled in beside my husband when there was a soft knock on the door.

"Mom," said the voice on the other side. "It's Samuel. I've forgotten how to sleep."

Lonny looked at me and smiled. Then his eyes grew round as saucers. I could read the look in his eyes: BE LOVING BUT FIRM.

"I love you, dear Samuel. But you've slept every night of your life for eight years. You know how, sweet boy. Now go back to bed and Dad and I will pray that you'll rest."

Lonny smiled his approval but another knock came quickly. This time the voice was deeper.

"Dad, it's Grant. I'm stuck on a math problem."

I smiled at Lonny and bulged my eyes at him.

"Okay, buddy. Mark the problem. I'll help you with it in the morning. Love you, Grant."

"Okay, Dad." Footfalls. Away from our door.

I pushed into Lonny's arms and waited for the tap of our next visitor. But it didn't happen. And Lonny and I began to share. We talked a blue streak. Laughed out loud. Shared stories from our days. Took time to ask questions. Invested in our relationship without restraint.

"Perfect," I said, as we drifted off to sleep.

The Nine O'clock Rule rocked.

It's been a few months now, and Lonny and I are still doing our best to live by our rule. It's tough. We have to be creators and defenders of our time. But it's worth every ounce of energy and defense. The kids are used to the routine now, and I think that they, in their boyish hearts, appreciate our priority and the blessings that it brings.

It doesn't work every night. We have to allow for some grace.

But on most nights, I catch Lonny's smile across the brimming bustle of our home sweet home.

And I smile too, when he says, "It's nine o'clock."

~Shawnelle Eliasen

Virginia Beach Is the Limit

A fellow who does things that count, doesn't usually stop to count them.
~Albert Einstein

When I think about what makes me fall in love over and over again with my husband of twenty years, I know it's not the flowers he sometimes brings home for me. It's not the chocolates or cologne he surprises me with when he returns from a business trip. It's not the bracelets, necklaces or earrings he gives me on special occasions.

Don't get me wrong—I love all that stuff. But guys should be let in on Peter's little secret—the way to your special lady's heart is through her kids. Coming from a childhood where I saw my own father once a month, I know the priceless value of a hands-on dad. If the kids are happy, I'm happy.

I'll never forget the beautiful scene in front of me one afternoon when I opened my little girl's bedroom door to find her daddy sitting on the floor beside her, the two of them happily playing Barbies together—something she could not force her own mother or any one of her three brothers to do.

I don't at all mind cleaning the kitchen by myself if Peter takes our three boys to the basement to play a rough game of roller hockey at the same time. They're out from under my feet and the noise is contained down there. He even takes all four kids out shopping to the mall, a weekly event that I gladly sit out. I enjoy the peace and quiet at home.

Peter never looks better to me than at 5:30 in the morning, when he pulls on his jeans and sweatshirt, runs his hand through his hair and quietly pulls our happy nine-year-old son out of bed and off to hockey practice. What a dedicated daddy, I think, as I bury myself deeper under the warm blankets and fall back to sleep. Did I mention that he's the coach? No relaxing in the stands and drinking coffee for my guy. He also coaches our boys' baseball team in the summer, rain or shine.

When my siblings begged me to fly home for my mother's seventieth birthday, Peter insisted I go for a long overdue vacation with my family. I knew the kids would be well cared for in my absence and I was able to enjoy myself without any worries.

Last year, the perfect ending to a perfect summer vacation made me fall for Peter once again. Actually, it didn't seem perfect at the time. We had left the sun and sand of Virginia Beach behind us and stopped two hours later to get a good night's sleep before attacking Busch Gardens Williamsburg in the morning. We were short on vacation time so Peter planned on driving all the way back to Pennsylvania the following night.

"Where's Bunny, Mommy?" Janette asked, as she unpacked her suitcase.

I started to panic. Janette, at the age of ten, had never spent a night without Bunny in her life. I picked up the phone.

"Hello, it's Mrs. Smith calling. We just checked out a few hours ago. Could you please see if housekeeping found a stuffed bunny in room 110? Yes? Thanks."

I glanced at Peter, who was relaxing on the bed with three boys climbing over him.

"I wonder how much it's going to cost us to get Bunny couriered back home," I said.

"Back home? I need Bunny now!" Janette began to sob.

"You didn't miss her all day; you won't miss her for a few nights...." I argued.

Peter got up to hug a very distressed Janette and said: "We can't leave Bunny behind. Let's go."

So away they went. Peter drove Janette all the way back to Virginia Beach, got Bunny, and drove right back to Williamsburg. Janette slept most of the way, but of course Peter couldn't. He got a few hours of sleep at our hotel before spending the next day being dragged around from one roller coaster to the next by our eldest son, while I, with my fear of heights, relaxed in the shade and watched the younger three on the safer kiddie rides.

The six of us met up for lunch, and as Davie told his siblings how brave he was and what scaredy-cats they were, I enjoyed one of the most romantic lunches I've ever had. I smiled shyly and stared deeply into Peter's bloodshot eyes, hopelessly in love with the wonderful, self-sacrificing father of our children.

Twenty years ago I took a chance that a man who was a fun date and a good tennis player would prove to be a great husband and a loving parent, and I have hit the jackpot. Love me… love my kids. That's true love.

~Jayne Thurber-Smith

16

The True Gift of Love

What is bought is cheaper than a gift.
~Portuguese Proverb

I never imagined that I would find love again, especially with three children in tow and dating virtually out of the question. But while visiting my uncle on his farm I was invited to join him along with about a dozen of his neighbors for an afternoon of horseback riding, and there I met the love of my life.

Ours was an unlikely union. He had never been married and had never been around children. I was divorced with three. Everyone thought he was crazy, including me, when after a just few short months of seeing each other he asked me to marry him.

I remember asking, "Why would you want to do that? I have little or nothing to offer besides three small children and a lot of baggage."

Once upon a time I had had hopes of that storybook marriage to my knight in shining armor but now I felt totally disillusioned by marriage and had issues with trust and abandonment to say the least. But his simple answer bowled me over and sealed the deal. "You need me," he said quietly. I certainly couldn't argue with that.

I knew he had no idea what he was getting himself into, but for whatever reason he took it on, and through good and bad, we just kept plugging away at it as the years ticked by. Certainly it was not easy. But I'd venture to say our first years were harder than most. I am a firm believer that "there are no perfect marriages—just stubborn people."

He was raised on a South Georgia farm with a basic and simple way of life. He hunted and fished and learned to drive a tractor by the time he was ten. He was not one for making a big deal out of birthdays, anniversaries or even for that matter, Christmas. To him it was all a superficial waste of money.

And I admit the first few years of that were hard to take. I went to bed many a night and cried myself to sleep because he had yet again not forgotten, but "ignored," my birthday or another anniversary.

As time went by he saw that it bothered me and he tried, but his gifts, usually purchased in a panic at the last minute, left much to be desired. And after a while it just wasn't worth the fight and so I chalked it up to "that's just who he is" and learned to pick my battles.

As the years went by I began to realize that he gave me "gifts" all year long in his daily acts of kindness, like the hours he struggled with my son to build a Pinewood Derby Racer for Cub Scouts, and how fervently he cheered him on, and beamed with pride as my son took the first place trophy at his karate tournament.

I still laugh as I recall him trying to teach my sixteen-year-old daughter how to drive a car for the first time. He came bolting back through the door after one particularly nerve-wracking lesson yelling at the top of his lungs, "She thinks speed limit signs are merely suggestions!"

He walked my daughter down the aisle when she married the love of her life and then paced the hospital halls by my side for eighteen long hours the night she gave birth to our first grandson. Years later he and my now-grown sons worked tirelessly for months to build an apartment over our garage when my mother could no longer live alone. And I will never forget how he made countless heart-wrenching phone calls to relatives for me the night my mother passed away.

He has been by my side through job losses, surgeries, cancer scares, funerals and births. And not a day goes by that he doesn't tell me he loves me, kiss me goodnight or brag endlessly about a meal that I've just prepared.

We have laughed and cried and loved and fought our way through thirty-four years together, through the good times and the bad times but mostly through the everyday times. Love, I have learned, is not in diamonds and gold or a dozen long-stem roses sent once a year on a special occasion. Love is waking me up with a hot cup of coffee every day before work, warming my car up on a cold morning or rubbing my feet after a long hard day. These are the things that marriage is made of. These are the true gifts of love.

~Andrea Peebles

17

Our Second First Date

You know when you have found your prince because you not only have a smile on your face but in your heart as well.
~Author Unknown

"Well, hello Beth!" I stammered as I found my tall, blond friend from college standing on my doorstep. I hadn't expected company, but felt honored Beth considered our friendship close enough for her to swing by unannounced.

"What brings you to this part of town?"

"Oh, I just thought I'd drop in," Beth said as she stepped into the living room. I instantly morphed into a happy hostess.

"Won't you sit down? Can I get you anything to drink? How are classes going?"

Beth smiled as my husband, Jason, entered the room carrying our one-month-old son. After I chatted with Beth for a few minutes, Jason radically changed the subject with, "Kate, would you like to go for a walk?"

"Um… uh…" I hesitated, rather unsettled by Jason's lack of consideration for our guest. Beth had been sweet enough to come over. I didn't want to take advantage of her good nature.

In an effort to make up for my husband's poor manners, I opened the walking invitation up to Beth as well.

"Oh, no thanks," she grinned. "You guys go ahead. Really. I'll stay here with the baby."

"Well, are you sure?" I asked, still doubting the etiquette of the offer.

"Of course. You guys have fun!"

"Well, okay," I answered, determined to take just a short walk so Beth wouldn't regret her impromptu visit.

Jason drove me to Coolidge Park—a nearby recreational haven bordering the Tennessee River. I strode quickly around the green, so focused on returning home that I felt almost annoyed when Jason suggested we visit an artsy flower shop just across from the park.

"Alright," I muttered. "But only for a few minutes. I don't want to keep Beth waiting."

Jason smirked and opened the door for me. We ambled along aisles of pottery and paintings until we came to a display of orchids. Blooms of yellow, white, and purple dotted several shelves in the back of the shop. Soon I stood admiring a large fuchsia orchid.

"You like this one?" Jason asked.

"Oh yes. It's lovely."

Jason pointed to a small sign sticking out of the pot: "Sold."

Darn! I thought.

Then I looked closer. Printed on a separate label was: "Katie Mitchell"—my name!

I gasped in delight at Jason's thoughtfulness and intuition. But soon I pictured Beth trying to calm a fussy infant. We needed to get back.

Jason, however, took both my hand and potted plant and led me away from our car to a small café.

We didn't have time for lunch! What about Beth? She would never drop by again.

We followed the hostess to a table with a blue-and-white checkered cloth near the front window. I smiled uneasily and wondered at my husband—so attentive to me, yet so thoughtless toward our abandoned guest.

Then I glanced at the menu. My eyes widened. Tucked in front of the list of lunch selections lay a handwritten love letter from Jason.

It slowly dawned on me that Beth's "impromptu visit" had been planned all along by the amazing man sitting across from me.

I couldn't help tearing up at my husband's reaffirmation of his commitment to our relationship. The last month had been a taxing one, with the joy of meeting our first child, the duty of midnight feedings, and the recovery from my C-section. Our lives would never be the same. Yet this cleverly planned, postpartum date reminded me that while Jason and I were parents now, we were lovers first. By making our marriage a priority, I knew we would continue to be.

~Katherine Ladny Mitchell

The Teamwork of Marriage

Do not anticipate trouble or worry about what may never happen.
Keep in the sunlight.
~Benjamin Franklin

Last summer, my husband and I stopped at a lawn and garden center and bought ourselves an outdoor fabric gazebo. It was something we'd wanted for a while, so when they went on sale, we took the plunge.

Driving home, I could already envision sunny days and balmy nights, spent outside under the gazebo's shelter.

Back at the house, our enthusiasm was high, until we carried the box from the truck to the back yard and opened it.

For a moment, we didn't move. Our eyes were fixed on this single box, containing 162 pieces, along with a few pages of instructions for assembling the ten-foot-by-ten-foot gazebo.

After the shock wore off, we looked at each other, as if to say, "What have we gotten ourselves into?"

I was designated the official instruction reader.

"Okay," I said, and cleared my throat. "Step one says, 'Fix the Panel A on the Panel B by using M6X35 bolts and nuts, which is Part L. Repeat this three times.'"

Our eyes met. I raised one eyebrow in a question mark.

Stan laughed. "Well, I guess we need to look for Panels A and B."

Within minutes, my handy man had Panels A and B completely upright. That left the nuts and bolts, and since I was also the keeper of the plastic bag, which was officially called Part L, I cut it open and offered up the M6X35 nuts and bolts, precisely as directed. While I steadied the panels, Stan secured them with the hardware.

It got harder from there. We discovered a few of the parts were flawed, so Stan had to improvise. Then there was his tendency to skip ahead in his thought process, thinking he knew what was coming.

I found myself saying things like, "Wait on that part," and, "No, that comes later," or, "According to the directions, blah, blah, blah." Other than these exchanges, we rarely talked.

At times, I could feel my husband watching me impatiently, as I fumbled in search of some elusive piece to the puzzle. I pretended not to notice. Putting together a gazebo required my total concentration.

Other times, I stood back and watched him work, admiring how he smiled whenever another step was crossed off the instruction list.

In our long marriage, this was not the first thing we had attempted to put together. Through the years there were dollhouses and baby doll strollers, swing sets, and an entertainment center or two. We knew the drill.

All of these occasions had taught us a lot about how a partnership is supposed to operate:

1. It takes two participating individuals to make it work.

2. There's a right way to do things, and there's a wrong way. (Do it the wrong way, and you'll wish you hadn't.)

3. If you want to see the end results, you have to stay with it. (And that's the tough part—sticking it out when all you really want to do is split the scene.)

Marriage is a lot like that. It takes both of you to make it work. There's a right way to treat each other, and there's a wrong way. And if you give up when the going gets rough, you'll never know the joys that come from having hung in there, even when you wanted to quit... especially when you wanted to quit.

Three hours after arriving home with a cumbersome box of assorted parts, my husband and I high-fived and stepped back to admire the fruits of our labor. It no longer mattered that Part F and Part J did not measure up appropriately, nor that one of the nuts fell through a crack in the patio. The gazebo was standing tall and firm. Together, we had made it work.

Smiling, we admired our creation. Finally, we had our very own backyard gazebo—a place to enjoy morning coffee and evening conversations, and every time I look at it, to this day, I remember that we are a team.

~Dayle Allen Shockley

A Steamy Romance

*Those who bring sunshine to the lives of others
cannot keep it from themselves.*
~James Matthew Barrie

Walking in the back door, I kick off my shoes and throw my purse on the counter. I can't wait to sit down. Pulling off my socks, I uncover four raw blisters—badges of pride for a full day on my feet. Although exhilarating, my new job as a substitute teacher is an adjustment after ten years as a stay-at-home mom.

Searching the cupboard for Band-Aids, I notice the clock: 3:30. In just half an hour, my younger daughter will bound off the school bus, bustling with cursive handwriting papers, tales of gym and recess, and complaints about her grumbling stomach.

Rummaging through the cupboard, I find my salvation—a lone bag of microwave popcorn peeking from behind a bag of stale pretzels. Snack dilemma solved, I walk into my bedroom to change into jeans and collect two overflowing laundry baskets. Though I'd love to read a magazine or watch *Oprah*, I know I'd better throw in a load of my husband's Dockers and Polo shirts. How much longer can I ignore my daughters' hampers, overflowing with grimy jeans and spaghetti sauce-stained sweatshirts?

Guess I'd better wash the jeans before dinner. I can do the whites later.

Just as I'm about to drown in self-pity, I stop dead in my tracks.

I rub my eyes to make sure I'm not seeing things. Could that be a row of clean, perfectly pressed pants hanging in my closet? Weren't those the same Dockers and jeans that sat crumpled in a heap before I left for work?

Pulling on a pair of crisply creased khakis, I hurry into the laundry room. Where are the piles of grape jelly-encrusted T-shirts and pizza-stained capris? Sunlight glistens through the window, spotlighting my glorious discovery: two baskets of spotless jeans, tees, and sweatshirts, lovingly folded and sorted, as if by magic.

I touch the clothes to make sure they're for real. The laundry is done. All of it.

A warm tingly feeling, not unlike puppy love, jitters through my veins. He did this, just for me. I'm light and giddy, like a schoolgirl with a secret admirer.

As soon as the garage door creaks open, I'm there, ready with a welcoming kiss. "You didn't have to do all the laundry."

My husband shrugs, as if washing clothes is some type of recreational sport. "Just threw a few loads in during lunch. No big deal."

No big deal? A mountain of mind-numbing whites, darks, and cool-water washables? Sudsing and sorting and ironing, too? For a girl pressed for time, this was beyond romantic. Forget the chocolates and roses. Turns out, Tide and Clorox emit their own type of pheromones.

After fifteen years of marriage, I've discovered the secret to romance: a husband who whistles while he Woolites. What could be sexier than a guy who knows the difference between the spin cycle and permanent press? Nothing beats walking into the bedroom and finding my husband plugged into his iPod, dancing around the ironing board and pressing his dress shirts.

Now that I'm a working girl, I know it's wise to accept help in the domestic department. A closet full of perfectly pressed pants is a fine surprise any day. As far as I know, there are no heavenly rewards for sacrificial sudsing and sorting. I'd be better off listening to E.B. White's words of advice: "We should all do what, in the long run, gives us joy, even if it is only picking grapes or sorting the laundry."

For me, laundry is arduous: a weekly mountain to climb when I'd rather be playing with my girls. Why not accept a reprieve from a man who looks awfully smooth moving back and forth behind the steam iron? Why not teach my girls that washing clothes isn't necessarily "women's work?" If I pass the laundry basket into my husband's able arms, my hands will finally be free: to hug my girls and maybe even relax with a good magazine.

Suds, steam, and heat are surefire ingredients for true passion.

Add an ironing board and a helpful husband for love that spreads far beyond the laundry room.

~Stefanie Wass

"Who needs a Prince on a white horse when you've got one who does the laundry and irons!"

20

The Grandpa Who Became a Daddy

How old would you be if you didn't know how old you were?
~Satchel Paige

One thing's for sure. When you marry a man seventeen years older than you, a man who's about an inch away from his fiftieth birthday, the subject of more children doesn't crop up in normal conversation. His six and my three from our previous marriages were quite enough, thank you. But surprise, surprise!

When the pregnancy test came back positive I was a little hesitant to tell Harold. Hesitant? I was terrified. How do you tell a man who's dreaming of early retirement that he's about to embark on eighteen more years of child rearing?

Almost apologetically I broke the news. The way Harold responded, you'd have thought he was a thirty-year-old who'd been trying to father his first child for years. That very afternoon he rushed out to buy cigars and started handing them out to his friends.

Perhaps he thought about how babies bring on a feeling of perpetual youth. Or maybe he thought that having one of our own would really solidify our marriage. He'd probably seen that old Lucille Ball movie, *Yours, Mine and Ours*. Perhaps he was just glad he still had what it takes to become a father. Whatever it was, dear

Harold stomped through the tulips with glee when I told him the news.

For the first two and a half years after we were married, Harold's job kept him in Wisconsin during the week while my three children and I continued to live in northern Illinois. Of course we were together every weekend, but when I became pregnant my heart broke when I learned the childbirth classes at our local hospital were only offered on Tuesday nights. Harold had never been present during the birth of his other six children and I wanted him to experience the incredible joy and miracle of childbirth. But unless he took childbirth classes, the hospital staff wouldn't consider him fit for delivery room duty.

Undaunted by the miles and the three-hour-drive between us, Harold signed up to take childbirth classes by himself at a large hospital in Milwaukee. There he was, fifty-one years old, already a father to six and grandfather to six more, graying around the temples, sitting alone on the floor, week after week, learning how to pant and blow, pant and blow. He had to do some pretty fast talking to convince his classmates that he even had a pregnant wife.

When Andrew was born, Harold was a trouper. He coached and encouraged me through labor. In the delivery room he all but delivered the baby himself... even talked the doctor into letting him cut the umbilical cord.

For a man who had paced the hospital halls with a headache during the birth of his other children, I was extremely proud of his delivery room technique. He held our son, posed for pictures and developed a bond with Andrew within minutes of his birth.

As Andrew grew I noticed that although Harold did not get down on the floor and roughhouse with his young son as much as a younger man might, he and Andrew maintained that closeness initiated at birth.

Harold survived the terrible twos and the temper-tantrum-threes better than I did.

Perhaps it was innate grandfatherly wisdom that reminded him that all stages, no matter how exasperating, eventually pass.

Harold also remembered what it was like when his first brood was at home. Trying to support six children under eleven years of age on a 1950s teaching salary of about $5,000 a year gave him ulcers. But as a newly promoted high school principal he didn't have to worry whether his paycheck would cover the grocery bills.

When Andrew started school, his dad entered a new phase of life—senior citizen discounts. But in spite of his advancing years, Harold had no trouble keeping up with the younger generation. In the summer he and Andrew visited the zoo, took walks along the lake, and played catch. In the winter Harold instructed Andrew on the fine points of giving Dad good back and foot rubs in front of the TV. Andrew's reward was usually a big bowl of popcorn and then a piggyback ride to bed.

Naturally, there were days when Andrew put a vise-like strain on Harold's good nature. Like when Andrew hauled out his toy guitar and drums during the ball game on TV or during one of Harold's favorite old-time movies. Or when Andrew's unbridled energy and unreserved playtime sound effects broke the sound barrier. But then those were the times Andrew drove me up a skinny-limbed tree, too... so Harold's age was not a factor there.

Sometimes, though, Harold would think wistfully about retirement. Many of his contemporaries were planning to retire in four or five years. They talked about traveling and taking life easy. The words condominium, Sun City, and motor home punctuated their conversations. But not Harold. As he approached sixty he was still traveling to Little League games, music lessons, parent/teacher meetings and the orthodontist.

Often when Harold ran into an old friend the conversation usually went something like this:

"This little guy your grandson, Harry?"

"No, this is Andrew, my son."

"Oh, ya? Heh, heh, heh."

Harold just laughed it off. Sometimes he laughed so hard he cried. Sometimes he just said, "Why me, Lord?"

Everything considered, I'd have to say that a man in his fifties can definitely father a child with little worry about whether or not he can handle it. Harold always remembered the old saying about "Age is simply a matter of mind. If you don't mind, it doesn't matter."

~Patricia Lorenz

Author's Note: When Andrew was nine years old, his sixty-one-year-old father died of leukemia, a disease that can strike at any age. But in spite of losing his father at a young age, Andrew has good memories of his older dad... the grandpa who became a daddy... and loved every minute of it.

21

Private Displays of Affection

A wise lover values not so much the gift of the lover as the love of the giver.
~Thomas à Kempis

I have never seen my parents kiss. Not once. Not even a peck on the cheek. I would imagine that they have—at some point. There must have been some romance during their courtship. But publicly, no one, as far as I know, has witnessed a display of affection between my mom and dad—except for the day they were married.

My mom has tolerated my dad's disinterest in all things amorous for almost thirty-five years and has rarely made mention of it. I'm sure that she would like to have some daisies on her birthday or a box of chocolates for Valentine's Day, but she is past the point of turning something frivolous into an argument. On more than one occasion, she has told me, "I know how to find the candy aisle in the store. No big deal."

"Well, that's not how it will be when I got older," said a younger, much more naïve version of myself. "My husband will bring me flowers every afternoon when he comes home from work. I will get sparkling jewelry for no particular occasion, cuddly puppies on Valentine's Day, and expensive European chocolates at least once a month."

My mom smiled and said, "That sounds nice, honey."

Today, my mom and I are a lot alike. We both enjoy travel, a well-written book, a delicious meal, and jobs that offer intrinsic rewards. We are also married to very similar men—men who don't have any interest in shopping for flowers, planning a surprise party, or holding hands in the middle of a crowded street.

Funny how things work out, huh?

Interestingly enough, they are working out—quite well. My husband Craig and I were married almost six years ago. He did kiss me during our ceremony but I felt him cringe just a little. After all, a lot of people were watching. I could probably count on my hands the number of times I have received flowers from him, and I have only gotten jewelry once, other than my wedding ring.

I don't have any stories to share about a romantic wedding proposal, a surprise trip to Tahiti, or a Christmas puppy with a red ribbon around his neck. I live a modest life with few surprises and minimal luxuries. But here's what I do have:

I have a husband who always consults me before making major purchases. I have a husband who is not afraid to take on a load of laundry or cook a meal when I'm knee-deep in lesson plans. He has even tackled the bathrooms when I have been incredibly swamped with work. He does what needs to be done around our house and he never complains.

Last year, I commented that I was tired of getting wet grass on my shoes when walking from our house to the detached garage. The following weekend, Craig spent six hours building me a walkway. He carefully dug up the earth and arranged large bricks in a semicircle that led from the driveway to the garage. It was a beautiful gesture and my shoes have remained dry since. But I must admit that my eyes were a little wet when I first saw his work.

A few months ago, I was almost in tears from the effort of trying to organize my closet. I was having a lot of trouble finding what I needed to get ready for work. My closet has always been my worst enemy and I wanted desperately to have more space for my favorite garments.

Without being asked, Craig came into the bedroom and offered suggestions that would make better use of my space: labeling shoe boxes, stacking slacks and sweaters, putting purses in crates, and storing rarely worn items under the bed. He helped me finally win the battle of the closet — I had been fighting it for years.

Just recently, Craig sat beside me in the emergency room while I waited for test results. He pretended to haphazardly attach various monitors to my body and examine me with several instruments. We were laughing so hard when the doctor finally returned that I was afraid I might be admitted — to the psych ward. Craig always finds a way to bring humor into the most stressful situations.

Craig is patient, supportive, respectful and kind. He is a true partner and a friend who improves my mood and the quality of my life. He may not kiss me in public, but that's okay. Those moments are ours, just between the two of us.

Valentine's Day will be rolling around soon. I know a lot of women will probably unwrap some pretty jewelry or receive a bouquet of flowers. Craig might get me a card. He might not get me anything. But I will not feel any less loved. I never have.

Sure, there are some days when I wouldn't mind having a sparkly bracelet or a box of candy. But fortunately, I am a lot like my mom. And I have known my way around the mall for a long time.

~Melissa Face

Married *Life!*

Chapter **3**

Because You Loved Me

When one is in love, a cliff becomes a meadow.

~Ethiopian Proverb

22

Loopy Love

If you tell the truth you don't have to remember anything.
~Mark Twain

"And then, they took me into the intimidation room where they... they pulled out this big scary machine and started to torture me," he said as his eyelids drooped slowly again. I held his hand and brushed my fingers gently over his forehead and back into his hair.

"That must have been so scary, honey!" I said as I winked at the nurse checking his vitals. "You're so brave, sweetheart."

My husband Jim had gone in for a medical procedure and was now in the recovery room waiting for the anesthesia to wear off. He was normally strong, coherent, and rational, but today he was a groggy, grown man sitting like a toddler, wrapped in a blanket with both legs out straight. His tennis shoes were untied and dangling off the bed and he had both hands wrapped around a 7UP he was happily slurping from a bendy straw.

When I first walked into the recovery room, he was mimicking a fighter pilot with his arms out—floating over a terrain of twists and turns, dipping his head to go down into valleys and then nodding his chin upwards toward the hospital ceiling to fly over the imaginary peaks.

Every five minutes or so, he'd ask how I was, wondered about the dog who happened to be waiting in the car, expressed his deep desire for pizza, and told me about a nurse who apparently had very hairy arms. Each round of questioning brought him a step closer to consciousness as I assured him once again that the dog and I were both fine, pizza would be the first stop on the way home, and it wasn't nice to talk about someone's arms that way.

Internally I giggled at his imaginative and expressive stories and secretly wished I'd brought the video camera so he could laugh along with me once he finally came back to earth. His ability to make me laugh, even in the most trying circumstances, has been a form of anesthesia that has served to ease some of the pain felt over the years from lost loved ones, unexpected illness, and a multitude of other nuisances life has thrown our way. It has been a glue formed by a mixture of secret stories, inside jokes, winks across a crowded room, devilish smirks in the middle of dinner with the grandma, and end-less silly pranks.

Though generally his teasing and trick playing are benign, I wasn't so sure about the effects of the medications he was under at the moment. So far, the anesthesia had been a truth serum, rendering useless any filtering devices that would have normally kept his ran-dom and sometimes inappropriate and socially awkward comments in check. For a moment I worried that it wouldn't be long until he started in on how much weight I'd gained since we got married, how horrible of a cook I'd turned out to be, or any of the other countless quirks I contribute to the marriage.

But he never mentioned any of that. Instead, he jabbered for a while about pizza and the dog and then remarked that the scrubs one of the nurses was wearing were so blue they hurt his eyes. I tried to shush him, but he turned towards me and mentally stopped dead in his tracks.

"You are so beautiful!" he exclaimed through the glaze in his eyes. I started to blush and then noticed a shade of worry suddenly panning across his face. He leaned close and whispered, "Am I a good husband to you?"

"Oh, honey." I smiled, feeling a piece of my heart melt. "Of course you're a good husband! I could never ask for anyone better," I promised.

"Are you sure? I mean, I don't ever want to sell you short," he said.

Then, with intense concentration, he grabbed my hand and pulled me close to him. I bent down and waited expectantly for another heartfelt sentiment. He thought deeply for a moment and then said, "You know, on second thought, I think I'd like a milkshake instead of pizza." He mused, sitting back and falling into his trance again.

"Sure, sweetie." I laughed and thought I should have seen that one coming. "We can get you a milkshake."

Though he doesn't remember anything from that day, I will always look back and smile when I think about it. We left the hospital with more funny stories than I can count, but what sticks with me a few years later is the fact that even the most powerful drugs couldn't keep him from pronouncing his care and concern for me. When his inhibitions were lowered and the verbal filter was broken, he was still gracious, kind, and compassionate towards me. Amidst the conflict between a milkshake and pizza and imagining airplanes and intimidation rooms, deep down in his core, there was a man who still cherished me above all else.

~Kara Johnson

My Long-Suffering Co-Pilot

If we are facing in the right direction, all we have to do is keep on walking.
~Buddhist Saying

It's hard to quantify how lousy my sense of direction is. If I had to guess, I'd venture to say that, at fifty-three, my frequent navigational goofs have added up to a total of five solid years of my life spent completely and hopelessly lost. And that's just while driving. If you factor in false steps on foot, you're up to seven years.

The two years squandered getting lost on foot I can live with. After all, the average adult spends two years of his life just waiting for the guy ahead of him at the post office to pick between the American flag or the Legends of Boogie-Woogie stamps.

It's the five years lost in my car that makes me melancholy. After countless misguided journeys left me older but no wiser, my wife and long-suffering co-pilot, Sherry, suggested I keep a travel journal to chronicle trips of various durations, monitor driving patterns and—hopefully—learn from my mistakes.

Submitted for your amazement and pity are a few excerpts from that journal.

Orlando, August 2006
While driving from our hotel to a nearby attraction called Church Street Station, my wife and I become lost. What

makes this unremarkable event remarkable is that once off the highway we actually see Church Street Station. In fact, we see it several times at close range as we drive from block to block. The problem is that a series of one-way streets keeps us from making the turns we want to make and soon Church Street Station disappears into the night.

Just when it appears things can't get worse, the lighted, paved road we are on turns into an unlighted, dirt road and dead-ends abruptly at a metal gate by some rundown warehouses on the outskirts of the city. My wife, who has been uncommonly quiet for the last few minutes of our descent into oblivion, turns and says: "Is this the part where we stumble onto a drug deal going down and are bound and gagged while they take our car?" She's such a kidder.

New Jersey, October 2009

While back in my home state for a cousin's wedding, I decide to show my wife some of my old stomping grounds. Things go pretty well at first as I successfully find my way back to my first apartment, the office I worked at right out of college, and the state park where I use to hike. But heading back to the hotel it all unravels. It seems that some of my "old stomping grounds" were stomped on by other people in the years since I left. Their overzealous and gratuitous stomping resulted in new roads, new scenery, and more opportunities for me to get spectacularly, irreversibly lost.

Soon, we find ourselves in a gritty, bars-on-the-windows kind of town with the gas gauge almost on empty, darkness falling fast, and the sound of broken glass crunching under our tires as we stop for a red light. My wife, who has been uncommonly quiet for the last few minutes of our plunge into purgatory, turns and says: "Is this the part where we run out of gas, are taken hostage by a drifter named 'Skunk' and are featured in a story on *Dateline* entitled 'Last Exit to Horror Cabin'?" I'm telling you, she's such a joker.

Tijuana, April 2011

While sightseeing in California in our rented van, I accidently cross the U.S./Mexico border into Tijuana. At the border checkpoint, my wife and I explain our mistake to the Mexican crossing guard, asking if we could simply turn around and head back to the U.S. side. As he confers with another crossing guard, both gesturing disdainfully in our direction, we get the idea that "simply turning around" is not in the cards.

"You must drive through and follow signs back to border," the guard snarls, motioning vaguely in the direction of downtown Tijuana.

As we forge on to find our way along Tijuana's turbulent streets and alleys, we realize that following signs back to the border would require several things we don't have going for us: luck, a sense of direction, and the ability to speak Spanish.

After plenty of wrong turns, we somehow wind up in a restricted commuter lane as we head back to the border. A pack of crossing guards converge on the van.

"W-w-what's wrong?" I stammer, taking care to keep my hands where they can see them.

"Silence!" our friendly crossing guard erupts. "You are not authorized to use the Sentri commuter lane. Out of the van!"

My wife, who was uncommonly quiet for the last few minutes of our south of the border adventure, turns and says: "Is this the part where we're taken off to a Mexican jail?" Such a wacky imagination, that wife of mine has.

So what have I learned about my horribly deformed sense of direction from my travel journal experiment?

I've learned that when I come to an intersection and confidently go left, I should have gone so far to the right it would make a conservative Republican proud. I've learned that when I decisively go straight ahead, I should have turned twenty miles back while there were still useful landmarks like buildings and living people. And I've learned that I can continue to count on being an accidental tourist, paying tolls on roads I shouldn't have been on, and asking directions at gas stations so far removed from where I'm going that the name of my destination is "a new one" on the locals.

Just last night, coming home from work, I got detoured into an unfamiliar neighborhood and lost my bearings. As I circled the same streets for the third time, I could almost hear my wife say, "Is this the part where we decide to buy a home here and start life fresh instead of trying to find our way back out to the main road?"

My wife. She sure makes a lot of sense sometimes.

~Alan Williamson

He Knows Me Well

*One thing you learn in a long marriage
is how many sneezes to wait before saying, "Bless you."*
~Author Unknown

Years ago, shortly after my second child was born, I took up swimming laps to get in shape. I bought a Master padlock for my swimming locker. It was a beauty—a brilliant red body with black lettering and a shiny silver hasp. Seems like a strange thing to grow fond of but a red padlock is a whole lot more zippy than one of those plain silver ones. Plus it was really easy to pick out as I staggered around the locker room at six in the morning.

A few years later, we bought a little farmhouse out in the country and moved out of our city house. My swimming habit died out with the distance. My poor lock went into the junk drawer and over time I forgot the combination.

One day, while cleaning up a pile of paperwork, I found the magic numbers. Excited that at last I could once again use my scarlet beauty, I immediately went to the Rolodex and filed the little laminated chunk of paper.

Months later, my daughter needed the lock for school. I nearly cackled in my glee, "I know where the combination is!" and ran to the Rolodex.

I started with L. No combination. I tried M for Master. No combination. I tried C and P too but there was no combination to my padlock anywhere. I went through it again. Not under lock. Not under combination. Not under Master. I absolutely knew I'd filed that slip of paper. I just didn't have a clue what letter I'd filed it under.

I stomped into the kitchen. Bill was working away at the counter on supper and I let loose, telling him all about how I was certain I had filed the missing combination, and now it was nowhere to be found. Bill got a little smile on his face.

"What?" I said irritated.

"Have you checked under R for red?" he asked.

I rolled my eyes. "Why would I file it under that? That's goofy."

Bill shrugged. "I'm just saying maybe you should check under R."

"Sure," I said and stomped out again. There was no way I'd filed those numbers under red.

Later that night, I was addressing some cards and had the Rolodex out. Maybe I should go through it one more time, I thought. I pulled up the cards under C for starters. Nothing. Next I flipped through to L. Not a number to be had. Since I was right there in the alphabet, I continued through the M's. Nope. Bill's words went through my head, "Maybe you should try R for red."

Now I knew that made absolutely no sense. But I also knew that those numbers were in that Rolodex somewhere; all I had to do was find them. I flipped to the R's.

The very first card under R was written in my handwriting. A small laminated form with a series of numbers was taped to the card. In big letters at the top, it said Red Combination Lock.

I walked into the kitchen where Bill was measuring out coffee for tomorrow's brew. He looked up at me as I came in, eyebrows raised.

"You were right," I said. "I filed the combination under R for red."

He started to laugh, which got me started too. Then he gave me a hug.

"How did you know?" I said. "That makes absolutely no sense."

He went back to setting the timer on the coffeemaker, shrugging as he said, "I just know you."

Yes, he does.

You know what one of the best things about being married is? If you ever forget who you are, there's always somebody around to help you figure it out.

~Theresa Woltanski

Mamas Don't Get Sick

You can give without loving, but you can never love without giving.
~Author Unknown

This has been the longest winter of my life. It started the day I remarked to a friend how healthy the kids had been. Now, I can't remember a time when one of them wasn't sick with something. They started with the nasal cruds. They all had it and passed it back and forth for a few weeks. It traveled from their sinuses to their chests and back again. We played musical humidifiers and bought Kleenex by the case.

From there we had a bout with a relentless stomach thing. We went from forgetting what the inside of our pediatrician's office looked like, to a standing appointment every Monday. (What is it with sick children and weekends?)

About the time we were back on solid foods, we began our strep throat marathon. Every few days, just as I began to breathe a sigh of relief, I'd hear the words I'd come to dread. "Mommy, my throat hurts."

But through it all, I'd managed to keep myself well. And, at last, I could see the light at the end of the tunnel. The kids were back in school and the baby was on a semi-normal schedule. That's when it hit me! The flu! I can't do this, I thought. I'm the one who keeps this show on the road. I don't have an understudy! I tried ignoring it.

It came on with achy muscles, cold chills, and hot sweats. It drained me of my energy and completely shut down my brain. All I could think about was crawling under the covers and never coming out. I'm not sure how I made it through the morning. The afternoon was a blur. By four o'clock, I used the last bit of strength I had to call my husband David at his office. My plan was to beg him to come home and bury me in a shallow grave in the back yard. As soon as he heard my voice, he said, "I'll be right home." I would have cried if I'd had the energy.

I collapsed on the couch where I could see the kids and waited for the crunch of his tires on the driveway. As soon as I heard it, I lurched toward the bedroom and aimed myself toward the bed. When I opened my eyes, again, it was dark outside. The house was quiet. I listened for the sound of "Daddy play." You know how it works. They start off wrestling. The noise level gets louder and louder. Then, someone gets hurt or too sleepy or overly excited and everyone runs for Mom. I waited for the stampede to head my way and started mustering the strength to resume my duties.

I must have dozed off again, because the next thing I knew, it was morning. I felt human, again—even hungry. Must have been a twenty-four-hour bug, I thought. Thank God! I headed out of the bedroom bracing myself for the mess that awaited me. The family room wasn't bad. My eyes scanned it critically. Those blocks didn't go in that bucket. I walked into the kitchen and saw the pots washed but still sitting in the dish drain. David had swept the floor but left the broom and dustpan leaning against the kitchen wall. Then, I saw the kids sitting around the table. David, who to my knowledge couldn't boil water, had thrown together a breakfast of eggs, bacon, toast and orange juice. Molly was dressed in an outfit she'd outgrown last year. She looked like she'd brushed her own hair and Haley's shoes were on the wrong feet. They spotted me and began to smile. David stood with a skillet in one hand grinning, as though he held a dozen roses. Shame on me for picking apart his efforts.

No, the house wasn't the way I would have had it. But he'd taken the time to straighten it up. He'd kept the kids quiet so I could sleep and he even cooked. The man who never misses a day of work was standing in front of me on a Wednesday in jeans and a sweatshirt ready to spend the day filling my shoes. Suddenly I felt loved—completely, unconditionally, and profoundly loved. I'd hoped to feel indispensable. But instead I felt appreciated. I'd tried to be disappointed. But instead felt lucky—lucky to have been sick, lucky to have a family that loves me so much, and was glad for a chance to prove it.

I'm back on my feet now and waiting to find out to whom I've passed my flu germs. I have my thermometer ready and have restocked the Kleenex supply. Bring it on, whatever's next. We can handle it. Summer will be here, soon, and with it the end of the longest winter of our lives.

~Mimi Greenwood Knight

My Nights in a Tent

How glorious a greeting the sun gives the mountains!
~John Muir

Once a year my husband and I enter that storage unit most of us have called the "garage," to revisit all those treasures we thought we just couldn't live without. He wants to throw out those bottles I have saved for the day I might make flavored oils. I want to toss those small jars he saves for that oddball screw, nut and bolt. We anguish a little, laugh a lot, and end up pitching it all.

Then there's that shelf with all the camping gear we never use. The Coleman stove for wonderful outdoor cooking, the coffee pot for hot chocolate, the special toaster that fits on the grill, the sleeping bags, and of course the tent made for two.

My husband grew up camping. His stories are colorful and fun. They are fun to hear, but I think my allergies act up just listening to stories about being one with nature.

Every year I feel guilty as he scans the shelf, looking at it with such longing. I immediately start planning our next vacation to Europe, Hawaii, Mexico, a cruise... anything to take his mind off that tent.

For many years I've dodged the word camping. Last year the guilt finally set in. I poured a glass of wine, took a deep breath and told my husband I'd love to spend some time in a tent with him. You'd have thought we were going on an around-the-world cruise.

For me it was an "open to buy!" I went to the 99¢ Only Store and bought a plastic container, filling it with tablecloth, silverware, knives, pans, detergent, sponges, etc. All the things I thought I might need to set up housekeeping outdoors. I do love to cook so I filled the cooler with chops, steaks, sausages and all the wonderful foods I felt we needed for our camping trip my way… "gourmet."

The hours my husband spent planning our destinations was a treat in itself. I knew I had made the right decision. I hoped and prayed I'd made the right decision.

Our trip was to be two weeks: some camping, some hotels thrown in because I was such a "great wife," and then some more camping.

Living in California we headed for Las Vegas. We stayed the first night with friends and hit the casinos. That wasn't bad. I was going to like this. Then on to Utah! It was September and all the leaves were changing. It was so beautiful. My husband found a wonderful camp-site near a lake and set up my kitchen. As I prepared pork chops for dinner he set up our tent. The lantern was hung from a tree near the stove and as I watched the bugs fly around that light all I could think of was "how many are falling into this food?" Dinner was just as he had described, with everything tasting better over an open fire. I made s'mores and felt young again. We spent the evening huddled close, sharing stories of our youth. That night, our first night in a tent, was COLD. But it's amazing how warm two bodies are when they are snuggled in a sleeping bag.

We went to Fort Bridger and Fort Casper in Wyoming. We wandered Deadwood, home of Calamity Jane and Wild Bill Hickok. We marveled at the wonder of Mount Rushmore. We saw the progress of the mountain carving of Crazy Horse. We traveled to Little Bighorn and onto Yellowstone. Old Faithful was faithful and the geysers were a sight from prehistoric times. We picnicked in the fields below the Grand Teton National Park. We even cowboy danced in Jackson Hole, Wyoming.

That shelf in the garage holds new meaning for me. It's no longer a shelf I'm longing to clean out, but a shelf I love to visit, even silently by myself.

And I truly love that tent!

~Kristine Byron

Along Came Leonard

Success in marriage does not come merely through finding the right mate, but through being the right mate.
~Barnett R. Brickner

My first adventure as part of a couple lasted thirty-three years and was a traditional marriage for its time (Dick and I were married in 1953). He commuted to work in the city while I taught school in our neighborhood. When I became pregnant with our first child I retired, because "a mother's place is in the home." Dick agreed with me. In our world, daddies earned the money and mommies took care of all things domestic — the cooking, cleaning, laundering, childraising, and nursing whoever was sick on any given day. Mommies didn't get sick — they never had the time.

Because we'd both grown up with this model, my husband and I felt comfortable with the pattern and it worked for us. Dick's advances in his career were not considered his alone. They were our victories. His disappointments were not his setbacks, they were ours. We thought of ourselves as a single unit. When he died, I felt like half of me had died with him.

Life went on. It had to. But I didn't believe I would ever be whole again. Food lost its taste — talking to an empty chair over dinner added no flavor. There was no laughter in the house.

Friends included me in their social activities as before, but I was the zombie in the crowd. Still, it was a life, and after about two years it felt normal to me and I saw myself continuing that way forever.

Then the phone call came. Hal, a fellow educator, now retired, wanted me to have dinner with a friend of his. The man had recently lost his wife to the same cancer that had claimed Dick. Hal thought we could help each other. I didn't think I needed help. I'd settled into my routine. I did not want my life disturbed again. I said no.

"Just have dinner with him… for me," Hal urged.

Reluctantly, I agreed. Maybe I could help this newly widowed man. I'd walked the lonely road he traveled now.

"His name is Leonard," Hal said. "I gave him your phone number. He'll be calling you."

We had dinner and played "who do you know," since he had recently retired from the school district where I still worked. We found we had many of the same friends, although our own paths had never crossed. We shared school stories and laughed. We talked about the trauma of losing our mates and fought back tears. We lingered over dessert, engrossed in conversations of discovery. By the time we said good night, I felt I'd known him all of my life.

Many more dates followed. After a while, it seemed as if we were spending all our available time together, even when our interests didn't match. Leonard was a runner; I was a couch potato. I learned to half walk, half trot my way through competitive races so we could do them together.

Baseball bored Leonard, but I was obsessed with it. He'd join me, a magazine tucked under his arm, so we could share peanuts and hot dogs for our dinner. He enjoyed his reading material while I rooted for the home team.

Leonard was a political conservative; I was a flaming liberal. We talked politics by taking good-natured pot shots at each other.

We were so different; what was the attraction? We didn't try to figure it out. All we knew was that we felt whole again in each other's company, and that was enough. We married during my winter break from school, with all of our grown children there.

We would use my two weeks off from work for our honeymoon.

I looked forward to it, remembering my first one. It was my model for what a honeymoon should be. Dick and I had gone to a luxurious resort hotel in the White Mountains of New Hampshire, where we lazed in the sun by the lake or pool, staff people always ready to fulfill our every wish. We slept late and had room service bring us breakfast. We dined on elegant cuisine in the dining room every evening, followed by a show or dance orchestra to entertain us. I felt like a fairy tale princess. I was more than ready to relax into another such honeymoon.

But Leonard's idea of a nuptial trip was different than mine. He flew us off to the Pacific Rim on the longest airplane ride of my life. We rose early each morning and ate modest meals on the run as we trekked around Malaysia, Thailand, Singapore, Macau and Hong Kong on our own. He had been to these places before and was eager to show them to me. I'd forgotten to tell him I was the stay-at-home type who liked the familiar.

In the end, it didn't matter. The sights and sounds, the tastes and smells of cultures so different from my own became addictive. I learned to use toilets that consisted of a drain hole in the floor. I survived wild rides in tuk-tuk taxis — rickshaw type carriages attached to motorcycles whose drivers sped through Bangkok's traffic so perilously close to cars and buses that a bent arm could have cost me an elbow. In another part of Thailand, I was fascinated by the boats of the floating market, laden with their flowers and produce for sale.

In Malaysia, I replaced my tank tops with blouses that had sleeves because I felt conspicuous having uncovered arms in that Muslim country. I was careful in Singapore not to drop a tissue on their spotlessly clean streets. By the end of our honeymoon, I had caught Leonard's lust for travel and adventure.

It was hard to get up and head off for school on my first day back at work. My desk was piled high with tasks and I was interrupted constantly by teachers and fellow administrators dropping by with congratulations, chatter, and problems to be solved. I stayed long after the last bell of the day to catch up with the most urgent matters on my desk. It was close to 6 p.m. when I arrived home, exhausted.

Something strange was going on. Mouthwatering aromas were coming from the kitchen, where I found Leonard tending to pots heating on the stove. The table was set with napkins, dishes, silverware and wine glasses.

"What's going on?" I asked.

Leonard looked up. "I'm making dinner," he said.

"Why?" I asked, still astounded at the sight of a man in the kitchen.

"Why not?" He looked surprised that I would ask. "You're working, I'm not. Sit down, food's ready."

I pulled out a chair and obeyed. Pot roast, mashed potatoes, carrots, and a tossed green salad magically appeared in front of me. Leonard sat down and poured the wine. We clinked glasses. "To us," we said and took our first sips. I lifted my filled fork to my lips and ate.

The kitchen had always been my domain. Obviously, this new husband of mine did not follow the traditional marriage model. Here was another difference between Leonard and me, but this one was deliciously easy to accept. It took no adjustment at all.

~Marcia Rudoff

Bright and Shiny

Gratitude is the best attitude.
~Author Unknown

As Christmas approaches, I usually start hinting to my husband about potential gifts for me. I'll say things like, "Gee hon, that's a lovely necklace they have over at the mall." Or, "There are a ton of new books at Barnes & Noble I'd love to read."

But over the years, I have learned that this tactic is not an effective one. For many years I struggled to understand my husband's lack of ability to understand "hints." Was he just being stubborn? Were the items too expensive? Did he need to have his hearing checked?

It was last Christmas, when I finally began to understand my husband. Under the Christmas tree, was a large box wrapped with beautiful holiday paper. I was stunned. What could it be? I was pleased that my husband had finally thought of me. He wrapped the present slowly and carefully. This was unusual as gifts from my husband usually come in plain envelopes or white plastic shopping bags.

Was it a music box, a snow globe or perhaps a lovely figurine?

"Nope," my husband said. I would just have to wait to find out.

On Christmas morning, I eagerly opened the present to see what my thoughtful husband had so carefully selected for me. I ripped off the paper, tore open the box and starred at my present with disbelief. Inside the box, sat a beautiful... colander.

I looked curiously at my husband. Was this a joke? Was my real present cleverly concealed underneath this kitchen utensil? No... nothing underneath.

My husband looked at me and smiled, quite pleased with his purchase, certain that I was going to love it. Now, I must admit, it is the most beautiful colander I have ever seen. It is shiny and metallic, almost too expensive-looking for draining pasta or washing lettuce. It sparkles under the light.

"I know you need one," Pete said, "and this one looks so pretty. When I saw it, I thought of you."

It was then that I realized how fortunate I am to have this wonderful man in my life. He does not place value on material things. He does not try to impress others. He sees the beauty in things that appear ordinary. But most importantly, he knows just what I need, whether it is a long silent hug, some straightforward advice or just a single comment that breaks my tense mood and makes me laugh. By embracing the beauty of this simple colander, he made me realize that he is the perfect father to our children and the perfect husband for me, for he truly sees what others cannot.

I realized that like this ordinary colander, I too am an ordinary mom with an ordinary function. But to my husband I am not like this colander because it is ordinary, I am like this colander because I am an ordinary mom who is also bright and shiny. To him, I sparkle. To Pete I am one-of-a-kind and for that, I am grateful.

I use this colander a lot, and every time I do, I laugh out loud. I think it is hilarious how this shiny, beautiful, ordinary kitchen utensil that I use every day is what made my husband think of me.

Now, while I do appreciate my one-of-a-kind colander, this year I have a new tactic for Christmas, I handing him a picture of a lovely diamond necklace.

I hope this time he gets the hint.

~Lisa Peters

29

Incompatible

Music is what life sounds like.
~Eric Olson

It's 3 a.m. and I'm lying in bed beside him thinking how totally incompatible we are. We went to a brilliant play this afternoon—*Brief Encounter*—with some of the most creative staging I've ever seen, and he thought it was "boring." And we came home and watched a gripping *Brothers and Sisters* episode on television, and at every commercial he switched to the Knicks game. How could he not be able to sit through one of my TV shows once a week without interrupting it with bits and pieces of a basketball game? What ever made me think we were suited to each other?

A song begins to run through my mind... "Incompatible... that's what you are; Incompatible... though near or far..." What was that song and who sang it? It suits us to a "T."

"Are you awake?" he asks.

"Yes, and I'm trying to think of a song that goes tum de dum de dum, that's what you are..."

"What time is it?" he asks groggily.

"Three a.m. and what is the song that goes tum de dum de dum... that's what you are? It was sung by a famous black singer... I can't think of his name."

"Are you trying to think of his name or the song?" he says, beginning to come awake.

"Both. Tum de dum de dum. His daughter sang it with him after he was dead."

"Um, yes. I've got it. Cole Porter."

"Cole Porter was not a black singer and his daughter didn't sing with him when he was dead."

"How could she sing with him if he was dead?"

"Never mind that. She just did. All right. I'll tell you the words and they apply to you. Incompatible... that's what you are..."

"You're lying there in the middle of the night and singing a Cole Porter song that says I'm incompatible?"

"It's not a Cole Porter song... it's this famous black singer...."

"Should we get up and look it up on the Internet?"

"At three o'clock in the morning you want to get on the Internet? Yes, I think we should."

We get out of bed and feel our way into our office, each going to our own computers.

"How do you look up tum de dum de dum?" he asks.

"No, look up famous black singer."

"I think his name is Cole something."

"He's not named Cole. Whose daughter sang with him after he was dead? Look up that! And then look up the name of the song... "Incompatible... that's what you are!" I sing it again for him. "I will go crazy if I don't think of the name of the song and the singer."

"Are you sure it's not "Uncompatible... that's what you are?"

"It's IN..." I scream. "In-compatible!"

"Is it Nat King Cole?"

"Yes, that's it! That's it! That's it!"

"And his daughter Natalie?"

"Oh, yes, yes. Thank God, that's it!"

"And was the song 'Unforgettable... That's what you are?'"

"You've got it! You've got it! You're wonderful. Amazing!"

"And not 'Un-compatible?'" He leaned across to my computer and kissed me.

"In-compatible. No, you're incredible."

He sings, "It's three o'clock in the morning. Can we go to bed now?"

I follow him back to the bedroom and I curl around him, spoon style.

"Am I still incompatible?" he whispers.

I think for a minute. Who else would get up at three o'clock in the morning and look up a black singer whose daughter sang with him after he was dead?

"No, you're unforgettable! Go to sleep."

~Phyllis W. Zeno

30

Reforming a Road Runner

I travel not to go anywhere, but to go.
I travel for travel's sake. The great affair is to move.
~Robert Louis Stevenson

Sunday mornings with my wife are nice. We make eggs sprinkled with cheese, then linger over coffee and the Sunday paper… the concerns of the world far away.

Oddly enough, the scene makes me think of Lionel Richie. The man who sang "Dancing on the Ceiling" doesn't typically utter deep truths about the human condition, but he got it right in the song "Easy." Being easy like Sunday morning, to sit and be still, to be at peace and in the moment, is indeed a good way to be.

I like to think I'm easy like that, but part of me wants to move, to get going somewhere. I'm plagued by wanderlust. A Sunday morning is about the routine and familiar, about feeling at home, but deep down inside, I long to live new experiences, wake up in unknown places, and see things I may never see again.

In short, I want to hit the open road.

I've tried to suppress that feeling. Before I got married, I took two long road trips by myself. I'm settling down with a great woman, I thought. I can't keep wanting to drive off somewhere. I've got to get that out of my system.

The first trip was a three-week-long excursion through the south.

I hit sixteen states and drove more than 6,000 miles. The second trip was out to Iowa and Nebraska, destinations chosen for the simple reason that I had never before been there. That trek was about 4,000 miles.

My days were filled with rest stops, gas stations, and greasy spoons, and I spent my nights in cheap motels and friends' spare bedrooms. The road is about freedom and possibility, and with my car filled with maps, music, and junk food, I truly felt alive. The trips only fueled, not eased, my roadrunner instincts.

But through the miles, my future wife wasn't far from my thoughts. I missed her, and I made sure to call every night. We talked about her day, about my day and what I had seen, and about our future plans together. Before hanging up, we said that we loved each other.

We married in 2006. As we've made a life together, my feelings of wanderlust remain, though the last few years have begun a slow process of domesticating a wandering cowboy and bringing him in from the range.

In 2007, for instance, I got a real job. For a while, I was a full-time freelance writer, which represents the ultimate in freedom. You have no boss and no schedule. The world is your office.

Unfortunately, it doesn't pay very well, and before I got married, I actually moved back home with my parents to save money. Of course, as a married man, that was no longer an option, so I now work in an office and wear a tie.

In 2008, I got a new car. My old 1992 Nissan Stanza was pushing 170,000 miles and my wife thought I should get rid of it. The time had come, she said.

She was ultimately right, but men become attached to their cars, especially the reliable ones. The Stanza had been on many adventures. I felt sad to let it go.

Then this summer, my wife and I took the big step of property ownership. With our new condo, we have put down roots and staked our claim.

And so goes the slow march to responsibility. The only thing left to complete my transformation from wanderer to respected grown-up is children, and I'm not sure how I feel about that possibility.

I don't doubt that kids are fulfilling, that they make the world new for you again as they venture out into it, but at the same time, you grow selfish as you grow older. The longer you don't have children, the more you think about the changes they would bring to your life and what you'd be giving up to have them. Pondering children, I think about my freedom, and I think about the road.

But you can't stay on the road forever. Bruce Springsteen sings about being "born to run," and while that sounds great on the highway with the wind blowing through your hair, the truth is that you can't keep running.

Sooner or later, you must park the car. You must grow up, take a chance with someone, and be a part of something. You don't want to be John Wayne at the end of *The Searchers*, standing in the doorway, unable to come home and be at rest.

That's why I make sure to appreciate Sunday mornings. I still may have lingering thoughts of the road, but Sunday breakfast with someone you love is comfortable, nice and easy. Lionel was right.

~John Crawford

Married Life!

Chapter 4

Why Do Fools Fall in Love

*Love often makes a fool of the cleverest man,
and as often gives cleverness to the most foolish.*

~French Proverb

31

Critical Condition

Only two things are necessary to keep one's wife happy. One is to let her think she is having her own way, the other, to let her have it.
~Lyndon B. Johnson

Back when Erica, my wife, was merely Erica, my girlfriend, she was much more tolerant of my faults. My faults, in the beginning, were really just "foibles," "quirks," and "slight imperfections." But as time went on and various rings were purchased and distributed, things began to change. More and more, I began to hear about how things I'd done could have been done "differently."

Erica is a woman who is not afraid to speak up for herself and that's one of the things I love about her. If I'm really messing up, I appreciate being "kept honest." If, for example, I were to get drunk at a bachelor party and somehow charge ten thousand dollars at a gentleman's club, I'd be disappointed if she didn't at least say, "Hey, that's not cool."

But there are some things that she chooses to point out that I think just aren't worth the effort. Like when I use a paper towel in a situation where a napkin might be more appropriate. Or a napkin when she would have used a tissue. Or a tissue when I should have used an industrial strength power cleaner.

What bothers me most, however, is when I'm criticized for things for which I believed I deserved praise. While some husbands might get nagged for never doing the dishes, or for doing the dishes but not using enough soap, I get berated for doing the dishes and using too much soap. I've been reprimanded for taking out the garbage before the bag is completely full. I've been scolded for bringing my wife a glass of cold water that was "too full"—and by that I don't mean that it was overflowing, just that it was 11/16 full, while she was hoping for 5/8.

A few years ago, when the iPod just came out, she wanted one for Christmas. Not anticipating the popularity of this product, by the time I went shopping for it, it was completely sold out across the city. The iPod display cases at most stores looked like they had been in a nuclear attack. I managed to get one, however, from someone online. When Erica opened her gift, the first thing she said was, "When did you get this?" As lying is not one of my faults, I said "A couple of days ago." "Where did you get it?" When I explained the story about my adventure, she was not amused. I used to think that the problem was that my wife's expectations were too high. Now I realize that the problem is that they're way too specific.

Before getting married, I'd envision how thankful my wife would be when I volunteered to do some household chore like going grocery shopping. Now I dread shopping since Erica seems to see it as forty-seven opportunities for me to screw up. I'm given a list and I dutifully check off items as I shop. Most of the items, I have no trouble with. One jar of chunky peanut butter. Check. Four cans of tuna in oil. Check. I inevitably run into a few snags. I'm supposed to get cilantro, but I can't distinguish it from the Italian parsley. Then there are some items that they don't seem to have. Sometimes I'll call from the store and say, "I don't think they have Israeli couscous" and she'll respond "yes they do" as if I'd said they don't have any butter.

Rather than make that call, I'll sometimes get the thing that is most similar to what's on the list. I see on the list something like "toasted unsalted almonds." On the shelf I'll find two things that are close, but not exactly. There are raw unsalted almonds or toasted salted almonds. I need to make an executive decision about which is the more vital adjective. Contemplating which wrong item to choose is like choosing if you want to be executed by firing squad or by lethal injection.

Then there are the subjective things like "one medium sized onion" or, the worst of all, "something yummy for dessert." Finally, there are the things I don't even understand. Once when I was really cranking on a particular shopping spree, I was derailed by the mysterious word "mirepoix." (In case you are wondering, it's chopped up celery, onions, and carrots.)

Knowing that communication is very important in a marriage, I eventually confronted Erica with my concern. "I'm not asking you to never criticize me. But maybe you could only criticize me about twenty percent of the time that you're tempted to." She solemnly responded, "I already do."

A few years ago, there was a movie, *As Good As It Gets*, where Jack Nicholson tells Helen Hunt, "You make me want to be a better man." That's how I feel about my wife too. Maybe then she'd stop criticizing me.

~Gary Rubinstein

"I'd tell you why I'm mad, but It's difficult to translate into 'man'."

32

The Matchmaker

He that would the daughter win, must with the mother first begin.
~English Proverb

With the hairdryer going during our phone call it was possible that I hadn't heard her correctly so I turned it off in time to hear her say, "So I gave him your number and he'll probably call you on Sunday evening."

"Mom," I said with quiet anger, "who exactly will be calling me?"

"You'll love him. He's delicious," she cheered.

I turned the hairdryer back on, first to muffle the rest of the conversation and second to dry my hair so that I could leave my apartment and go over to my mother's to kill her.

At twenty-one, I had been on my own for two uneventful and relatively successful years, although according to my mother I was living like a rat in a dark hole.

Yes, my studio apartment had a shower stall in the kitchen and yes, my laundry basket doubled for my bookshelf and coat closet, but I was living without any parental assistance (financially at least) and working my buns off to stay proud and independent. I often times reminded my mother that it was her splendid job of raising me right that had given birth to this competent and newly minted young adult.

For some reason though my mother lacked confidence in two of my abilities—choosing the right foods and choosing the right men.

I'll give her the one in the nutrition department as I lived entirely on pasta and peanut butter. After all, they provided the necessary protein without the unnecessary expense.

When it came to the romance department however, I was never quite sure what she was quibbling about.

After all I had had just two boyfriends in my life thus far. Kevin, my first true love, forgot to mention to me that he was gay. When I chased him half across the country to find out what was bothering him he introduced me to Paul and told me I was the problem. You can't fault me for this outcome though somehow my mom managed to question my judgment as if I should have figured this all out at the tender age of sixteen.

The second love of my life, my boyfriend Wally, loved me through senior prom weekend and then decided (with urging from his mother) that he was too young to go steady and needed to play the field.

It was then and there that I developed this strong belief: true love existed only in the minds and imaginations of talented authors.

When I arrived at her apartment, my mom was humming softly while braiding my younger sister's hair.

"Hi honey, I didn't know you were stopping by."

"Could you please leave the room?" I asked my younger sister. "I need to talk to Mom alone." I realized I couldn't kill her… yet. After a heaping serving of meatloaf and mashed potatoes I calmed down long enough to listen to her story.

"I was attending a meeting at the local library and the moderator asked for comments and questions after his speech. This very handsome young man raised his hand and said some things that sounded as if they had come directly from your mouth. I couldn't believe my ears! The two of you have so much in common and I thought that you absolutely have to meet." I left without saying goodbye but I think (although I'm not 100% certain about this) I called her to complain again as soon as I got home.

When I regained my composure the following week I found out more details. My mom had become enthralled with this mystery man and approached him near Biographies as he was preparing to leave.

I'm aghast at what supposedly took place next. She signaled for him to come over with the "bended and slightly moving pointer finger gesture" accompanied by the "psssst" sound.

Apparently, (whether through kindness or embarrassment) he walked towards her and the following exchange took place.

"I have a daughter you would love."

"Thank you but I'm really not in the market for dating right now."

"You're not married, are you?"

"No, actually I'm recently divorced from my childhood sweet-heart and I have two very young children as well."

I guess he thought the above information would be substantial enough to send my mother home.

Oh no, not my mother. She proceeded with gusto!

"You seem very bright and I love what you said in there."

A nod from the kind stranger.

"May I ask how old you are?"

"I'll be thirty-two."

"My daughter is only twenty-one but she's incredibly mature for her age and I would love for you to meet her. The two of you seem to have so much in common. Here's her phone number. Why don't you give her a call next Sunday evening? She's usually home by seven or eight."

"By the way my name is Beth and my daughter's name is Lisa."

"I'm Stu. It was nice to meet you."

He didn't call the following Sunday (much to my mother's chagrin) because I imagine he wanted to avoid any daughter whose mother had to go out canvassing for her love life.

Unfortunately for all concerned though, they met up again two weeks later and this time there was no avoiding the inevitable. Stu approached my mother first and assured her he would be calling soon.

He called three days later. I thought he sounded very nasal (which I dislike immensely) and his name reminded me of beef. Nothing he said sounded remotely like anything I would ever think or say, so the "you have so much in common" comment lost its credibility. We agreed to meet the following evening at a local café.

I decided that I would have to prevent any future matchmaking attempts on the part of my mother. My plan was to embarrass and humiliate myself so that my mother would be embarrassed and humiliated too, and would never try to be a matchmaker for me again.

The evening of the dreaded date I borrowed a top from my landlady who just happened to be sixth months pregnant at the time. It looked like an elderly woman's housedress and managed to cover up any shape I might have had. Next I proceeded to plaster tons of hair gel on top of my head, creating a Mohawk effect, and then I tied my long hair into a tight ponytail to accentuate the look. I used enough black eyeliner to be competing with Morticia of *The Addams Family* fame. For the finishing touch I wore striking red lipstick that would have made Bozo proud.

Stu did not describe himself and my mother's description of him could not be trusted, so I sat in the predetermined location to be sure we spotted one another.

An unappealing man walked in, so I figured it was Stu. But he passed me by. One bullet dodged; one to go.

Moments later in walked the man I wished my mother would have realized was my type—rugged and muscular, with blue eyes and a boyish grin.

"Lisa?"

I looked directly at him.

No way, I thought. This can't be happening.

"Stu?" (I think I whispered but I can't be sure.)

He smiled and shook my hand.

I excused myself and bolted to the ladies room. Down came the hair. Off came the eyeliner. On came a delicate shade of pink lipgloss. The muumuu had to stay. That or risk indecent exposure.

I think I tried to breathe deeply. I don't think I was successful.

It was too crowded in the café and Stu suggested the diner across the street.

We sat for four hours and shared our life stories and even some of our secrets.

He told me he gets cold sores every few months. I told him I would never marry a man who gets cold sores and drinks chocolate milk.

He told me he hadn't asked me to. I told him he would.

There were no future matchmaking attempts on the part of my mother. She got it right on the very first try. This year Stu and I will celebrate our thirty-third wedding anniversary. The children Stu had mentioned to my mother so very long ago are now forty and forty-three with five magnificent children between them. Stu's childhood sweetheart (and ex-wife) is one of our dearest friends.

And the woman who made all this joy possible for me will turn eighty-eight this month.

And don't think she doesn't remind me on a regular basis what a marvelous job she did indeed.

~Lisa Leshaw

33

Chicken Soup
for the Soul

The Perfect Pair of Sunglasses

If men liked shopping, they'd call it research.
~Cynthia Nelms

Mike, my husband of thirty-plus years, said he needed to buy new prescription sunglasses and he said he wanted a pair that resembled his best friend Doug's non-prescription wraparound 1960s-style black ones. Mike thinks Doug is cool... very cool. I could tell Mike had his heart set on wraparound glasses but I couldn't help thinking, "With your strong prescription, astigmatism and narrower face you will have a very tough time finding glasses that fit and that will work, but you go, guy."

I said, "Mike, go ahead and do your research; then I'll go to the store and help you decide which pair to buy." After many years of marriage I had finally figured out an approach to shopping that makes him happy and saves my sanity; he works alone, at least at first. No matter what Mike decides to buy these days he does Internet research first; he investigates all possible models of whatever it is he needs, often creating a spreadsheet to more easily show me the possible choices and the pros and cons of each. In his next phase he visits actual stores; he checks out the different models, debates the merits of each with any and all available salespeople, then he leaves, empty-handed, returning home to ponder what he has just learned.

He will modify his spreadsheet to reflect newfound factoids, then share them with me. This process can go on for days or months, depending on the cost of whatever it is he's shopping for. Higher cost? More time spent in the research phase. Meanwhile, I stay home and do something more interesting, like pick cat hairs off my black coat.

My husband—cautious, frugal and a very deliberate decision maker—immediately did what I expected. He fired up his computer and researched sunglass frame possibilities for himself on the Internet. He figured out what size frame he needed, what size lenses (width and depth) he required for his progressive lens prescription, and what manufacturers made the size frame he wanted. He spent hours, many hours on the endeavor. Then he showed me his Internet-found frame selections.

"All good," I said. "But what store in our area sells these?"

Mike stared at me, wordless, then he retreated to his computer to do more research. He made a list. He called stores in our area. He called stores out of our area. He visited small boutique eyeglass stores in our area to talk with the people who worked there. No one carried the frame selections he'd seen on the Internet, but Mike, bless him, talked to a lot of salespeople trying to find a store where he could buy wraparound prescription sunglasses for himself.

One evening a few days after one of his eyeglass store forays, Mike told me he might just buy the frames online, then get someone to make and insert the lenses. I wondered out loud if the stores around here would fit frames that he hadn't purchased from them. He stared at me, wordless, then he retreated to our home office.

Still wanting one of the perfect frames he saw online, Mike returned an hour later and said that maybe he'd order the whole frame/lenses combination online. I put down my magazine, looked at him and said, "Sure. Okay."

Mike returned a short time later and said, "I can't order online; it won't let me. I'm getting a message that says I can't use those frames with my prescription."

I stared at Mike, wordless, and he retreated to our home office to think.

A few days later Mike asked me to go to the eyeglass chain stores in our area to check out what frames they had in stock that might fit his face, prescription, and desire to have wraparound sunglasses. Sensing the end was near, I said yes. Off we went… store after store. His combination of narrow face, strong prescription and desire to wear wraparound sunglasses just didn't work.

At the end of the day, Mike found a pair of sunglasses that he liked; they reminded him of wraparounds, but the frames flatter his face and work with his prescription. After more than two months of searching, researching, talking, debating and shopping, Mike had cool new black prescription sunglasses and I had my husband back, until he decides he needs to go shopping again.

~Darlene Sneden

34

The Lottery

Forget the lottery. Bet on yourself instead.
~Brian Koslow

We left the Virgin Islands in 1995. We sold Valkyrie, a very sad time indeed. Many of you have heard the one about "the happiest part having a boat is when you buy it and when you sell it." Well, I must say it depends. We lived on this boat for ten years. It brought us through some pretty dangerous yet unforgettable times. We loved her.

But we decided that we had played enough. We had worked hard but had little to show for it. We were going to find a job driving a boat for someone else. We were going to grow up and go to work!

We stacked all our belongings on a four foot by four foot pallet, had it shrink wrapped, and sent to Florida's east coast. From there we had it trucked to Judith's parents' vacation home in Cape Coral, Florida.

Judith's parents were in Michigan, so we had the house to ourselves. In the evening we would sit down after dinner to watch television. When we were in the islands, we had rabbit ears on a 9-inch black and white TV with two stations available. On a windy night the boat swung around on the mooring so that the picture came and went often. Back in civilization, TV was a great new distraction. This one particular evening the news people were talking about the Florida Lottery that had reached somewhere in the $75 million area. I happen to mention to Judith, just for the sake of conversation, that maybe we should get a ticket. You wouldn't believe the next fifteen to twenty minutes. Judith went into lecture mode.

"My father was a gambler." "He lost everything." "I would never gamble." On and on and on. I listened for a while, finally had enough, and when she was between breaths I made a dash to go buy a newspaper. I mean, give me a break; this was probably the second or third lottery ticket I had ever considered buying in my life. I walked up to the local Circle K convenience store on the corner with my hands over my head repeating "Serenity now," "Serenity Now," and bought the paper. I also bought a lottery ticket. Reflecting back, I guess it was an act of defiance. We men have to fight back once in a while to resist our inevitable fate, while involved with a female, of becoming a nonentity. After completing my little walk I went back home to the TV. The lecture was over and peace had returned.

In the course of the evening, I daringly mentioned that I had bought a lottery ticket. Surprisingly the lecture did not continue, and Judith asked me about the ticket. "What numbers did you get?" "Did you play my birthday?" "Did you play your kids' birthdays?" This was from the person who had just given me a lengthy sermon on gambling.

I finally got tired of all the questions and gave Judith the ticket. She studied it for a few moments, lost interest, and haphazardly threw it on the coffee table. I thought it kind of strange that she hadn't been more careful with the ticket. I took the ticket, folded it and put it under the coaster in which I had my glass of wine. Everything was cool and quiet until the news anchor came on and said the drawing was in ten minutes.

Judith asked if I had the ticket. It was time for a little payback. I said, "You had it last. Remember you asked me for it; what did you do with it?" I love myself sometime.

Judith looked everywhere; she was obsessed. I, of course, helped her by saying things like, "I can't believe you lost it!" At one point she actually picked up the wine glass and exposed the ticket but she was in such a frenzy she didn't even notice it. I went to bed. I could still hear her as she watched the drawing on TV, "I think there was a six and a thirty-two."

The next morning I woke early, as usual, and went to the Circle K to get the newspaper. I asked the clerk if he would check to see if my lottery ticket won. It hadn't, as I expected. Then I had a great idea. I bought a new lottery ticket with the winning numbers from the prior night. I put the ticket under the couch knowing that Judith would find it. It was one of the most rewarding moments in my life. She still hasn't forgiven me, but there are no more lectures.

~Robert Campbell

35

Sneaking Up On Commitment

A man without a wife is like a vase without flowers.
~African Proverb

Forever can be a long time. For many people, the idea of committing to something or someone for forever can be so right-in-your-face intimidating, it's often easier to avoid it at all cost. This was certainly the case for me when Ann and I first met.

Ann and I met in the hallway prior to a workshop entitled More Money. Our homework assignment was to list 100 things we wanted to do, be or have. I listened as Ann shared with another participant two items on her list: a committed relationship and a romantic relationship. As a way to enter into the conversation (in my own smart-ass style), I asked her why those were two separate items? Didn't it make more sense to combine them into one—a committed and romantic relationship?

I then made sure I sat next to her in class, since being in a committed relationship was on my list as well, and I found her to be cute and very engaging. A few weeks later, after going out on three or four dates, I informed her I was ready for a committed, romantic relationship and asked if she was ready as well.

I still remember the shocked look on Ann's face as she backed away from me saying, "Whoa, whoa, whoa—not so fast! If I was any good at committed relationships I'd still be married to my first husband."

Well, I could understand her point of view. I'd been through not one, but two divorces of my own and had a long list of other failed attempts at committed relationships. Thinking fast on my feet, I made a counter offer.

"Would you be willing to go for a twenty-four-hour committed relationship?" At first, she thought I was joking so I repeated, "Let's go for a twenty-four-hour committed relationship. Surely we can make it for twenty-four hours, right?"

So we agreed.

The next day, twenty-four hours later, I called to congratulate her. She asked, "What for?"

"Congratulations on your first successful, committed relationship. Now, are you ready to try for another one? How about one for forty-eight hours? Forty-eight hours isn't that much longer than twenty-four hours, right?" She agreed once again.

Sure enough, we made it through the forty-eight-hour one and also a seventy-two-hour committed relationship. As our confidence grew, we decided to take on a much longer stretch of time. We enrolled in a five-day personal development retreat together. The entire trip would take ten days, so we committed to staying together for the whole time.

Midway through the retreat we were sure we'd sabotaged our relationship. The program brought up all our ugly stuff—the stuff you really don't want someone else to see, especially the person you've just started dating. While neither of us was thrilled revealing that side of ourselves, we hung in there, and by the end of the program we announced to the entire group that we were committing to a six-month relationship.

After completing the six months, we made a second six-month commitment. During the second six months, as we sat on the deck of a restaurant overlooking the San Francisco Bay Bridge sipping mimosas, Ann proposed to me.

We've now been married for over twenty years. Some commitments are worth sneaking up on!

~W. Bradford Swift

36

Taking His Measure

A good time to laugh is any time you can.
~Linda Ellerbee

For nearly two decades I'd dallied on the dating block, so by the time I got around to saying "I do," the adjectives "blushing" and "young" had expired. I was, at best, a "new" bride. As my friends would attest, I undertook my new wifely duties like any other job I'd ever had—I was going for employee-of-the-year. During my reign as dream wife I pledged to concoct culinary pleasures the likes of which would make Julia (if she were alive) weep; I vowed to out-Martha Martha as the diva of domestic decorating, and finally I swore I'd buy my guy some new drawers—underwear that is. His briefs were the ten-year-old leftovers from the days he'd lived at home and his mother had bought them.

I paused to think about my "for better or worse" vows. Clearly this couldn't extend to underwear so I called my husband at work with that nauseating niceness of newlyweds.

"Hey sweetie, I'm going shopping today—thought I'd get us both a little something. I'm thinking thoooongs," I said in my breathy voice.

"There's two feet of snow on the ground; I don't get it—why flip-flops?"

"Hoooney, panties—you know lacey, naughty, sexy, maybe even peek-a-boo panties."

"Oh yeah, fine, good."

"Is that your calculator clicking in the background? Are you working?"

"Uh yeah, that's where you called me."

"Never mind. Anyway, you need new underwear."

"Yeah, get me some Calvin's size 32 with the extra large pouch. Gotta run, hon, catchya later."

I jumped on the subway and headed to Saks Fifth Avenue straight to the men's underwear department.

"Where can I find Calvin Klein jockey shorts, please? I'm looking for size 32."

"Right this way."

"Calvin's got some real estate here," I said, trying to sound clever as I eyed the square footage of underwear racks rivaling the size of my New York City apartment. And then the packaging sucked me in with such magnetic force, that a tiny "Oh my" slipped out.

Headless male hunks in skin tones ranging from honey to espresso shamelessly showcased their chiseled six-packs and heaping doses of manliness. It was enough to make a new bride dizzy. But since I was in hot pursuit of the wife-of-the-year crown, I concentrated on the labels. There was the Classic, the Body Brief, the 365 Brief, the Pro Stretch, the Cotton Modal Rib Brief, and the Pro Rib Brief. Why were these starting to sound like entrees at a steak establishment? And the Micro Modal… (yuck, what could that mean?) Anything micro in a pouch couldn't be good. Poor guy. I imagined his agent calling.

"Hey great news. You landed the underwear ad for Calvin—from here on out you'll be known as Micro guy."

While I felt for Micro guy, I was more troubled by not finding the package with the extra large pouch. The sales associate was nowhere to be found so I whipped out my cell phone and rang up the hubby.

"Hi there, listen I am at Saks and I can't find… oh wait a second, here's the guy…."

"Excuse me, I can't find the ones with the extra large pouch."

"Rita," he yells across the aisles. "This lady is looking for the extra large pouch."

With my ear still firmly against the phone's receiver I heard a thud. It sounded like my husband and his phone had crashed to the floor.

"Honey, honey," I said. "Oh my God, are you having a heart attack?"

He was snorting between frantic desperate dying gasps for air and I was picturing my sudden widowhood for which I would be able to use the adjective "young." Finally, with one labored raspy gulp of air, his death rattle changed to the recognizable sound of hysterical laughter. My husband was laughing at me. He was laughing so hard that it finally dawned on me.

"Heh heh, gotta love those new bride jokes," I said, with the heat rising in my cheeks. Then I smoothed my skirt, lifted my chin and stared the clerk straight in his eyes, "Sir, I'll take a week's supply of underwear… just, please, make sure they're the Micros."

~Tsgoyna Tanzman

37

First in Line

There is no feeling more comforting and consoling than knowing
you are right next to the one you love.
~Author Unknown

We had finally chosen a destination for our quick vacation getaway. I booked reservations at the Polynesian Resort, scheduled a flight, and we were off to Disney World.

We entered the park. Our eyes did not know where to focus first. We were so excited. We strolled through Disney World holding hands, stopping at favorite rides and exhibits as we roamed.

This was everything we had heard about and more.

Mickey Mouse walked with us and Sleeping Beauty greeted us in a way that almost seemed enchanted. This was fantasy in its purest form.

Before we were about to take the movie studio tour, I told Richard that I had to use the ladies' room and to wait for me. I left him sitting on a bench near the ladies' room entrance.

When I came out, Richard was gone. I thought perhaps he had gone to the bathroom so I sat down on the bench to wait for him. I waited for quite a while before I got up and started pacing while calling his name, at first in my normal volume. As time went on I walked farther and was now calling out his name at the top of my lungs. People were looking at me with sympathy.

Suddenly a woman approached me, put her hand on my arm

and in her most gentle and soothing voice asked me if I had lost Richard. I noticed her badge and realized she worked at the park.

"Yes," I answered almost in tears. "I have lost Richard." By now she had her arm around me and was gently rubbing my back.

"Don't worry. We will find Richard. Tell me please, how old is he?"

That question threw me. "He is fifty," I answered.

That answer threw her. "Fifty?"

"Yes, fifty and when I find him…"

"But I thought you lost your child," she said.

"No, just my husband," I answered.

"We will find him. Follow me."

She took me through an employee-only door that led to a platform. Climbing to the top I scanned the crowd control maze of people in line waiting to enter the studio. There at the head of the line was my husband Richard.

Did he think he was saving a place for me? Did he expect me to say excuse me to over 600 people in order to eventually reach him in line? And how was I supposed to know he was in line when I had asked him to wait for me on the bench?

The Disney employee took me through a shortcut to my waiting husband.

"Richard, you know those leashes used for children?" I asked. "That is my next purchase." My husband looked embarrassed but proud that he was first in line.

~Elynne Chaplik-Aleskow

38

The Door Bell

Laugh at yourself first, before anyone else can.
~Elsa Maxwell

We had just moved into our new house—our dream house. Finally our family had room to spread out and each of us—my husband, our three sons, and I—had enough space so that we weren't stepping all over each other all of the time. What a luxury! It was a wonderful two-story house and each boy had his own bedroom. My husband and I had a wonderful bedroom upstairs right at the front of the house.

I was busy trying to get unpacked and put things away but with three young sons, all under the age of eight, it wasn't easy. My husband helped as much as he could but he was working during the day and by the time he got home and we had dinner, neither of us wanted to unpack boxes. It was taking us a while to get settled.

One night, after dinner, after the kids were in bed, Frank decided he would just go upstairs to our bedroom and take a short nap. Great idea. Now I love my husband and I love being married but I also like some time to just be by myself—to think and relax. If he were to go and take a nap that would give me some of that alone time—all-alone time—for the first time in our new house and what a rare opportunity that is for a mother with young children. So what did I do? I took off my clothes, put on my robe and decided I was just going to relax. No television, no book, no telephone, no nothing. Just me... and the quiet.

It was an unseasonably warm evening in January in California. The temperature was probably still seventy degrees at 9 p.m. and rather than sit in the house, I decided to sit outside in the back yard. I didn't even want the dog to come outside with me, so much to her annoyance I made her stay in the house. I just wanted to be alone. All alone. And alone I was. Completely. Totally. I opened the kitchen door and walked outside. The evening was divine; the air was not only warm but there was this amazing aroma of orange blossoms. I was in heaven. It was absolutely still. I relaxed and although we had been in our new house only a few weeks, I knew we would be happy here.

After an hour, it was time to go back in. I walked to the kitchen door and turned the handle. Nothing happened. Tried it again… still nothing. Was the door stuck? I pulled and pulled. Nothing. I knew I left the door unlocked when I came outside. Suddenly I realized that, in her great effort to get outside to be with me, the dog had somehow pushed the knob in and locked the door. And I was stuck outside. In my robe.

But not to worry. I knew the two younger boys, Mike and Rob, would already be asleep but my oldest, John, would probably still be awake. He could come downstairs, unlock the door and let me in. I took a handful of pebbles and threw them at his upstairs window. "John… John… are you awake?" I listened. Nothing. I tried again. All was quiet. I had three choices: I could spend the night outside, but it was starting to get chilly. I could go knock on my neighbors' door but I felt silly going to their house. First of all, underneath my robe, I was… naked! We had just moved in and I didn't know them, hadn't even met them. What kind of a first impression would I make if I knocked on their door like that? So that left option number three: I would try and wake my husband.

There was one small problem with that option… my husband doesn't take kindly to being awakened from a nap. But what choice did I have? So I walked through the gate to the front of the house and walked up the front steps. The front steps and front door are visible to the entire street but thank goodness no one was outside at this hour.

Our mail slot was located in the middle of the front door so I sat down on the step in front of the door, rang the bell, opened the mail slot and very gently called, "Frank." Then I put my ear to the slot and listened. All was quiet; there was no response to my call. So I rang the bell, opened the mail slot again and this time called a little louder, "Frank." I jerked my ear around to the slot and listened. Surely he had heard me this time. No response. Then, being the adult that I am, I started to laugh at the absurdity of it all. Picture this. Here I was sitting on my front steps, in my robe, ringing the bell and talking into the mail slot in the front door. The more I thought about it, the funnier it seemed to me. The funnier it seemed, the harder I laughed. But, you've got to know that it's not a good thing to laugh if you are trying to wake Frank. Not a good thing at all.

I tried again. I rang the bell over and over, opened the mail slot but this time I yelled and laughed at the same time, "Frank!!" I quickly put my ear to the slot and I... wait, I heard something. What was it? It was Frank calling... to me. "Barbara." I was frantic. I had made contact with the sleeping bear. I needed to keep going before he fell back to sleep. Again I rang the bell over and over, ding-dong ding-dong, and yelled/laughed, "Frank... Frank!!" I was laughing hysterically into the mail slot. Then I heard his voice: "Barbara, Barbara... the door bell is ringing. Someone's at the door. GET THE DOOR." Now I completely lost it. I couldn't breathe. Tears of laughter were streaming down my face as I gasped through the mail slot one last time. "FRANK... I AM THE DOOR!"

And that's when I heard it. The man I married, my knight in shining armor, my savior, my protector, my hero came stomping down the stairs, threw the door open, glared at me as I sat on the front steps, in my robe, in hysterics and said, "Well if it's so damn funny, you can just sit there all night!" He turned right around, stomped back up the stairs, fell on the bed and promptly fell back to sleep.

I came inside, closed the door and tried to stop laughing. It took me a long time to be able to breathe normally but finally I calmed down. And the best part of this whole story is that the next morning, when I reminded Frank what had happened, he didn't remember it at all. Nothing. He thought I'd made the whole thing up. Ah… married life!

~Barbara LoMonaco

A Couch for Two

Rise to meet him in a pretty disorder—yes—
O, nothing is more alluring than a levee from a couch in some confusion.
~William Congreve

My husband and I have been married for four decades and we have learned each other's preferences and dislikes. Sometimes they compliment each other, sometimes not. We know that we both don't care for surprise parties, for instance, not for us or for our friends. It doesn't mean that we won't attend one when invited and have a good time, but our children know better than to throw one for us. We also know that he likes action pix and I don't, but as we are both fond of going to the movies, we'll check out the reviews and pick a film that appeals to us both. We usually can find a way to cooperate.

One of the things we don't do well together is shop, and shopping for furniture is one of our least favorite things. We have different taste and agreeing on something is not an easy task. I like unusual; he likes classic. I prefer clean lines; he gravitates to curves. Yet sometimes we switch sides and confuse each other, like when I fell in love with an old-fashioned settee upholstered with medallions and swirls for our spare bedroom, and he took to a Danish modern table with no-frills chairs for our breakfast room. Our home reflects our eclecticism.

So when the day came that our old den couch needed replacing we knew we were in trouble. Someone would need to compromise.

We started out by checking home magazines for ideas. When I found something I thought had possibilities, I brought it up for discussion. Our conversations went something like this:

ME: What do you think about this sofa? It looks like a cross between seventies funk and Grandma Moses.

HIM: I hate it!

When he found something he liked, he showed it to me.

HIM: Here's a nice traditional couch. It would look great in the den.

ME: Let's keep looking.

The magazine route obviously wasn't working. So we decided to brave the furniture stores. This was a major decision for both of us, given his aversion to shopping and my habit of always wanting to go to just one more store. I didn't want to miss anything.

The first store we checked out was just down the road but it set the tone for the others.

ME: Wow, this is great! It explodes with color. What do you think, hon? Hon?

My husband was already off to another section of the store. I took it as a sign that we hadn't found the "right" couch yet.

Over the course of a week we must have seen every couch in every store in and around our neighborhood with pretty much the same result—no purchase. And the thought of extending our search was getting us both a bit ornery.

ME: Why don't you like anything I like?

HIM: I do, just not in our house.

We were getting desperate.

"I had enough," my husband said. "I could live with the old couch."

Only that wasn't an option. The problem was that we had given away our old couch. Our search continued, now out of necessity.

We found a couch (sort of) that we both thought we could learn to like. So we bought it and hoped for the best. It was delivered the next day.

"What's that smell?" I asked when the deliverymen removed the plastic coating.

"What smell?" said my husband.

I stuck my face into the fabric.

"That smell," I said.

"You're imagining things," he said.

Maybe I was. For two days I pretended everything was fine. By the third day, I was wheezing and had a violent headache. There must have been some kind of finish on the fabric that I was allergic to. Fortunately, there was a satisfaction guarantee from the store; the couch went back.

My husband groaned. He knew what was coming. The search continued.

"There's one more store we haven't seen," I said. "Let's give it a try."

He reluctantly allowed himself to be led into the store. A salesperson met us at the door and asked us what we were looking for. We were silent for a moment. Oddly enough, we had never really thought about it. The priority was just something we both liked; we hadn't defined it.

"Well," she said, "do you have any style in mind? What colors do you like? Do you want a cushy couch, one you can sink into, or a firmer one?"

We hadn't a clue. We just wanted what we wanted. Now what was it?

"It has to be deep enough," my husband said at last.

The salesperson looked at us with a question in her eyes. But I smiled because I knew what he meant.

"Yes," I said. "That's exactly right."

It was less a matter of style, though we did have our outer limits in regard to that, than of room. What we wanted, we suddenly knew, was a cuddly couch. We liked to snuggle up together at night to watch TV. Our couch had to accommodate our reclining, cuddling bodies. And even though we are both small, the two of us together needed a bit of space.

Now that we had a focus, our search through the store was easy. We passed on any couch that lacked that cuddle-ability.

We eventually found a simple Italian contemporary couch with sufficient definition to suit my husband and enough simplicity to satisfy me. To make sure it had the right cuddle factor, we tested it out in the store when we thought no one was watching, lying down side-by-side to make sure it was a good fit. It was perfect! We bought it on the spot and walked out of the store holding hands.

And it wasn't even a compromise. All we had ever needed was a couch for two.

~Ferida Wolff

"This was designed for people who have mastered easy chairs and want to attempt something more difficult."

Perfect

The trouble with, "A place for everything and everything in its place"
is that there's always more everything than places.
~Elayne Bundy

As a husband, you have to be really careful what you say because your wife might just take you to task—literally—based on nothing more than a simple statement like: "I'm going to golf all day Saturday; then Sunday I'll do whatever you want to do, dear."

"That's what you said," my wife reminded me, handing me a hammer.

"What I meant was we could go to lunch. Grab a crab melt at Moby Dick's out on Stearns Wharf or something. Watch tourists try to park their Hummers in those compact-car-only spots. That's always fun. Maybe someone interesting will show up—like the guy who lets the pigeons eat breadcrumbs off his head. You know he hasn't had dandruff in years? Or hair for that matter. Plus he never needs a hat because of the sunscreen effect of all that guano. Whataya say we check that out? Doesn't that sound like fun?"

"Sure," my wife said.

I smiled at my own resourcefulness.

"Right after we finish redecorating the house."

This confirms one of my many profound theories about married life. See, I believe that if a wife only had one wall and one thing to hang on it, she'd still want to rearrange it on a regular basis. It's in the genes. This differs from most guys I know who would only take down a piece of their art to put new batteries in it so the word "cerveza" would light up again.

"Why am I moving this painting that looked 'perfect' over the fireplace—your word, not mine—just a few months ago?"

"Because it's summer and this will look much nicer up there."

"You want to put a blanket over the fireplace?"

"It's not a blanket. It's a handmade Pennsylvania Dutch quilt. It's art."

"Taxidermy is art, too. Why don't we get a moose head? We wouldn't have to move it from season to season, just decorate it with different hats and funny signs and stuff."

I waited for the accolades of approval. Instead my wife handed me a curtain rod and I began my long ascent up the stepladder.

Did I mention the fact that we have cathedral ceilings? I believe these too were invented by wives, for wives. Because no guy in his right mind, who knows he is eventually going to have to repaint his "kingdom," wants ceilings that soar to the nosebleed section.

"Higher," my wife said.

"I'm already standing on the step that says do not go above this step. What if the home repair police show up and cart me off to homeowner's jail. Then where will you be? Huh?"

"Higher," she said again.

I took another step up, cursing the existence of Pennsylvania Dutch culture on the way. "Oh look, an eagle's nest," I said.

I looked down. My wife looked like an ant.

"Perfect," she yelled.

It took about fifteen minutes to get the blanket—excuse me, art quilt—perfectly straight, then another fifteen minutes to put the painting that had been over the fireplace over the couch.

"Left. No, right. No, left. No, right."

"You know," I said. "If you ever want to try a different career. You'd have a real future leading parades."

"That's funny. You should write humor."

I thought I noted a bit of sarcasm in that statement, but before

I could respond, she said: "Okay, now all we need to do is take the two landscapes that were over the couch and put them in the dining room and take the watercolor that was in the dining room and put that in the guest room and then take the photos that were in the guest room and put them in the hall and then..."

Impossible as it must seem, I finally did get this all done. And, after a few minutes of agonizing scrutiny, my wife smiled and said: "Perfect."

I sighed in relief.

That's when the front door opened and my stepdaughter Christy walked in.

"What's that?" my wife asked.

Christy—the artist/troublemaker—held up her brand new oil painting.

"Boats!" my wife exclaimed. "I love boats. It's going to look perfect over..."

"Don't say it," I begged.

"... the fireplace," she finished.

In my next life, I'm going to be the pigeon guy.

~Ernie Witham

41

The Long Way Around

Soul mates are people who bring out the best in you.
They are not perfect but are always perfect for you.
~Author Unknown

My husband and I are soul mates. We also have completely opposite ways of coming up with solutions to problems that arise in our lives. While I, the former preschool teacher, use my college training class method of K-I-S-S (keep it simple stupid), my husband comes up with the most time-consuming and detailed methods he can possibly dream up.

My wonderful significant other was shopping with our daughter and grandson and found us a new bed set. You know the kind: dust ruffle, comforter, shams and decorative pillows. We had needed a new set for a long time.

It's a very nice set. Since it was in a clearance bin, it was a real bargain. He wanted to surprise me. So as soon as I walked in from the day job, he made me close my eyes and he guided me into our bedroom.

I was quite pleased—but a bit taken aback by how massive our queen-sized bed appeared. Being a mere five-foot-one-and-a-half-inches, I already had to sort of boost myself up onto the mattress. Now, the bed stopped at my waist!

Being the curious type, I asked why we suddenly had a resting place right out of *The Princess and the Pea*.

His answer: "The dust ruffle was too long. I had to go to the store and buy bed frame extenders, so it wouldn't drag on the floor."

Six inches worth! This wasn't where it ended either. Oh no.

My husband then realized that he had to raise the headboard, the picture just above it and last but not least he built extensions to our nightstands. Then came the "sad" part — he told me he was going to leave the TV stand and the bureau on the other half of the room at their original height.

Next question — did the extenders include a stepladder? No, but my darling did realize that having a "height-challenged" wife meant he'd have to purchase one.

How would a wife have handled this problem? If I had found the bargain bed set and saw that the dust ruffle was six inches too long, I would have taken it to my dad, the retired upholsterer, and had him hem the darn thing. Yes, I would have had to wait a couple of weeks, but heck, what's time?

That's why our marriage is so strong — my husband is a dear, I love him with all my heart and he makes me laugh. The thought he put behind our "Land of the Giants" bedroom is worth every penny he added to his shopping spree.

~Carine Nadel

42

Newlywed Lock Out

A good laugh and a long sleep are the best cures in the doctor's book.
~Irish Proverb

had insisted that the city was too big for me, and my new husband tried his very best to understand. We would be married soon and his plan was to move us to a large city, one of the many that he had lived in while growing up.

My husband's childhood was vastly different from mine. He had moved over ten times while growing up, while my family only moved once, when I was five years old. The thought of trading our small-town life for the big city was overwhelming.

Finally we had agreed that once we were married we would move to a smaller city. Bigger than the small town that I was used to, but large enough that we would have more work opportunities.

We settled into our two-bedroom apartment. We loved our new life and we were thrilled to be alone in our very own place. Our apartment was sparsely furnished with my parents' outdated kitchen table, a TV, my old beanbag chair, and a blow-up couch that a friend gave us as a gag gift at our wedding!

The only problem in our newlywed bliss was that my husband's job demanded that he work until the late hours of the evening. It was during those hours alone that I would imagine all kinds of intimidating scenarios involving the dangerous people that were in this "huge" city, and heaven forbid even in our building!

It was on such a night that my imagination had run wild and I found myself pacing in the living room. "What would I do if something terrible happened?" I decided to go and make sure that I had locked the door. I did, but just to be extra safe I put on the chain link lock as well. My nerves settled when I heard the chain fall into place. I went back to the living room and put on a movie to try and distract myself. I lay down, and before I knew it I had fallen sleep.

I was enjoying a nice deep sleep, but somewhere in the distance I was certain that I heard my husband shouting. I tried to respond but he continued to rant about something. I was unclear as to what he was shouting about! As I rubbed my eyes I decided that he was being unreasonable and told him that I was going to bed. I started to march towards our room, but not before I told him that he had some nerve to come home and shout at me the way he was. I felt justified in what I said, and as I climbed into bed I made up my mind that I'd "let him have it" in the morning. I was too tired to complain so I went right back to sleep.

The next morning came and I immediately remembered what had happened the night before. When my husband turned to me I made a point to dramatically roll over in the opposite direction.

"What's wrong with you?" my husband asked.

"Are you really going to ask me that," I said, "after the way you behaved last night?"

"You really don't remember, do you?"

"Remember what?" I snapped.

"Remember locking me out?"

My husband explained the whole story to me. When he had come home from work that night he was unable to open the door because of the chain lock! He had banged on the door and shouted out to me, and when I did not answer he really began to get concerned.

Worried, he climbed up the building to our balcony desperate to ensure that I was okay. When he looked in our patio window he was shocked to see me lying on the couch resting peacefully. He proceeded to bang on the door, and shout my name in the hopes of waking me.

In the end, he had to walk over to his cousin's house and ask for bolt cutters. In the middle of the night my husband had to cut the chain lock off our door.

No doubt he was shouting when he finally got inside our house! To this day we still laugh when we remember that night. Most new brides greet their husbands lovingly at the door after work—I locked mine out of our house instead!

We've been married eleven years and my wonderful husband still knows that there's no use trying to talk to me when I am almost asleep, half asleep or just waking up. And needless to say we have never had a chain lock on our door again!

~Brenda Redmond

Married *Life!*

Chapter 5

What's Love Got to Do with It

Marriages are not as they are made, but as they turn out.

~Italian Proverb

Hats Off to Romance!

A woman wears many hats in one lifetime —
why shouldn't one of them be a crown?
~Annie Jones

he smooching in the sketch meant that I needed to find a married couple to act in the drama that Sunday morning. Not having any married couples on our church drama team, I recruited my somewhat reluctant but good-natured husband to join me on stage.

The theme for the day was the Roles of Women, and we'd picked up on Amy Grant's song, "Hats," to write a hilarious sketch based on some what-ifs. What if a woman *literally* had to change her hat every time she "changed hats?" Within the span of a fast paced, five-minute sketch, "Millie" gets up in the morning, meets briefly with God, provides breakfast for her family, packs their lunches, sees them out the door, goes to work, and has lunch with a friend. She returns home to children with homework, one with the flu, supper to make, church choir practice to lead, and so on. Throughout the day, she keeps returning to a large hat box placed center stage, where she finds the appropriate hat for the task at hand—sometimes wearing two or three at once but never doing any one job well. By the end of the day, things have gotten totally out of control. As an exhausted Millie is frantically sifting through the box searching for her "nurse" hat, her husband walks in wearing a grin.

"Look what I found hidden away in the back of the closet," he announces, blowing dust off a hard hat. "Your LOVER hat!"

To which Millie's only reply is an exasperated "Lover hat?" and she faints into his arms as the lights fade. We knew it would be a big hit with an audience who could easily identify.

My husband agreed to dust off his business suit for the role, but didn't bother to try it on until Sunday morning. Uh oh... it seemed to have shrunk a little while it hung in the closet. There was no time to do anything about it. The show had to go on. And it did. I played my part with enthusiasm, allowing my character to get more and more crazed as the story unfolded and built to the big finish when my knight in *binding* armor would sweep me into his arms right there in front of the entire congregation! And he did... just as his pants split right up the back, revealing to the crowd his white undershorts as the lights faded and our audience burst into gales of laughter and applause.

I went home and put on my mending hat.

~Terrie Todd

Neither Rain Nor Snow

A person often meets his destiny on the road he took to avoid it.
~Jean de La Fontaine

Darryl and I met one summer between college semesters, when we both had summer jobs in Colorado. In his spare time, Darryl was building a tree house in the woods. I knew then he was my kind of guy. His dog accompanied us on our first date... a hike. She ate the cherries that we picked from a sunlit orchard, and spit out the pits! I was impressed.

We dated just four weeks. Then I left for a semester in Europe and Darryl returned to graduate school in another state. We married less than five months from the day we met. We'd never seen each other without a suntan, or with a runny nose. We had two cars, but no bed. For Valentine's Day, Darryl bought me red knee socks and a kitchen sink trap. I baked him crunchy granola.

We scraped, painted and papered our first tiny house. We camped in the mountains, fished at the beach, planted a vegetable garden, raised two geese, provided a foster home for pound puppies until they were old enough to be adopted, and bottle-fed an orphaned raccoon.

We made four beautiful babies, enjoyed ice cream cones and some great laughs in three dozen states and five countries, started two businesses, won a jitterbug contest and bought land and built a cabin in a remote mountain valley. We held hands at funerals for his mom, both our dads and my grandmother, and prayed for our children in waiting rooms in four different hospitals.

We've been a team now for thirty-four years. Darryl's still my sunshine. I'm his old flame. He's my one. I'm his only. And we thank God for what we've shared with each other.

But things could have turned out much differently... because when Darryl asked me to move to California when I got back from Europe so we could be together, I mailed him a letter telling him all the practical and sensible reasons why I could not—like how a friend was counting on me as a roommate, that I didn't even own a car and how I couldn't possibly pay out-of-state tuition to continue my college education in California.

When he called, I stalled by saying, "Just wait until you get my letter; it will explain." But being practical and sensible on paper was one thing and SAYING the words I had so painstakingly written to the guy my heart yearned for was another. While waiting for him to receive that eminently reasonable and responsible letter, my heart won over my mind.

We'd been married two months when the weary, bedraggled envelope in which I'd sent that letter finally arrived. The envelope was empty. A handwritten note by an unidentified postal clerk explained that it had only recently been discovered, in its woebegone condition, in the bottom of a bin at a faraway post office.

~Lynn Worley Kuntz

45

Roving Eye

To avoid mistakes and regrets,
always consult your wife before engaging in a flirtation.
~E.W. Howe

The first time it happens, we've only been married a couple of months and we're driving to the beach. Everything is going splendidly. We're chatting about this and that, the meeting he had the other day, the new book I'm reading, whether or not we'll stop for ice cream later.

And then, just like that, the conversation comes to an abrupt halt. His head swivels toward the open window, his eyes riveted on some passing distraction. Despite the new bride beside him, he lets out a long, low whistle.

I take a deep breath as I scan the sidewalk for the object of his attention. Is she a blonde? A redhead, perhaps? Sleek and sophisticated? Wild and crazy? But all I see are two men in business suits talking on their cell phones and a guy in a muscle shirt with tattoos up and down his arms.

"Sweet," my husband says.

That's when I catch a glimpse of her. She's sleek, all right. It's hard not to notice how he looks with longing at the bold curve of her front, the subtle tilt of her rear. Her long nose goes with her lean body. She is classy. She is polished. She is... a roadster.

It has taken me a while to grow accustomed to these stolen glances. How the shiny flash of chrome and steel lures his attention away without as much as a moment's notice. How the purr of an engine causes him to halt mid-sentence and forget what he's even talking about. Forget everything around him.

Except for her. The fast one coming up behind him with her top down.

All these years later, I've become used to my husband's love affair with cars. It is what it is. I never give it more than a passing thought.

But then, one sunny afternoon, we're wandering down the street enjoying the scenery with no particular destination in mind when he abruptly stops. He turns and faces me.

"I've got a question for you," he says.

"Sure," I say, wondering what could change his mood so suddenly.

"If you were going to buy a Jeep CJ-5 and it were only available in two colors, say bright yellow or dark green, which would you pick?"

I start to laugh, but the sincere look on his face tells me he expects an answer. Doesn't matter that we're not in the market for a car. Doesn't matter that I have no idea what a Jeep CJ-5 looks like. Just answer the question. Let me see. I like green. I like yellow. Don't think. Just pick.

"Yellow," I say.

"Great! So far, so good," he says. He claps his hands and smiles. "Now, let's move on. Mercedes 500. Midnight blue or red?"

"Blue."

"That's it. That's the right answer!"

"It is?"

"We're definitely on the same wavelength."

"We are?"

Now that I've passed some sort of marital compatibility quiz, the kind they must publish in *Motor Trend* or *Car and Driver*, we walk off happily into the sunset.

Until a few months later when we're actually shopping for a new car. I'm sitting in the dealer's office, sandwiched between my husband and a car salesman, and somehow color doesn't seem to be at the top of anyone's list. Except possibly mine.

"Four-wheel drive?" asks my husband.

"Of course," replies the dealer. "4-WD all the way."

My husband's eyes light up. "How's the compression ratio?"

"Excellent. Coefficient of drag is decent. Torque's right up there, too."

"MacPherson struts?"

"Absolutely."

"Rack and pinion?"

"Definitely. And check this out," the dealer says, pointing to a photo in a brochure on his desk. "GPS navigation system. Accurate to 1.3 meters, give or take a centimeter."

"Cool."

"Yeah, well of course, there's ABS."

"Wheels?"

"Low-profile eighteen-inch alloy rims with five spokes."

"What do you think, dear?" My husband turns to me, searching my face for some sign of approval. The dealer waits anxiously for my reply.

I want to say something like I want a car that starts up when you turn the key. I want a car that's good for hauling the kids and groceries. I want a car I can drive without a degree in mechanical engineering.

I want to. But the words won't come. So I just smile a low-profile-kind-of-wife smile and say to my husband the only thing I can think of:

"It all depends on if you know the right answer to my question."

"What's your question?"

"Moonlight silver or jet black?"

~Rita Lussier

Reprinted by permission of
Marc Tyler Nobleman ©2001

46

Pantless in Puerto Rico

If a friend is in trouble, don't annoy him by asking
if there is anything you can do. Think up something appropriate and do it.
~Edgar Watson Howe

We were nearing the end of our Caribbean cruise. My wife Carol and I were aboard the MS Windward, escaping the wrath of winter in Canada. We had spent the last seven days celebrating our twenty-fifth wedding anniversary, along with our friends Jim and Meada Hunter, also celebrating their twenty-fifth. It had been a wonderful experience, from the accommodations to the dining and shows; shipboard life was luxurious and we had a terrific time touring the islands and sunning on the beautiful sand beaches of the West Indies. But now it was time to return to reality... or so I thought.

Our ship would be docking in San Juan, Puerto Rico, in the early hours of the morning. Every one of the 1,300 passengers on board would have to clear U.S. Immigration before being allowed to disembark for the airport to catch their flights home. This sounds like a simple process, but in fact, it is a very complicated operation that involves careful planning and coordination by the ship's crew and the full cooperation of the passengers—1,300 passengers generate about 5,000 pieces of luggage. Somehow, it must all get off the ship and onto the same airplanes as its owners. To facilitate matters, the passengers are required to place their luggage in the passageway outside their cabins on the last night at sea. Before retiring you lay out your clothes for the morning, keep a carry-on for the trip home and put everything else out in the hall. While you sleep the stewards collect the bags for shipment to the airport.

Our last evening was outstanding! After a sumptuous dinner, we caught the finale in the lounge, spent some time in the disco and then hit the casino in hopes of recouping some of our losses. We partied until the wee hours, dreading the mandatory muster for immigration clearance at 6 a.m. Jim, Meada and Carol wisely decided to head for our cabins to grab at least a few hours of sleep. But I had consumed enough piña coladas to convince myself that if I played blackjack just a little longer, I would end up ahead. My companions abandoned me to my folly.

I had a wonderful time winning and losing and winning again, just barely accomplishing my goal. I finally quit while I was ahead and at about 5 a.m. crept quietly into our cabin and crawled under the covers to snatch at least a little sleep.

Carol took no pity on me and shook me awake at 5:15. She was already dressed and anxious to leave for the immigration screening in the main lounge. I groaned, pleaded for a little more sack time and pulled the covers over my head. She relented and left to visit Jim and Meada in the adjacent cabin, threatening dire consequences if I wasn't up when she returned. Carol was back before I knew it and woke me again. She was very upset. Thinking my tardiness was the cause I started to beg for mercy. But, that wasn't the problem.

Carol explained that in the Hunters' cabin she had found Jim missing and Meada in tears, clad only in her underwear.

Her initial thought was that something had happened to Jim or that Meada was ill, but thankfully neither was the case. The problem was—Meada had no pants!

I started to laugh! Carol frowned and tried to voice her disapproval, but she too couldn't keep a straight face. Apparently after last night's revelry, in her hurry to lay out their travel clothes, pack everything else and get the bags out into the companionway, Meada had forgotten to keep out a pair of pants to wear home. Jim was fully dressed and so was Meada, except for slacks.

Meada didn't discover her error until she started to dress for breakfast. Jim immediately went to see if he could get access to their baggage, but it was already on the dock. Next he tried the on-board Duty Free shops they were required to stay closed when in port. He tried the Purser's Office too, but they could not help. Finally he sought out the Officer of the Deck to seek permission to go ashore. Permission denied! No one was allowed to leave the ship until they had been cleared by immigration. He reminded Jim that the process would soon begin. All passengers were expected to gather in the grand ballroom by 6 a.m. sharp. Jim returned to the cabin to find Carol consoling Meada. When he delivered the bad news she broke down completely. She was pantless in Puerto Rico!

With all avenues of hope exhausted Carol explained that the tentative plan was for Meada, passport in hand, to appear before the Immigration Officers wrapped in a stateroom blanket. We knew from experience that she could not skip out because the ship would not be cleared until every single passenger was accounted for. Indeed on our last cruise we had watched with amusement when ship's security arrived escorting a young couple, still dressed in their pajamas, whose absence had delayed the ship's clearance for about thirty minutes. The electronic ship's chime sounded and the fateful announcement, requesting all passengers to attend the Crystal Ballroom, was made. That was my cue to get up and Carol pointed to my traveling outfit hanging in the closet.

I reluctantly removed the bedcovers and revealed the solution to Meada's problem.

I was still fully dressed. Carol grabbed my traveling slacks from the hanger and ran to the rescue.

I must say, that when we arrived in the Ballroom we presented quite a picture. Carol and Jim were impeccably dressed, while my clothes clearly reflected the fact I had slept in them. Meada's attire was unique; blue pants, legs folded and pinned way up, baggy in the crotch and butt, cinched tightly at the waist and all nicely set off by a white blouse, lime green jacket and black loafers. We passed muster, made it off the ship and returned safely home.

But to this day, whenever our group gathers to reminisce and the talk turns to our anniversary cruise, Carol pipes up and revels in retelling the story of how she saved the day by helping another woman get into her husband's pants!

~John Forrest

47

Put On Something Else

Clothes make the man. Naked people have little or no influence on society.
~Mark Twain

"You gonna wear that?" is the question I have asked my husband many times over the span of our marriage. After twenty-two years of marriage I find it amazing that the man thinks a pair of clean underwear and a new tie meet the business casual dress code requirements.

Once again the other night, getting ready for an evening out I looked at him and asked, "Are you gonna wear that jacket?"

"I was planning on it. Why? What's wrong with my jacket? You told me you like this jacket."

"Yes, I told you I like the jacket back in 1980 when I met you. Now it's old, worn, faded and small on you; besides I thought we got rid of it—where did you find it?"

"I found it on the floor of my closet. I forgot it was there until today when I decided to clean out my closet rather than listen to your constant nagging one more minute."

"I only nagged you to pick up your underwear since you ran out and the pile on the floor was obstructing the television. It was a choice of doing laundry or running to the store to buy new underwear."

"Oh, that reminds me, next time you go to the store pick me up some underwear."

"You gonna wear those sneakers?"

"I was planning on it; they're my dressy sneakers. Why? What's wrong with my sneakers?"

"Well, since tonight is formal you should wear shoes. I don't remember those sneakers. Where did you get them?"

"I got them under the jacket in the closet."

"Oh."

"Do you think I should give the jacket to our son?"

"No, he won't want it."

"Why won't he want it?"

"Well, for one thing, he has taste. We can bury it tomorrow along with the sneakers. Now go put on a pair of dress shoes."

"I wear dress shoes to work."

"Yes, dear, I know, but you work from home now, remember?"

"Yeah, so now there are boxes of untouched shoes in my closet."

"You gonna wear that tie?"

"I was planning on it. It has some green in it, which matches my shirt. Why? What's wrong with my tie?"

"It has green in it because it's a Christmas tie decorated with Christmas trees."

"Well, you gave me it to wear."

"Yes, at Christmastime, not the middle of July. Put it back and pick out a different tie. Hey, where are you going with the tie?"

"I'm planning to go to the bathroom to hang myself with it before you look at the red socks I'm wearing that you gave me for Valentine's Day."

~Cindy D'Ambroso Argiento

A Weekend of Freedom

*The reason women don't play football is because
eleven of them would never wear the same outfit in public.*
~Phyllis Diller

I'm not showering this weekend. I'm not shaving, either. I'm not doing a lot of things. My wife has gone to visit her parents, so I'm going to park myself in the recliner and watch football. I'm not talking about one little game here, either. I'm talking an entire weekend of gridiron action. I'm talking forty-eight hours sprawled out in the La-Z Boy, armed only with a remote, snacks, and a cooler full of beer. I've got two full days to myself, and I'm going to make the most of it.

Yes, it's time for a husband with floors to vacuum and windows to wash to cast all of that aside and tune into football. The next forty-eight hours will either be spent watching a game, recovering from a game, or preparing for the next game. I plan to stay in an adrenaline-laden state of bliss the entire time. I'll eat what I want when I want, and wear the smell of body odor like other men wear cologne.

My selfishness will be breathtaking.

My wife doesn't like football. Actually, she hates it. She and football mix like nitroglycerine and band camp. Whenever I ask her to watch a game with me, she gets a look on her face like I just asked for a bowl of baby toes.

"I've got better things to do with my time," she says with irritated sarcasm. "Like clean the toilets."

"Football is great," I explain. "It builds stamina and character. It produces the qualities we look for in our leaders."

She laughs in response, gives a caveman grunt, and makes a few derisive remarks about blood lust. My wife doesn't care who wins or loses the game, or even if the entire stadium collapses at halftime, killing everyone. But I certainly do. I think football is about the finest spectator sport ever invented. Much like a Whitman's Sampler, it seems to offer me a bit of everything.

That's why a spouse-free weekend is the best marriage therapy money can buy. My wife goes to visit her family, and I watch football. It's a win-win situation.

So here's my plan: I'm going to flick on the television and start enjoying myself any minute now. What about cleaning the bathrooms? Ha! Forget it. Bathroom cleaning will be unthinkable. I'll sweep every room with a glance, whisking by the untended laundry and the sink full of dirty dishes on my way to the couch. I'll become the anti-Martha Stewart.

Let other men be whipped slaves to their chores, living on a short leash with a massive honey-do list. Those kinds of guys have about as much spontaneous mobility as, say, a lump of cheese. I'll meet every day as a new adventure. My only decision will be what football game to watch next.

Heck, I might even wear my team colors if I get the notion. I'll put on face paint and haul out my Styrofoam finger. Other fans will be all sizzle, no steak; big Stetson, no herd; wild horses, no rope. In spectator terms, I will stride the earth like a colossus.

What's that? The lawn? Forget the lawn. I'll mow it when I get around to it. Back off, will ya? Live-for-the-moment dudes like me sometimes don't feel like mowing lawns.... Okay, at the moment my lawns are mowed. But that's because I chose to mow them.

There is one embarrassing part to this entire football weekend I'll tell you about, but only if you promise not to let it get around. It confirms people's worst suspicions, is the thing. And it doesn't make me look very cool.

I haven't actually watched one single game yet. I thought I'd change the sheets on the bed and do the laundry before I get started.

But I absolutely refuse to fold the clothes. Not folding clothes doesn't rattle a carefree guy like me. I never worry about such nonsense. Not when there are more exquisite forms of fun straight ahead.

Also, before I get settled into the recliner, I thought I would head down to the grocery store and get the shopping done for next week. I might even trim the hedges and change the oil in the car.

But like I said, keep quiet about this, okay? It takes a while to warm up to this kind of freedom. Besides, there are just some things people don't need to know.

~Timothy Martin

49

Order

Why does a woman work ten years to change a man's habits and then
complain that he's not the man she married?
~Barbra Streisand

I have a deep need for Order in my life, and so, to my packrat chef husband's ultimate dismay, I alphabetized our spice shelf.

The idea of having a shelf dedicated entirely to spices and herbs struck me as strange, but then again, I'm not a chef. In my obviously sheltered existence, my mother's spices were simple: salt, pepper, chili powder, cinnamon.

In short order, I sorted, disposed of, combined, consolidated and coordinated the shelf: caraway seeds, cardamom, cinnamon, cloves, coriander seeds, cumin. Two half-filled jars of paprika almost the same color seemed wasteful, so I combined the two, pleased with my progress.

Hmmm, bay leaves, several varieties—Indian, Greek, California. Should I or shouldn't I?

The Family Chef arrived home as I was finishing and stared—open-mouthed.

"What are you doing with my spices?"

"Last I looked, they were our spices."

"Where's the fenugreek?" he wailed.

"Probably in Athens by now. Nah, next to the fennel seeds where it belongs."

"It took me a year to get that shelf organized the way I want it!"

"Oh please. It looks better already."

"Yep, Miss Organization, that's you," he declared, as if this skill was beyond redemption.

"I'm a Virgo. What do you expect?"

"Is that an excuse or your horoscope?"

I grimace. "Some of these look positively ancient. Fingerprints from…"

"They're not ancient, they're… seasoned."

Now it's my turn to laugh. "You wouldn't eat ten-year-old food. Why'd you want to use ten-year-old spices? The jars are old and cruddy, labels smudged, it's disgusting."

"You don't understand.…"

"What, that boll weevils live in our spice jars?"

"They do not. Boll weevils feed on pods of cotton plants."

"By the way, why do you need so many different kinds of salt?"

"What do you mean?"

"What do you mean, what do I mean? Sea salt crystals, sea salt granulated, sea salt coarse, fleur de sel salt, sea salt light, Fumee de Sel salt, sea salt flaky."

"Stop it!" he says.

"What'd you do before you met me? Go on a tour of the Dead Sea?" I doubled over, laughing my head off.

"Nothing worse than a person laughing at her own bad joke." He rummages through the neat rows of jars. "What'd you do with the mace?"

"In the glove compartment with the flashlight."

At least he was laughing. "The spice, mace!"

"Oh, that mace. Say, what is mace?"

He rolled his eyes.

"Mace is a spice made from the waxy red covering of nutmeg seeds. It's a flavor similar to nutmeg with a hint of pepper but with a subtler note. It's overwhelming though if used by, shall we say, heavy-handed cooks."

"Oh," I said. "Two questions: why do you talk like that and why don't you just throw a little pepper in the nutmeg and forget about the mace?"

He has to sit down at this. "You seem to be dedicated to the proposition that all spices are created equal."

"See, there you go again. You sound like Thomas Jefferson."

"Don't get me started on Thomas Jefferson," he said, hand over his heart like he was about to say the Pledge of Allegiance. "I'm going to the garage. I can't face this."

"Hey, where do you want the saffron?" I called to his retreating back. "Next to the sesame seeds?"

"What? We have saffron?"

~Gretchen Houser

50

Those Doggone Socks

At the height of laughter,
the universe is flung into a kaleidoscope of new possibilities.
~Jean Houston

S tanding outside our first apartment watching the moving men unload boxes, I almost had to pinch myself to make sure this wasn't a dream. For the first six months of married life three thousand miles separated us, courtesy of the United States Navy. Not to mention that the two years prior to our wedding found Joe on one coast and me on the other for many months at a time.

I stood on the threshold of my new career as wife and homemaker eager to unpack boxes and turn our first apartment into our first "home." The only thing missing was a string of June Cleaver pearls and an organdy apron. No worries though, they were packed in a box somewhere.

The morning after arriving I woke up just as the first light of day crept through our bedroom window. With a stretch and a yawn I tossed the covers aside, hopped out of bed and slipped into the white chiffon peignoir robe that matched the gown my mother had given me at my bridal shower amid the winks giggles of many.

I tiptoed quietly lest I wake my adorable husband from his slumber. When I reached the door I stole one last glimpse at him snuggled under the comforter of our little love nest.

As I opened the bedroom door I realized a dirty sock was wedged between the door and the carpet. Poor thing! Joe was so tired from unpacking boxes he must have dropped his socks on the way to the hamper. I picked up the socks and dropped them into the hamper. Then off I went to prepare breakfast and pack my sweetheart's lunch. What a thrill to be taking good care of my handsome husband.

When Joe was off to the Navy base I finished unpacking the boxes, hung a few pictures and prepared a sumptuous dinner of roast chicken with all the trimmings. We toasted our new home with chardonnay at dinner, ending another perfect day.

The next morning as I made the bed and was tidying up I noticed dirty socks on the floor once again. That was a little disappointing, but probably just a fluke.

By the third day I was officially annoyed. At the end of three weeks I was ready to spray paint his feet black so he'd never have to wear socks again.

"What is it with you and the socks?" I blurted out one morning at breakfast. Joe looked down at his feet and then at me. "What do you mean? What's wrong with my socks?"

"Nothing right now. They're still on your feet."

"What are you talking about?"

"Your socks, buster! I've noticed they've never, not ever, not even one time navigated from your stinking feet to the clothes hamper. Surely you're aware of this."

"So you pick up my socks. So what? What's the big deal?"

"The big deal is that I am not the maid. Not now, not ever. So you'd better teach your socks how to launch from your feet to the hamper all by themselves or you'll find them some day in the last place you'd expect and I'm pretty sure you won't be happy about it."

I had laid down an ultimatum and meant it. But I had no clue how I'd follow through. Joe huffed out the door for the first time in our four weeks of marital bliss.

That night, dinner was quiet except for the gnashing of teeth. We successfully avoided each other all evening and I turned in early to get a head start on feigning sleep, then ended up tossing and turning all night. In the morning I got up and headed toward the bedroom door, once again treading on the dreaded dirty socks.

I don't know how many people were sitting at the table when Joe bit into two dirty socks on rye with extra mayo but I bet none of them kept a straight face. I wasn't really sure what to expect when he came home, but when we looked at each other neither one of us could stop laughing. That was twenty-six years ago. Near as I can figure, I've picked up roughly 18,980 dirty socks since that day, give or take a leap year or two.

I can't complain though. Joe is a good provider and a mighty pleasant fellow. He's always quick to unload the dishwasher and throw in a load of wash when necessary. In fact, now when his socks come off he lays them right on the dog's back. Then Sammy our Yorkie dutifully trots over to the hamper and rolls over on the floor depositing the socks right next to it. After twenty-six years I'm confident that's as close as socks are ever going to get to the hamper in this house. You can't teach an old dog new tricks.

~Annmarie B. Tait

Reprinted by permission of Off the Mark
and Mark Parisi ©2011

Sweet Discovery

Our mouths were filled with laughter, our tongues with songs of joy.
~Psalm 126

On the morning of my birthday, I caught my newlywed husband hunched over our kitchen counter, carefully studying the directions on a box of cake mix.

Scott and I had been married less than a year. His military duties had taken us far from our Yankee roots. And, when it came to celebrating our birthdays, even the warm Georgia sunshine couldn't take the place of our families back in Pennsylvania. Scott did his best to fill the void with kindness.

What my sweet husband lacked in baking experience, he made up in tenacity; he was determined to make it a memorable day. Decades later I still cherish his impish smile as he mixed up my birthday surprise.

Scott neared his final preparations with an air of satisfaction. His dimples deepened and he flashed me a broad smile. His warm brown eyes sparkled with the joy and spontaneity of a little child, as if to say, "Look what I did." I laughed out loud, tickled by his thoughtfulness, thoroughly enjoying his sense of accomplishment. His face shone as he carried two pans of cake batter to the oven.

It was then that I realized that Scott mixed his cake with love, goodness and a few other things. Sharp points protruded from the batter in the center of each pan. Seeing my quizzical expression, Scott assured me of his attention to detail. "The directions on the box say

Sweet Discovery : What's Love Got to Do with It   171

the cake is done when a toothpick stuck in the center comes out clean."

I wrapped my arms around this precious man, still staring at me with puzzled eyes. Gently, I explained that toothpicks are inserted at the end of the baking, to test the cake's doneness, not during it. As the smile I'd been trying to stifle met Scott's, we burst into uncontrollable laughter; it was one sweet discovery.

~Kathleen Swartz McQuaig

52

It's Really the Thought that Counts

I love being married. It's so great to find that one special person
you want to annoy for the rest of your life.
~Rita Rudner

The men in my family have a long and sordid history of giving heinous gifts. The official records only go back a few generations but if we could see into history and watch my great-great-great-grandfather bestow a gift upon his pioneer bride it would probably have been Confederate war bonds, a tract of oceanfront property in Kansas, or a sixteen-year-old lame mule when she had asked for laying hens.

The first Christmas my dad celebrated with a new girlfriend he gave her a large wrapped box. As the paper came away she laughed and told her mother, "It's in a router box, how funny." That might have been hilarious if the box had contained anything but a router. Which it didn't. In my poor father's defense, she had said she liked woodworking. Or was that woodwork? Wood-burning stoves? Walking in the woods? Love can be just as deaf as it is blind some days.

Even once the first blush of love wore off, my father's gift giving didn't get any better. When presented with a lovely Ping-Pong table, my stepmother nodded, smiled, and resolved from then on to purchase her own gifts and just let my father sign the card.

It was evident the gene had not skipped a generation when my brother presented his wife with a Swiffer for Mother's Day. Not just any Swiffer. It was a special occasion after all, so this was the Swiffer that squirts cleaner with the flick of a trigger and even vacuums crumbs. His thinking was that his neatnik wife would like nothing more than something to make her job easier. Are you surprised he's no longer married to wife number one? Me neither.

The lack of talent for gift giving is carried on the Y chromosome and is highly contagious. So when my husband married into the family, it was only a matter of time before he became infected. It was our second married Christmas, I believe, when he did the bulk of his shopping at a small-town dollar store and presented me with... I kid you not... a plastic food scale. Were I a more gracious receiver, I might have taken it a little easier on him. Or at least kept my mouth shut. Instead, such marital hell rained down that we immediately made a trip to see Jake the Jeweler.

If it's the thought that counts, I hesitate to wonder what he must have been thinking about me when he made that choice! To help him focus during subsequent holidays, I created a list to help him choose a bit more wisely.

1. Think of me when I'm not with you. It doesn't count as a gift if I have to pull it off the shelf and hand it to you or, worse, pay for it along with my groceries. I'm happy to make a list, circle pictures in a catalog, register at Target even, but don't make me buy it myself.

2. Think not of anything pluggable. Electronics are fun but usually not gift-quality. iPods, maybe. Hard drives, DVD burners, SD cards, or clock radios are not. Coffeemakers, toasters, and mixers are fine if I happen to be a new bride, not an old wife.

3. Think not of you. Gifts for you are not gifts for me. Don't get me a new laptop because you want to use it to play *World of Warcraft* online. And we both know who enjoys lingerie more. Have you noticed that I don't

wear that sparkly bustier to soccer practice on Saturday morning?

4. Think not of making it yourself. Homemade gifts are acceptable from the children. But unless you're brewing a batch of boutique beer or have developed skill in building Amish furniture, don't go there.

5. Think not of critters. Pets are not presents. They are the opposite of presents. Cleaning up hairballs, scraping doo-doo off my shoes, or being gnawed on while I trim nails aren't usually effective marketing ploys.

6. Think of something new. Replacing the piece of my grandmother's china that you dropped or the cell phone that fell into the pool is not a gift. Yes, I would love it. The same way I'd love it if you wrapped up my favorite sweater, the dinner I just made, or one of our small children. It's already mine.

7. Think in advance. Internet shopping has opened a world of new stores to those of us living on the rural outskirts of nowhere. However, you must allow for shipping time. If you wait, you can choose to pay the extra to ship it fast or pay by sleeping on the couch when there isn't anything under the tree for me. Your choice.

My five-year-old son is already being trained to be a better gift giver than his forefathers. But if the electric lime socks I got for Mother's Day are any indication, his girlfriends and wives will suffer the same fate as the rest of the women in our family. It's okay. On their wedding day I'll slip her the number for Jake the Jeweler. He'll take good care of her.

~Becky Tidberg

Married Life!

Chapter 6

Love
Will Keep Us Together

The weather is always fair when people are in love.

~Italian Proverb

53

The Fan

There isn't a single professional sports season now that doesn't go on at least a month too long. Baseball starts in football weather, and football in baseball weather, and basketball overlaps them both.

~James Reston

"Throw it to Austin! He's wide open... nooooo! Interference! Where's the flag, ref? He was all over him!"

That nutty fan screaming at the television from the couch in the den is a fairly accurate portrayal of yours truly on any fall Sunday afternoon, but when I married Scotty ages ago, I was a TV sports virgin. Oh, I'd always played sports. I even went steady with a lineman on the high school team and played powder puff football, but watching sports on the tube was a foreign concept to me. So when the man I loved suggested we sit in front of the TV and watch the Cowboys play football on a fall Sunday soon after we were married, I was crushed.

I'd just started a job teaching school, and he was working on a graduate degree in accounting while holding down a part-time job. Sunday afternoon constituted a significant portion of our free time together. I thought he was already tired of me. Why else would he choose to watch a football game when he could be doing something fun with me? I vowed to win him back.

The next Sunday he turned on the game and I launched my campaign.

"Hey, sweetie, it's a gorgeous day, why don't we take a hike with the pups?" I suggested.

"Sure, babe, as soon as the game's over," he replied without moving his eyes from the screen.

Okay, score one for the Cowboys, but that was only the first down!

The following week I tried again.

"Scotty, you wanted me to help you reorganize the garage. I've got the afternoon free—no papers to grade, no lesson plans due."

"Great! Thanks, honey. We'll do it right after the game," he said as another handful of popcorn made the trip from the bowl to his mouth.

Second down! Score two for the noodle headed boys in blue!

The following week I played what I hoped would be my trump card. "It's such a cold day, Scott. Why don't we spend the afternoon in bed cuddling?"

Surely no red-blooded guy could resist that invitation!

"Ummm! I like that idea! The game will be over in an hour. You climb in and keep my place warm, okay?"

Well, that was it. Three tries and no first down meant it was time to punt. Even I knew that much.

Admitting defeat, I sat down beside him, leaned against his shoulder, and dug into the popcorn that was an inevitable part of the Sunday ritual. I could handle this. After all, football season only lasted a few months, right? Then I'd have his full attention on Sunday afternoons. I'd use football season to show him what a good wife I was and how lucky he was to have me. How many men had a wife willing to sit down in front of the television for a football game just for the pleasure of being with them?

So began the new order of things. Whatever happened Sunday morning, by eleven o'clock we'd be curled up on the couch with the popcorn trying to pull the Cowboys through to a win. Now that he had his game and my attention, Scott was in heaven. He explained the intricacies of football with patience, and I gave him my full attention.

I can't say exactly when it happened, but within a few weeks I became aware of something really strange. I no longer woke up Sunday morning dreading the game I'd be watching in the afternoon. What a nice surprise! A couple of weeks later I woke shuffling through my mind to remember who our opponent was that day, then found myself talking to Scotty over breakfast about what our chances were. It still came as a shock when I realized I was actually looking forward to game afternoons, but I really knew I'd seen the light when I volunteered to make the popcorn.

Once he had me hooked on football there was no stopping him. I soon learned that basketball season followed football season and that baseball filled the summer months. Should there be a gap between seasons there was always tennis or golf. The Triple Crown of thoroughbred racing captured our attention for three Saturdays in the late spring, and of course the Olympics came around every couple of years.

Although I never became a baseball fan, the two of us were pretty much in sync for a few years, but Scotty was like those early pioneers who heeded the call, "Go west young man!" He was always on the lookout for a new thrill, a new challenge, or a new pleasure. With the inception of video and computer games his loyalty to the Cowboys, the Mavericks, and the Rangers began to wane, and our Sundays in front of the television began to bore my husband. Ten minutes into the first quarter he'd begin to fidget. Glancing at him sideways, I'd notice his hands flexing as if he were working the joystick on a computer game.

"I think I'll go play on the computer," he'd mumble sheepishly.

"But this is such a big game! If we beat the Eagles today we'll cinch a berth in the playoffs," I'd remind him with the passion of the true fan.

"Yeah, well, keep me up to date on what's happening. I'll be in the other room," was his response as he stood to leave.

Before long any pretense of interest disappeared, and he'd head for the computer room as soon as I turned the TV on.

"Scotty, aren't you going to watch the game?" I'd ask.

"Nope, you pull 'em through for me. I'm gonna play on the computer a while."

After ten years of marriage I knew him. His loss of interest in watching the football game had nothing to do with me. In the "been there, done that" mindset that was so much a part of his persona, Scotty was simply moving on. Sadly, I faced facts. Our shared Sundays in front of the TV were over.

In spite of the disappointment I felt, I am aware that I am the one who benefits the most from my husband's approach to life. Scotty blazes the trail, trying anything and everything that comes his way. I follow a few steps behind, sampling each new game, challenge, or pleasure for myself, picking and choosing those that work for me. His passions blaze fiercely for a while and then fade into ashes. Mine are slower to kindle, but more lasting. For this reason, his full throttle approach to life enriches mine in ways I might miss without him. My life was full long before we took up scuba diving, motorcycles, and skiing, but it has been even better since these were added to the mix. Introducing me to the pleasures of spectator sports has been his greatest gift of all.

~Pam Bailes

54

Sweeping with the Enemy

Don't find fault. Find a remedy.
~Henry Ford

Forget the five teenage stepdaughters I had acquired—it was my new husband's adopted dog that frightened me. As Michael and I settled into married life, his Australian Shepherd became increasingly unsettled. Each time Michael snuggled up to me, Frodo emitted a visceral growl from the depths of his belly, warning me that he wasn't keen on sharing his master's affections.

"Don't worry. He'll warm up to you in no time," Michael assured me. But as Frodo lowered his shoulders, raised his hackles, and jostled between us, I remained skeptical.

"He just needs time to adjust." Michael stroked Frodo's head, and the dog stopped growling.

I pointed to my Collie who lay on the floor nearby. Dexter's tail thumped and his eyes gleamed. "Dexter's adjusted just fine. You don't hear him growling at anyone."

"Well," Michael said, "you can hardly compare the two. Dexter... well... he's just Dexter. Now Frodo, he's a guard dog. A real protector. Soon you'll be thankful he's here, keeping you safe."

A few days later, Frodo cornered me in the laundry room with his teeth bared. Thankful he's here? Keeping me safe? I would rather have taken my chances with an armed intruder, I thought, as I shielded my body with the laundry basket and jockeyed toward the door. Frodo followed me to the bedroom and stood nearby as I folded the laundry.

Every few seconds, a grumble of displeasure traveled the length of the room.

"What do you mean Frodo bit you?" Michael asked when he returned home from work.

"Just what I said. I was folding the kitchen towels, and he jumped up and bit me."

Frodo tucked his head into Michael's lap. The dog's stubby tail fluttered like a hummingbird while he licked Michael's hand. "I can't imagine Frodo biting anyone. Did you do anything to provoke him?"

I shot up from my chair. "So you're blaming me?"

Michael quickly backpedaled. "I'm sorry. It's just not like Frodo to bite."

Frodo inched his way toward me with his head bowed in submission.

"See," Michael said. "He's fine. Go ahead and pet him. Look, he's even wagging his tail."

My hands remained plastered to my sides. "Yeah, and a rattler shakes his tail just prior to striking his victim."

Whenever Michael wasn't home, I felt Frodo's presence from anywhere in the house. He was a ninja. Stealthy. Intelligent. Unwavering. I considered placing a cowbell on the dog's collar to warn me of his approach, to give me time to find an escape.

"I think you're overreacting," Michael said.

"Your dog stares at me. Follows me around. Taunts me. I swear he's plotting my demise."

Michael's laughter eased my tension. "Maybe Frodo senses your anxiety. Try loosening up a bit and see what happens."

For the next few weeks, I tried everything to gain the dog's approval: treats, praise, more treats. I fed him dinner, took him for walks, and threw his favorite ball. All things positive could be linked back to me, but he continued to bare his teeth, snap, and snarl. How could I tell my husband that I wanted to secretly do away with his dog? The same dog that Michael had claimed to be the best dog he'd ever owned, the dog that had pulled him through a bitter divorce.

Out of guilt, I stopped planning Frodo's unfortunate accident.

Several weeks later, while I was drying the dishes, I felt a pinch on my wrist and heard a "tink."

"Well," Michael said, pulling me close, "at least he bit your bracelet and not your arm."

I drew back. "He still bit me nonetheless."

"Technically… he didn't bite you. He bit your…"

"We've got to do something," I demanded. "I can't live with a dog that bites."

Michael suggested we take Frodo to the vet to see if a medical issue was at the root of the aggression. The medical tests came back normal, and the vet suggested we write down the events that led up to the biting to gain a better understanding of any precipitating factors.

The next evening, as I swept the kitchen floor, I felt the nip before the warmth trickled down my belly. Frodo cowered in the corner as if he knew he'd gone too far. As I washed the blood from my skin, Michael expressed his concern.

I took the vet's advice and jotted some notes: folding dishtowels, using the duster, drying the dishes, and sweeping or mopping the floor. Every act of aggression could be linked to household chores.

"What? He doesn't like a clean house?" Michael asked.

"I think he's been abused. You know, hit with the broom, snapped with a kitchen towel, or shooed with a mop. Frodo assumes I'm going to hurt him. You know… a conditioned response."

Michael looked at me with pained eyes. "That certainly explains some things."

Frodo settled down and lay quietly at Michael's feet. I waited a while before testing my suspicions.

When I picked up the broom, Frodo ran over, snarling and bristling then ripped it from my hands. After the broom hit the floor, Frodo stopped the attack.

"See?" I said.

"So, what do we do?"

"Well, I could always quit cleaning," I said, tossing Michael a smile.

"Uh… no."

"Darn."

That night, I planned a strategy to gain Frodo's trust while still tending to the household chores. Over the next few months, I kept Frodo sequestered while sweeping and mopping but let him watch from behind a gate while I performed the less threatening tasks of dusting or folding towels. He growled, jumped on the gate, and whined while nervously pacing back and forth, and I ignored him. When he stopped, I rewarded him with a treat, a kind word, or a tweak of the ear. Soon, Frodo watched me sweep and mop, earning the same rewards. Eventually, the aggressive posturing stopped, and he could stay in the same room while I performed all the cleaning.

As Frodo grows older, some of his grumblings have resurfaced. He recently whined and drooled as I retrieved the cleaning supplies, and I warned Michael of Frodo's regression.

"Well, we're not getting rid of him."

I leaned against the broom, and Frodo stood, perched for action. "Well, I'm not getting attacked again."

"A maid?" Michael offered.

"I don't see how we could afford…" Frodo's snarl drifted in my general direction. "To pass up such a wonderful idea."

~Cathi LaMarche

"Honey, did you walk the dog?"

The Proofreader

*Marriage is a book of which the first chapter is written in poetry
and the remaining chapters in prose.*
~Beverley Nichols

After years of odd jobs and raising children, I went back to my first love, writing. Finally! The perfect job for me! Words fly from my neurons to fingers to the keyboard at a dizzying pace, and when I'm all written out, I sink back in my chair, absolutely amazed at what my genius hath wrought. Except that once the glow fades, I notice a few teensy problems. Like a sentence that's three hundred words long. Or a character whose name, sex, and species change, all in the space of one page. So, okay, fine—I needed a proofreader, and I thought my husband would be perfect for the job.

See, I hadn't exactly turned a profit at writing, so free labor was a must. And I wasn't quite ready to show my work to the world, or even the next-door neighbor. The obvious choice was staring me in the face, if I leaned over the couch and pried apart the snoozing eyelids. Because there lay my helpmate, the man who promised to stand by me for richer or poorer, better or worse, dangling participles or split infinitives.

Not that my husband would actually know a participle from the past tense. He's a wonderful guy in a ton of ways, but technically, I wouldn't call him the "reading" type. He believes movies were invented so that humankind would not have to slog through something like *Toy Story*. He'll check the sports pages, and he'll zip through a paperback thriller in a year or so. But what he lacks in literary depth, he more than makes up for in convenience.

So, when I finished my first story, I headed to the couch to ask my hubby to give it a read. He seemed happy enough to oblige. His brow furrowed in concentration. He chuckled in all the right places. Afterwards, he even offered a gracious compliment. I asked probing questions about motivation and characters and such. He squirmed a little there, but managed one or two polite responses. In short, he was as perfect a proofreader as he could be, all things considered. I was thrilled!

So, a week later, I headed to the couch again with the second manuscript. My loving partner took one look, rolled his eyes, and sighed. Loudly. As if I'd asked him to read *Gone With the Wind* instead of a 3,000-word humorous, contemporary, swashbuckling, mystery/romance.

I pressed the story into his hands. His shoulders slumped, and he leaned over, groaning, with his tongue hanging from his mouth. But that's his usual routine when I ask him to unload the dishwasher. I wasn't going anywhere till he finished the proofreading job. He flipped the pages, scanning the words, with one eye focused on the game that was blaring from the TV. I didn't hear any chuckles, but I thought I spied a curled, sort of snarling/smiling lip. I moved on to the question part of the critique.

"Were you surprised? Did you get it? Did you like it?"

"It's fine," he said, in a Zombie dead tone. "I loved everything about it."

Not as thrilling an evaluation as I'd have liked, but I love a good challenge. So I worked on the story, editing this and polishing that, until I had a humorous, contemporary, swashbuckling, romantic mystery. Totally different.

It was around this time that my proofreader developed evasive maneuvers worthy of a CIA operative. Whenever I checked the couch to deliver my new and improved literary masterpiece, he was gone. One evening, I heard a strange, rumbling noise outside. My husband was in the YARD. He'd fired up the leaf blower and was actually blowing leaves off the driveway!

Two can play that game I thought, as I plopped my story onto his dinner plate. Hunger eventually drove my prey, er, man inside. He entered the kitchen and a moan escaped through his parched lips. He'd spied the typewritten paper blocking his path to gastrointestinal fulfillment! So he sunk into his chair, resigned to his fate. But his glance kept darting back and forth from story to stove. And he constantly sniffed the tuna burger-scented air. I just did not feel as if I had his complete attention. So I asked a few penetrating questions.

"Did you like it? Did the second paragraph make sense? Did you understand that the pirate woman is really his wife in a wig?" I hammered at him relentlessly. Nobody was eating till I had answers!

"What was the funniest line? Were you surprised by the first plot twist? What about the second plot twist? Did you know belladonna is a poison? Did you guess that the wife was the KILLER?"

He refused to answer a single question. Or eat the tuna burgers.

Anyway, we have since called a truce. He has determined that in order to continue working in his paying job (which supports me in the manner to which I've accustomed myself), he must have uninterrupted couch time. I have determined that my writing group, meeting twice a month in the local bookstore, is far more helpful in developing my writing genius.

But every once in a while, I write something scathingly brilliant, and need a proofreader right that minute. And then, I circle the couch—and the chase is on!

~Cathy C. Hall

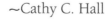

56

Giving and Taking

The difference between try and triumph is a little umph.
~Author Unknown

"Hmm," said Reverend Stevens, the man who was scheduled to perform the wedding ceremony for my fiancé, Bob, and me. He was reviewing the results from the personality test we took as part of the marriage class offered at our church. Since this was a second marriage for both of us, we wanted to get it right this time.

He placed the two printed pages in front of us so we could see the source of his concern. "This test is scored using four letters, each one representing a different personality trait."

Bob and I leaned forward to take a peek at what must surely be disastrous news.

"They're almost exactly alike," I said, grinning.

"Three of the letters are alike," Reverend Stevens agreed. "But one is different—very different—as far as you can get different."

Bob frowned. "Does that mean we shouldn't get married?"

"No!" replied the reverend. "It means you'll need to compromise—a lot—more than..." he caught my glare and decided to take a lighter tack. "Just a bit more than the usual give and take," he said, smiling.

"Hmm," Bob and I said in unison.

And so it came to pass that we were married and the giving and taking, or in our case, the tug of war began. Actually, it started the first weekend after we returned from our honeymoon.

Our most notable personality conflict turned out to be the fact that I couldn't stand clutter and frequently threw things out, and Bob felt the need to hang on to everything he'd ever owned.

His justification for hoarding, which he learned from his mother, was that he might need each and every one of those items "some day." I acquired my clutter-free tendencies from my mother, whose philosophy was, "If you haven't used it in a year, it's taking up valuable space. Get rid of it."

After we married, I moved into Bob's house. He'd been living there for six years and his double-car garage was packed with stuff, most of which was still in the original moving boxes. Since I wasn't accustomed to leaving my shiny new car outside under the broiling Texas sun, I laid claim to half the square footage.

Following a lively discussion about the value of things versus space, Bob reluctantly agreed to clean out the garage. He and his hoarding mentor, a.k.a. Mom, set out to complete this monumental, emotionally wrenching task. They both feared my "use-it-or-toss-it" tendencies, so I wasn't allowed to participate.

I watched from a safe distance as they dragged everything out to the driveway, opened the boxes, and took an extended trip down memory lane, examining each treasure. Then they dusted it all off, sorted it into even more boxes and put them back into Bob's designated half of the space. Apparently I misunderstood; he meant "clean off," not "clean out."

The contents were now stacked side-to-side, front-to-back and floor-to-ceiling in his half of the garage! I was speechless, but he and his mother beamed with pride at their accomplishment.

As promised, however, that evening I managed to pull my car into the garage and had just enough room to squeeze out and slide along the wall of teetering boxes to reach the back door.

But it was progress nonetheless, and the first in a long line of compromises that would test our vows to the limit. Year after year, as each conflict arose, we repeated our mantra, "Give and take, give and take."

After twenty-three years, it seems that this giving and taking strategy has finally taken hold. I've grown comfortable living with more, and Bob is agreeable to living with less.

~Gloria Hander Lyons

57

Hearts and Hurricanes

If you surrender to the wind, you can ride it.
~Toni Morrison

My husband and I are rookies when it comes to travel as a couple. We stay in the United States and have ventured to Mexico only recently.

In contrast, I grew up in a family where travel was one of the four food groups—good health demanded it. Summers were spent voyaging to Europe on the Queen Mary, picnicking in the English countryside and watching tremendous men throw logs the size of redwood trees at the Scottish Highland games. At six years old, I found nothing about this interesting, romantic or beautiful. I spent a lot of time just wanting a hot dog. The youngest of three children, I was squashed in the back seat between my brother and sister, feeling carsick and dreading the next castle. Inevitably I would feel lost in a large group of foreigners, listening to a French guide point to doorways and furniture in excited tones. Castles smelled like a mixture of my father's starchy shirts and musty closets. In between museums, my mother read to us from *Michelin* guidebooks as my father drove haltingly ahead on a different side of the road. Like the guides, she too would get very excited, interjecting, "Isn't that fascinating?" like a chorus hoping we'd sing along.

So now, decades later, I am trying to find my own sweet melody in travel—as my husband and I venture away each year without children. Our recent trip to the California wine country began with yellow sticky notes decorating the kitchen counter, as my son and daughter would be left in the care of a dear friend. The notes were yellow reminders about two tennis lessons, one dentist appointment, my son's volunteer work with developmentally disabled adults, two Halloween parties, one school field trip, garbage pick-up and plant watering. Puppy care, bunny care and fish feeding had their own full page. The puppy goes to Canine Campovers and I had to remind my friend she gets car sick so to avoid stop and go traffic.

My careful note taking occurred before a couple of last-minute emergencies threatened to scuttle our vacation plans. A Florida hurricane hit my son's university and my father-in-law had triple bypass surgery.

Suddenly my organized sticky notes provided no comfort, no direction. When I was making reservations at our Mendocino bed and breakfast, I hadn't taken into account old hearts and young hurricanes. Our family looked like the route map in an airline magazine — my son was driving north, my father-in-law was ailing in the south and we were considering going west.

My father advised, "Go west, your son will be fine."

My mother said, "Stay home, you should be there."

My husband was pondering traveling to a southern ICU, and I was left with a lot of cross-outs on sticky notes. My heart told me we needed to get away. I'd recently had a dream in which my husband and I stopped in the kitchen to talk to each other! Obviously our lives were moving too quickly. As I zipped my suitcase, guilt was stuffed in the corners next to a good novel and my running shoes. We were going anyway, with charged cell phones, Internet access and the hope our self-care wouldn't impinge on dying hurricane winds and recovering hearts.

We landed on a rainy San Francisco runway. The Hertz lady said we needed a six-cylinder engine for the curvy wine-country roads. I was more concerned about the color of the car and was just happy to be standing next to my husband with no one asking me for anything. We weaved our way up north on Highway 1, listening a radio station that played old songs from when we were in ninth grade.

After stopping in Santa Rosa for tofu and vegetables, a shared glass of wine, a shared cup of decaf coffee, and a shared chocolate chip cookie, we were feeling like adolescents again. Without children, we were free to be children. The Mendocino coast brings together the redwood forests, rocky cliffs and a quiet blue ocean. The stillness of the forest on morning runs matched an inner stillness allowed by our solitude. In our regular life, my husband and I have gotten used to running separately. Young children demanded "revolving door" running. My husband would return through the front door and I'd head out the back. He usually did the early run just because he felt more comfortable with a headlamp — but no revolving doors in Mendocino.

Daily calls back to the "real world" kept us informed about heart and hurricane realities. Power to the university campus was restored; my father-in-law's pacemaker at full charge.

There are no sticky notes on vacation, and stepping out of a morning shower has no deadline. We hit more coffee shops and bakeries than wineries. Heading home, our suitcase zipped more easily because we had no guilt stuffed in corners. Everyone survived. And I am reminded of the importance of making the pace slower — it strengthens the heart in a marriage. So tomorrow when the winds blow again, we're that much stronger to take care and hold tight. And someday, we might even make it to a French castle.

~Priscilla Dann-Courtney

58

Sweet Thereafter

A bend in the road is not the end of the road...
unless you fail to make the turn.
~Author Unknown

I was eighteen years old when I met Daren, the man that I would marry, during a casual evening with friends. It felt like magic from the very beginning. I remember having an "ah-ha" moment when I saw him: we locked eyes and I thought to myself, "this guy seems important to me in my life." From that very moment, there was never another for either of us.

We moved in together after only three months of dating, and that's when the "honeymoon" period of our relationship abruptly came to a halt. Suddenly we were fighting about even the most mundane things. Still, there was a fire inside both of us to work it out, to stay committed, and we loved each other so much that we couldn't leave. Something very powerful attracted us to one another.

After five years of dating, living together, and sharing our lives, Daren proposed to me. Everything just felt right. We had come a long way in those five years. We had both grown up considerably in that time. Life felt entirely blissful as we planned our wedding and honeymoon. We knew that being together would not always be easy, but that it would be worth it because our love had grown and blossomed into something we had never expected.

The wedding felt like we were on own planet. The people, the music, the food—it was so perfect in every way I felt surely there was enough love to sail us into eternity. But after the wedding and the honeymoon, our lives changed considerably. I left my employment to become a full-time freelance writer, and Daren was running the home business, which is also largely seasonal. Since I had left my job, he was in charge of supporting our little family of two, and I think that the pressure of that coupled with the large amount of time we began spending together became overwhelming.

After nearly seven years together, redefining everything radically seemed an impossible challenge. Each of us was disappointed about the nature of things, and so we took it out on each other, not knowing what to do. I cried behind closed doors, and tried to cope with the changes. I felt misunderstood by the one person who was my shelter: my husband. Daren went into his own world. He was doing only what he had to, and nothing it seemed, of what he wanted to do. His unhappiness made my own unhappiness worse.

The fighting seemed to never end. The smallest mistakes turned into big fights. I wondered what I might be doing wrong. I wondered what he was feeling. I wondered most about when it would end... and how it would end; would we come out better and stronger than before, as we had in the past?

After a few months, I turned to him and said, "I think that you have lost your passion in life. You are unhappy." He looked at me, bewildered, and told me he almost couldn't stand to be around me. I countered, "That is because I do not let you run from your greatness." He said nothing. The next day I spent the day out with my mother. When we returned home, Daren was in the garage building speaker stands and a shelf for our stereo.

The following day, he was also very motivated... and so, too, the day after that. He was so motivated he even helped me reorganize my writing office. He looked at me—he kissed me. We danced together to our old music and experienced a new level of passion and energy.

We both knew that marriage wasn't going to be easy, but what we had forgotten about is the passion that is innate to life. There is a need for creativity, and positive reinforcement from our support systems—each other. For a small moment, life overtook us and we lost sight of our need to push each other as people, because that too is a form of support. Life is sometimes a challenge. Sometimes Daren and I feel it is hard to be honest with one another, but when we are, it yields the best results, even if we haven't perfected the formula yet.

~Billie Criswell

59

It's Not There

Language is the means of getting an idea from my brain into yours
without surgery.
~Mark Amidon

Cutting boards, jars, knives and a colorful mix of veggies cluttered the kitchen island. Minced onion, garlic, and ginger swam in hot golden olive oil in a pan. Following a sniff trail, my husband approached and gently brushed my hair aside to kiss my neck.

"Smells great. Tell me what I can do to help, hon."

"Would you mind going to the deck and getting the seasoning I left out there?"

He nodded and headed outside, only to return in under ninety seconds.

"I'm sorry. Can't find it. Where exactly is it?"

Concentrating on my prep work at the sink, I pressed the mute button on my "right-in-plain-sight-did-you-even-look-or-move-anything" thoughts and responded, "It's on the shelf in the corner. Thanks."

With a cheery "okay" he headed back to the deck. Four minutes later, he reappeared. Hearing him enter, I automatically stretched out my hand for the seasoning.

"Tell me again… where exactly?"

Did I have to be so precise? Our deck isn't a football field. I stopped myself from saying what I wanted to say, in the how-could-you-miss-it-do-I-need-to-draw-you-a-map vein. I must wrestle this communication snafu to the ground. After all, I am a marriage counselor!

"Look on the second shelf... the three-tiered glass and metal thing... next to the barbecue pit... where we keep the bug candles. Okay?" I separated my directions into chunk-size bits of detail. By this time, I could have crawled sideways there and back three times and been done with it.

He made his third trip, but returned empty-handed. I could sense he was frustrated, so I sweetly asked, "Would you like me to show you where it is, dear?"

"Sure, but it's not there."

I hooked my arm in his—by now we were each grinning in anticipation. I escorted him to the window overlooking the deck and pointed. "Can you see it now?"

"Well, duh. Why didn't you just say it was to the right of the outlet? I would've found it immediately."

We hugged and laughed over a humorous ending to a threatened mini-crisis of annoyance and bickering. I suppose a woman's clearly perfect directions can be clearly muddy to her husband. We can move on with humor and grace or spoil the moment with nitpicking words.

~Patt Hollinger Pickett, Ph.D.

60

The Sign Solution

What counts in making a happy marriage is not so much how compatible you are, but how you deal with incompatibility.
~George Levinger

When I joined the at-home work force, I thought my biggest problem would be the demands of the new job. Or maybe interruptions from friends or drop-in neighbors. Possibly even the rowdy antics of Sally, the crazy dog. But I didn't expect my number one problem to be my husband.

After all, it was my husband who encouraged me to take my free-lance writing bull by the horns. "It's time you gave yourself a chance," he said. "You have talent; now follow your dream!" he said. So I did. I followed that dream right into the room where my husband's home office was set up. That's where the old, extra computer happened to be situated. I dragged a file cabinet up from the basement, stuck a bulletin board on the wall above my computer desk, and voila! I was all set up for business.

"Are you going to be here ALL THE TIME?" my husband asked after the third day. Er, I thought that was the idea of working at home.

Here's the thing: my husband is an occasional work-at-homer, too. About every other week, he's on the road, doing his business thing all over the country. But those in-between weeks, he's at home, snug in his office, doing his business thing. Somehow, amidst all the encouraging words and merlot, he'd completely forgotten that he'd be sharing office space with me. And oddly enough, after twenty-five years of on-and-off the road connubial bliss, we found working together in VERY close proximity to be a bit of a strain.

The trouble started with music. My husband, a former DJ, loves rock music. Apparently, Led Zeppelin, playing at twenty decibels, is necessary for him to achieve optimal business efficiency. I, on the other hand, require absolute silence and a Zen-like atmosphere in order to achieve optimal writing brilliance.

Except for that golden moment after I've written something scathingly brilliant! See, I have to read my works-in-progress aloud — over and over and over again. Any writer will tell you that this is a necessary part of the process. My husband considered my reading aloud an extremely annoying part of the process.

You can see where this was going. The funny thing is, I didn't see where my husband was going the day he left the house and returned home with a spanking new laptop and printer. He carried them upstairs to my off-at-college daughter's bedroom. Well, I can take a hint. I relocated my business.

I'd barely figured out how to use a wireless mouse before trouble came knocking again. "Who's been working in my room?" said my little Goldilocks girl. She'd decided to move back home. Papa Bear groaned and Mama Bear packed up the writing stuff.

It was back to the corner in my husband's office. Week after week, the music blared and I glared. I read aloud, annoyingly, and my husband turned the music up louder. Neighbors hinted about a noise ordinance. If friends called, I didn't hear the phone ringing. Sally, the crazy dog, put her paws over her ears. It was the Battle of the Work-at-Home Spouses!

But as my husband had noted back in the early days, I had writing talent. So I got to work... and wrote up a sign.

"QUIET," it read on one side. "ROCK 'N ROLL" it read on the other. Now when my husband and I happen to be working at the same time, he can look on my bulletin board. If I'm doing research, or answering e-mails, or playing games (sometimes necessary to jump-start the creative juices), I'm happy to rock out. But if I'm writing, then I need quiet to make the big bucks (sometimes necessary to jumpstart connubial bliss).

And if I need to read my works-in-progress out loud, I wait until my husband goes to bed. Because let's face it. That reading out loud, over and over and over again… really is annoying.

~Cathy C. Hall

61

Little Black Book

Are we not like two volumes of one book?
~Marceline Desbordes-Valmore

"You don't want to date him," my ex-boyfriend Joe said. "It won't work. He's too predictable. Steady. Why, he probably carries a little black book in his back pocket. A schedule. A life-syllabus."

"He does not," I said.

"I'll bet he does. I'll bet it's a rule book. A rule book on how to do exactly everything in exactly the right way."

"Not true," I said.

We were talking about my new boyfriend, Lonny. Prince Charming. The man I eventually married. And spent the next several years trying to separate from the black book that lived in his back pocket.

It's not a little black book, really. It's more of a way of doing things. A way of living. It is, well, sort of like a set of rules. The way to do everything, just right.

Early in our marriage, this caused some struggle.

"Lonny, why is it taking a million years to paint the house?" I asked as I scrunched my toes in the too-long grass and peered up at my new husband, who was dangling, paint brush in hand, from a ladder that was propped against the peeling exterior of our very first home.

"There's a right way to do things," he called down. "And it involves many steps."

"What about the lawn?" I asked.

"If it's cut too short, it won't thicken up. It needs to be long. It's the right way."

"Oh," I said. A little hard for me to comprehend. I was a slap-it-together girl. A scrape here, a scrape there, fresh coat of paint. A zip here and a zip there, freshly cut lawn.

Easy. Simple. Fast. Free.

But for Lonny, this was wild. Reckless. Uninhibited. In a not-good way.

After we procreated, the chasm between black-book-living and life-on-the-wild-side deepened.

"Poor little Logan," I said, as I patted dry the sweet baby buns of our first little boy. I'd just pulled him from the tub and noticed a grisly, red rash. "Lonny, can you please hand me the diaper-rash cream?"

"Sure thing," Lonny said. He retrieved the cream from the closet and read the back of the tube as he padded across the nursery floor.

I unscrewed the cap and allowed a liberal amount to goosh over our baby's diaper area while Lonny tickled Logan's tummy and peered over my shoulder.

"Um, Shawnelle, the tube says to apply to affected area," he said. "You've gotten a little medicine where there's no rash."

"It's all good," I said. "Won't hurt him a bit." I slathered a little more cream for emphasis.

"But the package says..."

I hushed him with a kiss. But I knew, that behind the smooch, he was still concerned about proper rash-cream application.

The years swept by. Lonny and I had four more sons. He learned to endure watching me shake detergent into our commercial-size washing machine without measuring. And I learned to zip my lips when I saw him measure exactly four cups of water into the saucepan, to boil, for the awaiting noodles of his mac-and-cheese. It all worked. Him living life his way. Me living life mine. Despite the differences, our marriage grew, stretched, developed, thrived.

Then one day, a few months ago, as Lonny and I prepared for little get-away, I had a surprise.

"Do you have the folder? With our itinerary?" I asked as I folded sweaters and jeans in the most pristine way. Stacked up, even and straight, just the way one's clothes should be.

"Sure do," he said. "What about the emergency numbers, for when the grandparents babysit the boys?"

"In the bottom of their suitcase," I said. "Under their pajamas. And toothbrushes. And tube of fluoride gel."

I zipped my bag closed and then reached for the notepad on our bedside table. Packing. Check. I picked up a Sharpie, snapped the lid on the end, where it belonged, and laid a thick, black line through the words on my list. Then I peered across the room at Lonny, working on his own list. Tidy socks, all in a row. I laughed out loud. It was a showcase moment, featuring how like-my-man I'd become.

"What?" Lonny asked.

"Nothing," I said.

We proceeded through the rest of our to-do chores, side-by-side, in sync, and then left for our romantic trip.

We had a blast.

Just as planned.

Looking over the years, I have to smile. Lonny and I have blended into each other. The things that once drove me crazy about Lonny have become (though diluted, of course) my own strengths. I know, in many other ways, I've seeped into Lonny's persona, too.

Kudos to Joe. I guess he was spot-on. About some things.

Lonny does enjoy living by his imaginary little black book.

But Joe was way-wrong about other things.

Lonny and I worked. I'm still madly, hopelessly, forever-in-love with my black-book spouse.

And Prince Charming's in love with his, too.

~Shawnelle Eliasen

Married Life!

Chapter 7

Crazy Love

Love conceals all of one's faults.

~Italian Proverb

Tabula Rasa

Everything should be made as simple as possible, but not simpler.
~Albert Einstein

Ever since I was a child, my parents fed my precocious reading ability. The real treat was every Thursday afternoon. My father and I would drive into town to make deliveries for his watch repair business and we would stop at Clay's News Agency. There, I would always choose the same thing: a coveted copy of *The Wall Street Journal*.

And ever since that childhood, I have been a newspaper hoarder.

As a child, each of those newspapers was a precious gift. The articles were written for and about important people — people who'd made something of themselves; people who made decisions and ran the world. I had to savor every succulent morsel of that paper. Even if it would take me the rest of the week, I'd read every article, sometimes three or four times. I'd internalize the business leaders and politicians and all the important decisions they made. I imagined what I would do in each situation, what decisions I would make in each case. As I devoured the contents, I dreamed that one day I would be among the decision-makers of the world. I would leave my parents' one-horse town and make my mark on society.

Each Thursday, when I brought home the latest edition, I couldn't bear to part with its predecessor. Not all the articles, the people, the friends I'd made in my mind as I travelled their lives with them! And so instead of discarding the previous week's edition, I stowed it under my bed.

Every week.

There they remained until my parents cleaned out my bedroom when I went away to college.

Fast forward some fifteen years, and I'm married.

In the apartment my wife and I shared, I could justify the stacks of newspapers: the apartment complex did not offer recycling, so we stacked the newspapers behind the door of our spare bedroom. When we had a trunkful, we drove to the recycling center with my precious cargo.

My wife never knew how much it pained me to recycle them. In fact, I'm sure she attributed my hesitancy to the physical labor involved in moving the stacks from our third-floor apartment to the parking lot below. Not wanting to scare my new bride, I never told her the truth.

But the truth came out nonetheless. When we moved into our first house, the recycling truck came by once a week. And it accepted newspapers.

Attending graduate school and working, I had little time to spare. The newspapers delivered each morning started to pile up near the front door. At first, with moving and packing, my wife was lenient. She understood that I wanted to catch up on reading before recycling the papers. She was content, at first, with the slow trickle of newspapers leaving the house. But with two papers delivered each day, they were coming in faster than I could read them.

"Just recycle them," she told me. "By the time you read them, it'll be old news. Start fresh with tomorrow's paper."

How could I explain to her that childhood feeling of solidarity I'd had with each news story and its participants? My engagement with the goings-on in the world had lifted me, inspired me to be the first in my family with a college degree, the first in my family with a job in the city. It was the stories of those business leaders and politicians, their successes and failures, which served as the foundation for my own decisions. They had given me so much. How could I simply abandon them without a second thought? I wondered as I gazed at the growing stack that had now intruded into the corner of our dining room.

It didn't take long for my wife to guess at my hoarding tendencies. Relieved that it was limited to newspapers, she allowed me to use our home's spare bedroom as my office, which she told me I could use for "newspaper storage." She promised it would be my own room and that, as long as the newspapers stayed there, she wouldn't bother me about them.

A few years later, a layer of newspapers lined the floor. Precarious stacks stood like unwieldy skyscrapers. There was a narrow and dangerous path from the door (which could no longer close) to the desk. But still, my wife kept her promise: she never bothered me about the papers.

That is… until the mice.

One autumn day, I heard a skittering about in the newspapers. Peering behind one of the piles, I saw that a family of mice had nested in the soft shredding of our paper shredder's basket. Peering back there, I saw that mice had invaded my office and found comfort in the stacks of warm newspapers and all the cozy nooks they offered.

It was when we covered the paper shredder, my wife and I, and drove out to the reservoir to release the mice back into the wild, that it dawned on me that hoarding newspapers might not be the best idea. We didn't tell my wife's parents about the mice, but we borrowed their SUV and cleared out the papers nonetheless.

I'll admit — it was difficult. As I watched those stacks disappear from my office, I felt like I was murdering a friend. Every now and then I'd read a headline of an ancient edition and say to my wife, "Maybe just…"

But she'd shake her head, pick up the stack, and continue out the door. "There's always the Internet," she said.

When the shock of it wore off, it dawned on me that I liked having a clean office, a room in which I could move about. Every now and again, a small stack would grow in the corner, but a certain look would come across my wife's face — for she now used the office along with me — and I knew it was time to recycle.

It is still a challenge for me, and I think it always will be. Each day when the newspaper arrives, I can't help but feel a tinge of that childhood adrenaline, the wonder at the possibility of the world. But then I think of how far I've come, how much I've learned of the world since leaving home, all the decisions I've made and people I've impacted. When I think of these things, it isn't so hard to make that trip to the recycling bin.

Besides, there's always the Internet.

~Eric Allen

63

Chicken Soup for the Soul

Six Parts of a Pot

It destroys one's nerves to be amiable every day to the same human being.
~Benjamin Disraeli

After dating for eight years, and reaching near-senior-citizen status, we find ourselves married and living together for the first time. It doesn't take long for our cohabitation incompatibilities to manifest themselves: me, the fastidious, orderly type; him, well… the opposite.

A few tête-á-têtes lead us to sharing the household chores, beginning with after-dinner cleanups. The fruits of his labor linger on the dish drainer. Reaching for a washed pot to dry and put away, I see… fruit. Caked onto the outside of the pot. So I ask, "Honey, did you just rinse this pot and set it here so you'd remember to wash it later?"

He says, "Oh, no, that's washed, hon. You can just put it away."

The same conversation takes place night after night. Each time, I think, no way is this cruddy pot going back into the cabinet where it'll surely breed salmonella and botulism. But not wanting to become a newlywed nag, I hold back my thoughts and rewash the pots—after asking the did-you-just-rinse-this-pot question, thinking he might eventually ask why I'm asking.

Weeks later, on an otherwise ordinary Friday night, I shriek like the Bride of Frankenstein. "Didn't your mother, or your first two wives, or your daughter, or anyone else ever teach you how to wash pots?" It's a rhetorical question, but he answers:

"No."

Okay, it's possible. Improbable, but possible. A problem-solver by nature, I assess the lack of training as an easy problem to fix. Falling back on old skills from my former career as a management trainer at the AT&T School of Business, I launch into a session of Pot Washing 101. I hold the questionably clean pot in my left hand as I point with my right index finger, like Vanna White showing us our vowels, and say "Pay attention," as I point out the six parts of a pot:

One: The inside bottom.
Two: The inside sides.
Three: The rim.
Four: The outside sides.
Five: The outside bottom.
Six: The handle.

"All you have to do is count to six to remember them. Make sure you put soap on the sponge, press hard on each part and rub until the food and smudges come off. Then rinse. Got it?"

He glares at me and mutters, "Yeah." I want him to demonstrate what he's just learned, but I cut him a little slack and let him get back to pushing buttons on the remote.

In the weeks that follow, it's as if the training never happened. I discover that if I make a loud noise by dropping a supposedly clean pot back into the sink, from a height of about ten inches, I get a reaction:

"Leave it, leave it! I'll take care of it!"

Twelve years later, the fruits of my labor unrealized, I share this lesson with new brides of all ages. It's what's on the inside that counts, in life, as in pots and pans.

~Marilyn Haight

My Fortune

Tell me what you eat, I'll tell you who you are.
~Anthelme Brillat-Savarin

One of the unspoken "duties" in a good marriage is to be there for your spouse. Whenever I had a work-related social function, my husband accompanied me. He'd smile and make appropriate small talk and I did the same for him. That's just part of married life.

I attended one such event after my husband Frank got a huge promotion at work. His employees loved him and before Frank left for his new position, they wanted to show their appreciation to him for everything he had done for them over the years.

The people in his old laboratory decided to take him out for dinner—and they invited me too. I was happy to go. They chose a very authentic Chinese restaurant that wasn't open to the general public. You had to know someone who knew someone who was friends with someone in order to even make a reservation. One of the people in the lab knew the owner and reserved a table for twenty.

The night of the party we arrived at the restaurant right on time. As the guests of honor, we were shown to our table—a table with just a white linen tablecloth on it... no silverware, no plates, no water glasses. Nothing. It was big round table with a Lazy Susan turntable in the middle of it. As soon as everyone was seated the waiter took our drink orders. Our drinks were the only things we would order that evening; there were no menus. The dinner was at the discretion of the chef.

First, tiny little plates, maybe four inches in diameter, were put down in front of each person along with a pair of chopsticks. Hot mustard, soy sauce, sweet and sour sauce and a few huge bowls of steaming white rice were put on the Lazy Susan. Our host—the woman who knew the owner—explained that the custom was to leave all serving platters on the Lazy Susan, take what you want from them and then turn the Lazy Susan to the right so that the next person could serve himself. Frank had warned me that there could be some strange things served at this restaurant. He told me to be careful, and look twice before taking food from the platters. I was a little apprehensive but my husband was watching out for me.

The first dish look familiar… and safe. It was some kind of egg roll. I liked egg rolls. And I knew egg rolls. I put some rice on my tiny little plate along with some mustard and sweet and sour sauce. When the Lazy Susan finally brought the egg rolls to me, I took one. It smelled so good—and I was hungry. I dipped it into the mustard and took a bite. Yikes!! Help!! The mustard was so hot. Breathe! I looked desperately at Frank but he was sitting across the table and couldn't do anything for me. There was no water on the table to put out the fire in my mouth and our drinks had not yet arrived. The tears were streaming down my face and I wanted to scream. But, this was a business dinner so I had to behave. Gasping quietly for air, I wiped the tears with my napkin and piled all of the rice on top of the mustard so I would not make the mistake of dipping into it again.

The drinks finally came, along with a procession of dishes with enough food on each platter to feed a small town. There was soup, many different chicken dishes, fish dishes, beef dishes, pork dishes, noodle dishes and more vegetables than you could imagine. There were also some mystery dishes. Those had to be the dishes that Frank had warned me about so I looked twice before serving myself from those platters. Some of the food was delicious; some of the food was… well, not so delicious. But I was a trouper; I tried almost everything. And it just kept coming. Due to the size of the tiny plates, we kept that Lazy Susan spinning around and around as people took seconds, thirds and fourths of the food.

I wanted more of the chicken dish that was across the table. So, I slowly rotated the Lazy Susan until that platter was in front of me. I moved the rice that was on my plate over, being careful not to uncover the mustard, and served myself another piece of chicken. Then I used my chopsticks to pick up the chicken. Frank, who can speak with his eyes, gave me this really strange look. What was wrong? Did I have sweet and sour sauce on my chin? Had I dribbled noodles down the front of my blouse? I started to raise the chopsticks to my mouth. His eyes opened very wide and he shook his head ever so slightly—no, no, no. I paused and smiled at him. What was wrong? Nothing that I could see. So, ignoring his pleading eyes and the cutting motion he was making with his hand across his throat, I moved the chopsticks up to my mouth, opened wide and took a bite of the chicken. As I was biting, I actually looked at it.

And the piece of chicken was… looking right back at me! I had selected the head of the chicken from the platter. And I had just taken a bite of… the beak! Yuck. That piece of the beak, although quite small, was in my mouth. Double yuck! I was panicked. Now what? Should I just spit and gag? Should I jump up and run away from the table—a table filled with Frank's employees? Poor Frank had seen what I was about to do and he tried to warn me. Why hadn't I figured it out? Why didn't I look carefully at what I was eating before I took a bite? Why wasn't he sitting next to me so he could have stopped me? My life was over—I had a chicken beak in my mouth.

So I did what a loving wife who was at a business dinner for her husband and who didn't want to ruin her marriage should do. I slowly and carefully, without spitting, gagging or making any unnatural sounds, lowered the offensive chicken head back down to my tiny plate. The whole time that damn chicken was looking right back at me. This was not acceptable so I moved him on top of the pile of rice that was covering the hot mustard. I could still see him—and he was still looking at me—so I took more of the steaming rice from the Lazy Susan and buried him… again! I then took a big bite of a wonton skin and proceeded to chew the small piece of beak along with the crunchy wonton skin so I couldn't tell which crunchy thing was which and, with difficulty, swallowed everything.

Poor Frank, he could feel my pain. I knew that if he could have helped me, he would have. I took a long drink of water and put my chopsticks down. I was done. Finished! No green tea ice cream, no almond cookie and especially no fortune cookie. I was completely grossed out and I already knew my fortune: "You will become particularly close to a chicken tonight!"

~Barbara LoMonaco

65

Glass Dismissed

No man acquires property without acquiring with it a little arithmetic also.
~Ralph Waldo Emerson

Peek inside the kitchen cabinets in our home and you'll come face to face with a disturbing secret my wife and I have kept for decades: a massive stash of drinking glasses that has spiraled out of control and continues to expand against all rhyme or reason.

I recently sat down and did the math: 124 glasses divided by two people equals sixty-two glasses per person. And that doesn't even factor in the countless glasses squirreled away in china cabinets, the living room wall bar, and boxes under beds, in closets and stacked out in the garage.

Our "glasses of mass consumption" surplus started innocently enough. When my wife and I first joined forces, I possessed a certain number of assorted drinking glasses (eight) and Sherry had a certain, somewhat higher number (fifty-eight).

As time went on, my glasses—which mostly consisted of sixteen-ounce plastic tumblers commemorating outdoor events at which I consumed a cold beer—were weeded out to make room for more respectable, stylish glasses that came in sets, had elegant stems, and illuminated alluringly when the light hit them.

Now, as best as I can figure it, here's where things started to get out of hand. During occasions when our "good glasses" played a prominent role in a social gathering at the house we became quietly and irrevocably identified by well-intentioned friends and family as "appreciators of nice glasses."

This led to our receiving sets of glasses as gifts on a regular basis. Red wine glasses. White wine glasses. Red and white wine glasses. Crystal dinner glasses. Smoked dinner glasses. Everyday dinner glasses. Indoor/outdoor glasses. Fancy coffee drink glasses. Holiday-themed coffee mugs. Coffee mugs from the White Castle Hamburger collection that, in spite of their blatant promotional purpose, are sturdy, first-rate mugs worth reaching around the more "respectable" mugs in the cabinet to get to.

On any given day, in fact, my choice of glasses follows a conspicuously narrow and predictable pattern.

Morning: I'll reach for a White Castle coffee mug or a mug that says "The Grand Village: Branson, Missouri." (I've never been to Branson, Missouri, but the mug evokes an odd sentimentality in me fueled by visions of an ancient Andy Williams singing the *Hawaiian Wedding Song* while I eat roasted chicken and mashed potatoes at a dinner theater with busloads of tourists.)

Noon: I'll reach for a twelve-ounce plastic tumbler that says "Promenade in the Park: The Family, Food and Fun Festival" or a sixteen-ounce plastic tumbler that says "It's 5 o'clock at the Quarter Deck Lounge."

Night: I'll reach for a tinted German wine glass with a green spiral stem or a goblet-style wine glass with grapes hand-painted on it by our friend Jane while she skillfully drank wine from another glass.

According to my meticulous calculations, that leaves about fifty-six glasses allotted for my daily use that are severely underemployed and deserve to hear the words "glass dismissed" any day now. Even if I quadruple my daily fluid intake, I'm reasonably confident that I could still get by with fewer than ten glasses, even if it meant resorting to more or less unlimited refills of the multipurpose "Promenade in the Park: The Family, Food and Fun Festival" plastic tumbler.

One consolation in all this is that during candid conversations with an intensely private married couple who prefer to remain nameless (Uncle Al and Aunt Jean), I've discovered that others have a similar baffling surplus. While the consensus is that it's nice to have extra glasses around for when you have company, Sherry and I don't throw the kind of get-togethers where 124 glasses are needed on standby to be called into active service.

Actually, in our marriage, Sherry and I don't throw the kind of get-togethers where twenty-four glasses would be needed. That being said, you never know when the national tour bus of a philharmonic orchestra might break down in front of your home and serving refreshments in paper cups would reflect poorly on your reputation for exceptional class and cultural sophistication.

In the meantime, please excuse me while I refill my "It's 5 o'clock at the Quarter Deck Lounge" plastic tumbler. It's not the most attractive glass in the house, but it holds a hearty sixteen ounces and when I accidently knock it over lunging for the last chicken wing, I can pick it right up, wipe it right off, and start all over again.

~Alan Williamson

66

The Odd Couple

*Things turn out best for the people who make the best out of
the way things turn out.*
~Art Linkletter

Bill likes everything to be in orderly fashion and he'll plan
months in advance for an occasion. I am impromptu
and can pack the night before a vacation. He has a need
to know facts, formulas and minute details about future events. I
wing it.

We were middle-aged when we met at a dance hall. He was a
genuine, respectful man. Neither of us was looking for a relationship.
After I'd known him about six months he invited me to his home
for lunch. I opened his pantry to retrieve a can of corn and thought,
"Oh boy! He and I would never work as a couple." His shelves were
aligned with rows of canned goods and healthy foods that were
sorted, alphabetized and neatly stacked. His half-eaten bags of chips
had decorative clip closers, and his plastic storage bags were seriated
from snack size to gallon size. My pantry was like my life: groceries
tossed haphazardly on a shelf, corn curls unraveling in cellophane
bags, and way more chocolate products than healthy foods. His sink
was scoured, not piled high with dirty dishes. There were stacks of
neatly folded laundry, not rumpled piles of clean whites in a busted
laundry basket in the bedroom.

This guy was too nice, too organized, too good a listener, too
perfect for me. His hands were too big, and his feet were as long as

carpet samples. His head was too round, his hair was too naturally curly, and his eyes disappeared into his face when he laughed. And he made me laugh… all the time. His laughing eyes peered into mine with sincerity. His head contained a methodical brain that knew a little bit about a lot of things, and he readily shared information and facts. Those over-sized feet had taken him to places I'd only dreamed about, and he never used them to kick people when they were down. His ears were big, but what a listener. I observed him reach out with his big paws to give people a helping hand, and when we danced and he held my small hand in his, I felt safe and protected. But I resisted affection. Friendship felt fine, but a relationship with an organized, intelligent, psychologically sound man—no way!

Our relationship progressed from seeing one another at Friday night dances to Sunday walks around Francis Park. I could barely make the one-mile lap by myself, but it seemed effortless when we walked together. Bill's large feet balanced his 6'4" frame. Like a gentle giant, he towered over my 5'4", but he never talked down to me. He was so genuine; he'd stop to chat with old timers sitting on benches, and he'd pat dogs on leashes. He was too good to be true. He didn't complain, raise his voice to make a point or express disapproval with a grimace. He had a positive approach to life and a wonderful personality. I had recently unraveled a twenty-five-year marriage, but no matter how nice Bill seemed, I wasn't looking to be tied down.

Sometimes, no matter how unintentionally you toss groceries onto a shelf, the two ingredients that work well together end up side by, like a package of spaghetti and a jar of Ragu. I decided to reciprocate the lunch with a meal: spaghetti, salad and garlic bread. I introduced Bill to my cat, the crazy dog and the kids, but I refused to let him near my pantry. I just knew if he saw how disorganized it was, he'd get a glimpse of the real me, and that would be the end of us.

When he discovered me rummaging in the pantry and complaining that I could not find the garlic salt, he didn't lecture; he merely said, "A place for everything and everything in its place."

As our relationship evolved, we spent more time together and eventually married. We were committed to one another, but neither of us could commit to the other's way of stocking a pantry. What worked for me never worked for him, whether it was in regards to groceries, luggage or lodging.

When we planned a trip to Colorado, he asked if I wanted to make reservations. "Why? Let's just drive until we get tired, and then find a place for the night."

He shrugged and said he'd give my way a try. He didn't tell me he could drive for hours on end. Neon NO VACANCY signs glared at us. By midnight we realized there was no room at any inn, so he pulled into the dark lot of a car repair shop and reclined his seat. He didn't complain. He snoozed. I rolled up a wad of twenty-dollar bills and hid them in the waistband of my shorts and lay there wide awake, worrying about being robbed. At daybreak, I spied a convenience store a block away and gently opened the car door. As I stepped out of the car, twenty-dollar bills started falling out of my shorts and down my leg. The wind whisked them away one after another. Each time I took another step another bill fell out. I chased them for half a block, peeling them off the damp pavement. When I looked up, Bill was watching me, and so were the workers in the weigh station across the highway. Sheepishly I returned to the car.

"It pays to have a plan," is all he said, with an ear-to-ear grin on his big Irish face.

He's right, and I have tried to commit to being more organized. When Bill buys groceries and shelves them, our pantry looks like the grocery store. When I stop at the store for a few things, he never knows what he'll find or where he'll find it when he opens the pantry door. My way makes him as crazy as his makes me. After seventeen years of marriage we're still crazy about each other. We allow each other space; his is organized and mine is cluttered, but we are still very committed to making it work.

~Linda O'Connell

67

Living in Hormone Hell

No one will ever win the battle of the sexes;
there's too much fraternizing with the enemy.
~Henry Kissinger

My wife and I had our daughter Sarah a bit late in life. Cheryl was thirty-eight and I was forty-five. We thought that was a good thing.

In many respects, it was. After all, as mature parents, we figured we would be better prepared to deal with the challenges of child rearing. And, for the most part, that's how it turned out.

Since we were older, we had fewer financial challenges. And having already settled into our careers, we had more time to devote to Sarah's upbringing.

What I hadn't counted on was that fifteen years later the numbers wouldn't add up in my favor. Cheryl's now fifty-three and Sarah's almost fifteen.

What that means is that, as a sixty-year-old male, I am caught in an estrogen-laced web spun by two hormonally challenged females. Sarah is riding the emotional waves of adolescence while Cheryl is buffeted by the ups and downs of menopause.

Dealing with one of them at a time is hard enough. But when they're both in full-blown hormonal overdrive, it can be a bit too much.

I can handle Sarah's mood swings and teenage angst on its own.

And I can survive Cheryl's mood swings and dramatic temperature shifts when it's just the two of us.

But put both of them together in estrogen flux and I haven't got a chance. No matter what I do or say, it's wrong.

Sarah wants to know if her new haircut looks okay. If I say no, she says I'm an uncool old geezer who doesn't know anything. If I say yes, she says I'm only saying that because I'm her dad.

Cheryl wants to know why the temperature is so hot. If I agree that it's hot, she knows I'm just trying to humor her and tells me to turn on the central air. If I tell her it isn't hot she says I'm an idiot and orders me to turn on the central air.

What's an aging befuddled father/husband to do? Avoidance doesn't work and silence is not an option.

One-on-one, I can often gingerly back out of the room and extricate myself from the dilemma. If I can make it down the stairs and into the basement TV room, I'm usually safe.

But if they're both assaulting me with no-win questions, I tend to just adopt a deer-caught-in-the-headlights look and hope for the best. Clasping my hands in mock prayer, I beseech whatever goddess governs matters gynecological to deliver me from their wrath.

Sometimes I'm lucky and Cheryl and Sarah lock horns and argue with each other. "You don't understand; you never understand!" wails Sarah. "I've asked you a million times to clean up your room and you never ever listen!" replies Cheryl.

When the two of them are in high dudgeon, I can usually quickly absent myself, with the emphasis on "quickly." For if I am not opportunistic and fleet of foot, they will ensnare me in their web of women's woes.

"Where do you think you're going?" says Cheryl. "Get back here. We have to settle this now."

"Dad, can't you see how unreasonable she's being?" says Sarah. "Make her stop."

This is the ultimate in folly. If I had any sense, I would simply run from the room, jump in the car and drive for as long as it takes for hormonal balance and sanity to return to the Martin household.

But no, I naively and stupidly believe that my rational participation in this dispute will result in a calm and logical resolution happily embraced by all. Needless to say, that particular result has occurred exactly zero times.

Initially, I figured that I would have to weather this storm and simply wait until Sarah had passed through adolescence and Cheryl had released the menopause button. But it turns out that I have my own hormonal challenges that allow me to join in as an equal partner in the fray.

As a male in his sixties, I am now experiencing the joys of something called late-onset hypogonadism, more commonly known as andropause. So now, when I am caught in an estrogen sandwich by my wife and daughter, instead of trying to argue or escape, I simply dissolve into tears. Then we all start crying, which leads to a group hug and the end of the current dispute. At least until tomorrow.

~David Martin

"When I said don't apologize, what I really meant was... apologize!"

Sirius Arguments

Country music is three chords and the truth.
~Harlan Howard

My marriage has dodged a major bullet. Our trial subscription to Sirius Satellite Radio just expired and I couldn't be more pleased. Don't get me wrong—I totally loved having hundreds of stations, knowing that my every musical whim could be satisfied at the touch of a button. But all the shoobie doos and sha la las, all the twanging and head banging, and even all the cheesy love songs in the world are just not worth risking my marriage.

You see my husband and I are a classic case of opposites that attracted. I am the positive to his negative, the yin to his yang. So far our marriage has survived his love of baseball (and my apathy to it), my political drive and involvement (and his apathy to that), and even the struggles in our earliest years between a dog person and a cat person. (I'm glad to say he's now a fervent convert, and we have four indoor cats.) Having worked those things out, I really thought our marriage could survive anything. Then, along came a free three-month trial subscription to Sirius satellite radio. It came with my new car and it almost broke us.

Mark is a 1980s guy. He loves the funky rhythms, the big-hair bands, the insistent guitar riffs, and even the fashions associated with that period. I, on the other hand, am a honky tonk and bluegrass girl. He may have played blocks to the sounds of Madonna and Duran

Duran, but I drifted off to sleep to Ronnie Milsap and Crystal Gayle. When Merle Haggard sang "Okie From Muskogee" he was literally singing my song. That's me — born in Muskogee Medical Center in Muskogee, Oklahoma. It's more than a birthplace — it's a heritage. Little did I know that even though "Opposites Attract" (Paula Abdul, 1989), our musical differences were threatening to cause a "D-I-V-O-R-C-E" (Tammy Wynette, 1968).

Long car trips, of course, were the hardest. We have a rule that whoever drives gets to pick the station. These past few months we've been arguing over who gets to drive rather than who has to. Even quick stops at a gas station were opportunities for the listener/passenger to pull a quick switcheroo. Upon arriving back to the car from the pump or restroom, someone was bound to be motioned from the driver's side to the passenger's side and a conversation something like this would ensue:

Delighted New Driver: Gee, honey, I thought you looked tired and might like it if I took a turn at the wheel... for your sake, of course. (Big grin)

Disgruntled New Passenger: (indistinct grumbles) Alright, but I'm warning you — one of the girls is probably going to need to stop in about thirty miles for a potty break, you know!

Our record was fourteen stops in 100 miles. Our children were confused, but happy, since each game of "musical drivers" generally resulted in the purchase of some type of snack or beverage. I gained three pounds, but got to listen to all the fiddles, banjos, and steel guitars that I could ever want. Mark, likewise, drank four Dr. Peppers and rocked out to no less than seven Cyndi Lauper songs, and a late Eagles hit that even I enjoyed. Thankfully, however, those days have come to an end. The subscription price to continue getting satellite radio coverage may only be $12.95 a month, but I hear that divorce lawyers are pretty pricey. Even if it never came to that, I don't think we can continue to afford the snacks. There's only one thing left to do — go back to disagreeing over talk radio. At least it's free!

~Andrea K. Farrier

69

Helping Harry

*A habit is something you can do without thinking—which is why most of us
have so many of them.*
~Frank A. Clark

I've spent the last twenty-two years searching for my husband's
keys. Seriously. Every day of my life, I get up, start the coffee
and look for Harry's keys. The problem is, I don't know why
Harry loses them so often. This is a man who can remember exactly
how much money we spent on our very first vacation together. I'm
not kidding. Frankly, if it weren't for the fact that we have a photo
album filled with pictures of the trip, I'd never remember going.

But he cannot remember where he left his keys.

I don't think I need to tell you that it's making me crazy. Look,
how many places can you leave your keys? It's not like we live in
Buckingham Palace. Although, if we did live in Buckingham Palace
chances are a butler would be in charge of Harry's keys and life would
definitely be easier.

That aside, I have tried to help Harry. Look, I don't want to
get up every morning and fling pillows around the family room in
a desperate search for his car keys. Or his house keys. Don't get me
started on that. I mean, the man cannot remember where he puts his
keys—so he has two key rings—one for his house and office keys
and one for his car keys. Please. Don't I suffer enough without having
to look for two sets of keys every morning?

Anyway, in an effort to preserve the remnants of my sanity, I have tried various organizational methods to help Harry. I cannot tell you how hard this is for me. I'm not the most organized person on earth. But I did it because, honestly, I was afraid that one morning I'd be looking for the keys and lose my mind instead.

For my first effort, I hung a little basket on the front door. Now the intent was that he would step into the house and immediately dump his keys into the basket. Then the next morning, he would retrieve his keys from the basket and go on his merry way.

Too bad we live in the real world. Because in the real world, Harry would come in the door and the basket would swing around and scratch the door. Then Harry would dump his keys in the basket, take it off the handle and put it somewhere else in the living room so it would stop scratching the front door. And then the next day, we'd run around the living room looking for the basket. All the while, Harry would be saying useful things like, "I put the keys in the basket; what more do you want from me?"

So I tried hanging the basket from a hook. This worked for about a week, then the basket collapsed. Turns out Harry had liked the idea of always having his stuff in one place, so he loaded the basket with his car keys, about a thousand receipts, two wallets, a business card case, his cell phone and about $400 in pennies and nickels. Personally, I think the basket was overworked and trying to escape so it broke off its own handles, but I could be wrong.

Next I tried a tray that sat on a small table in the entryway. Yes, that was soon overflowing with junk as well. The table legs started bowing, so I cleared off a section of kitchen counter. You can imagine what the countertop looked like after a few days. It was covered. Good thing I don't actually cook.

Finally, I found a device with a remote control that attached to Harry's keys. When he lost them, which he did every single night, I pressed a button on the main controller and his keys beeped. It was like a miracle. Every morning, his keys were found. And then one day, it didn't beep. We panicked. Why wasn't the remote working? Had it, like the basket, become overwhelmed by the amount of junk it was attached to? Not really. Turns out that if the remote falls off your keychain and is run over by your very own car, it has a tendency to never beep again.

But that's okay because I have a new plan. I'm just going to make 365 duplicate sets of keys and not worry about looking for them for a year. Hey, it could work.

~Laurie Sontag

70

No Doubt About It

Laugh and the world laughs with you, snore and you sleep alone.
~Anthony Burgess

No doubt you've heard of Doubting Thomas. I live with him. Or at least I'm married to one of his descendants, Doubting Dale. Let me just say that our wedding vows should have read: "for better, for worse, for richer, for poorer, in sickness and health, til snoring do us part." Because it did… part us. One part of us is positively certain that one of us snores. The other part sincerely doubts it.

For years, our morning conversation would go something like this:

"Honey, I know I don't snore, but did I snore last night?"

"No doubt about it, unless I dreamt that I was sleeping with Darth Vader… again," I'd reply. Soon my subtle hints took on a note of sarcasm.

"Honey, I know I don't snore, but did I snore last night?"

"No doubt about it, unless you think I actually prefer sleeping in the garage with a pool noodle wrapped around my ears." Then, since sarcasm seemed to be wasted on him, I tried telling him the truth: "Your snoring was so loud, it made the china rattle in the dining room buffet, next door at the neighbor's!" But he just wouldn't believe it, even after our neighbor moved to Calgary, three provinces away.

Needless to say, Dale's doubts were doing nothing for our relationship, let alone our sleeping arrangements. As time went on, the peace and quiet of our lumpy living room couch seemed more and more appealing. But first, I tried every anti-snoring gimmick out there. I wore earplugs guaranteed to muffle the sound of a jackhammer. They didn't work. I drank gallons of chamomile tea to make me fall asleep faster, to no avail. I sewed a tennis ball into the back of Dale's pajama top to make him roll over onto his side. It didn't matter. Apparently he can snore in any position. A real turning point came when I tried the "hands-on" approach. One night I pinched his nostrils shut and he came up for air, fists swinging. I just barely ducked in time. And then he accused me of premeditated murder. As if anyone could meditate in that racket.

Of course that little incident didn't do a whole lot for our relationship either. Something had to be done. That's when Dale signed up for an overnight stay at a "Sleep Lab." There, someone actually watches you sleep and records it on video. But first they have to hook you up to a computer that monitors your sleep patterns. Eleven wires were attached to Dale's head (with one up each nostril), four more were fastened to his chest and two were taped to his legs. Then they wished him, "Good night, sleep tight!" Yeah right! Most of us would be too wired to sleep a wink. Dale was sawing logs in five minutes flat.

In the morning he asked his favorite question: "I know I don't snore, but did I snore last night?"

"No doubt about it," the technician answered. Then they went on to tell him he has a mild case of sleep apnea and recommended him for laser surgery to enlarge the breathing space at the back of his throat. It wouldn't be one hundred percent effective, they told him, but the surgery could reduce his snoring by eighty-five percent. Dale decided to go for it.

After the surgery, his throat was very sore for about ten days. Six weeks later, however, I noticed little change in his snoring. So, back he went for more surgery... more soreness and then after six weeks... more snoring. At this point, I really didn't want him to go back, but Dale refused to give up. At his next appointment, the doctor sent him home with a CPAP (Continuous Positive Airway Pressure) machine for him to wear with a mask every night… and it worked!

No doubt about it, Dale's determination to make us an "overnight success" story has done a lot for our relationship. The sparkle is back and we're able to tease each other, again. Just the other morning, for instance, Dale said to me, "Honey, you sure had a good sleep last night. You were snoring to beat the band!"

"Very funny," I chortled, rolling my eyes. "I know I don't snore."

~Lisa Beringer

71
Chicken Soup for the Soul

Doing the Chicken Soup Dance

An expert is a person who tells you a simple thing in a confused way in such a fashion as to make you think the confusion is your own fault.
~William Castle

We met on Match.com on December 8, 2008. Harvey was in New York; I was in Florida. The odds of our getting together were almost unimaginable. Yet here we were, two eighty-two-year-olds who stumbled onto each other on the Internet and were instantly smitten. I tried to follow the rules of the dating service... no telephone numbers, no addresses, pure anonymity... at least until I was sure that I wasn't talking to an axe murderer, as my daughter suggested.

But Harvey was almost too good to be true. Handsome, witty, a former executive at CBS, a widower looking for love. Our e-mails via Match.com burned up the airwaves. We were writing day and night, and after a week, he was begging for my phone number and address.

"I need to hear your voice," he pleaded. And after a brief resistance, I gave him my phone number. He called immediately, and his voice was warm and reassuring. We talked for more than an hour... about our backgrounds, our families, our careers... then I took time out.

"I'll call you this afternoon," he said tenderly.

"I won't be home," I apologized. "I'm doing a book signing."

"What is that?" he asked.

"I have stories in two new *Chicken Soup for the Soul* books and I'll be signing them."

"You've written two books of chicken soup recipes? I'm impressed. You must be a great cook."

"I don't cook," I laughed, "and they aren't recipe books. They're part of a series called *Chicken Soup for the Soul*. One book is *Chicken Soup for the Soul: My Resolution* and the other is *Chicken Soup for the Soul: Tales of Golf and Sport*."

"Let me get this straight. You've written an entire book about your New Year's resolutions? I hope I figure in that. Have you resolved to keep writing me?"

"Well, yes, I have that, but this was written long before I met you. There are 101 stories for your mind, body and wallet."

"Hm, so my wallet figures in there," he said suspiciously. "I guess I'd better get a pre-nup!"

"Me, too. I have a daughter-in-law who's a lawyer."

"So you've made 101 resolutions?" he asked.

"Only two."

"What do you mean only two? What about the other ninety-nine?"

"Somebody else wrote them."

"You're signing a book that you only have two stories in? What do the other ninety-nine people have to say about that?"

"I assume they're just glad to have me selling their book."

"Okay. And what about the other book... the golf one. Do you only have two stories in that one?'

"One."

"You only have one story in the golf book, and you're signing it, too? Well never mind. I never figured you for a golfer, but I'm happy to hear that because I'm quite a golfer myself. Maybe we can play a game when I finally meet you."

"I'm not a golfer, and I did not write about golf," I sputtered. "I wrote about football."

"I see. So you play football. Now I'm really impressed. You wrote a story about football in a book about golf."

"Listen, Harvey, I really have to get out there and sell a few books. I'll talk to you tomorrow."

"Why don't I buy a couple of your books. How much are they?"

"$14.95 each."

Harvey mused a minute. "I don't want to be picky, but I was an accountant for CBS. How many words in the football story?"

I sighed. "Around 1,500 I would think."

"Wow! You are really well paid at $14.95. That's about a dollar a word. I guess that makes your Resolution book a real bargain with two stories in it. I'll send you a check for $30. How's that? What's your address?"

"Harvey, Match.com doesn't want us giving out our addresses."

"Shall I send the check to Match.com then?"

This man was really getting on my nerves.

"All right. I'll give you my address. But don't come stalking me."

"Stalk you? I'm going to marry you!"

"You are? All right. But first you have to buy my *Chicken Soup for the Soul* books."

"This is blackmail. Are you signing them for me, too? What are you going to write in the front of them?"

"Hm, let me think about that. In the Resolution book, how about, "To the most exciting man I never met?""

"That sounds good. And in the Golf book?"

"I'll write, 'The ball is in your court.'"

Harvey was thoughtful. "The word 'court' really applies to tennis, but we don't need to get technical. I'm writing the check now. Are you wrapping my books?"

"They're practically in the mail."

"That's great. And I'm practically on the next plane down there."

"In that case, why should I send them? Why don't I just hand them to you when you arrive?"

"Why don't you? And then I can write, 'To the most expensive date I never had!'"

•••

He did fly to Florida, and I did marry him, and he did buy my *Chicken Soup for the Soul* books... all of them!

~Phyllis W. Zeno

Married *Life!*

Chapter 8

Will You Still Love Me Tomorrow

The heart that loves is always young.

~Chinese Proverb

72

Homecomings

A happy marriage is a long conversation which always seems too short.
~Andre Maurois

he dress was cranberry and rust plaid, somewhat bold for me. It had been a splurge. I'd yearned to feel sophisticated, and this dress somehow did it.

There was a reason for the indulgence: I was a young bride about to meet my husband's college buddies at the big Rutgers University homecoming game. It all felt momentous in our brand new marriage.

We drove up the New Jersey Turnpike that day in our used Chevy convertible, but I wouldn't let Victor put the top down for fear of ruining my carefully arranged hair. I'd slept the whole night before in hair rollers to achieve just the right look.

I was nervous. At twenty-one, I barely knew myself, let alone how to behave in my new role as somebody's wife. "Wife" had such a grown-up ring to it, but grown up was not what I was feeling that day. Like a hapless eighth grader, I was worried about whether these guys—and their wives—would like me.

We climbed up to our seats, and there they were, six couples who all seemed perfectly nice. But I kept mixing up their names, and who went with whom. Besides, it turned out that the plaid dress itched.

That year marked the beginning of a precious marriage ritual for us—but we didn't know it.

We could never have dreamt, as we clambered up those stadium steps in those early autumns, that over five decades later, we would still be meeting. Who thought in decades? Back then, a year was an eternity.

Suddenly, we were all having babies, moving into split-levels in the suburbs, and realizing that we really didn't have to dress to impress at those football games.

No more Chevy convertibles either. We were at the stage of marriage—and parenthood—when a solid station wagon with faux wood sides was our vehicle of choice. Kids and convertibles didn't match.

Then one year, six couples had been reduced to five plus one widow. A horrible car accident had claimed one of our gang, and we young marrieds couldn't connect the dots: we were still young enough to feel invincible, yet death, which was supposed to be for our parents' generation, had intruded.

Our perfect little young-marrieds group would go through other losses and renunciations—the first divorce among us felt like a knife cutting through our former equanimity about life and love and the notion of forever.

Through the years of homecoming games, we measured out our own wins and losses. Marriage was no longer a given as yet another couple divided the sheets and towels and called it quits.

Our cars were getting smaller again as the kids we'd chauffeured to soccer practice and Scouts were suddenly, audaciously, leaving us for places with trailing ivy and grassy quads.

We didn't dash up the stadium steps anymore—my husband had fallen victim to a tricky back and mine wasn't terrific either.

Nobody can remember precisely when we slipped into sleek condominiums or when we stopped eating spicy foods and transitioned to decaffeinated coffee and herbal teas.

But we still went to those Rutgers games, by now climbing more slowly up the steps and into our seats in the stands. One year, my husband and I couldn't get to the game because we had a far more important commitment: a granddaughter's ballet recital.

Our marriage was at a vastly different stage by then—and so were our priorities.

There also was a new sensibility about how blessed we were—and how young and middle marriage eras had yielded to something brand new: senior status. It was both shocking—and enormously satisfying.

Those of us who had cheered together for the Rutgers football team for so many autumns were awash in new realities in a post-9/11 world. My husband and I clung closer, searching for meaning and connection in a world that had been inalterably altered.

Yes, there were grandchildren to sweeten this fourth quarter—undeniably, a bonus, and the source of shameless bragging. But not quite enough.

It was marriage, which now spanned five decades—a notion that took our breath away—that had become even more central.

Last fall, as we drove up to the stadium for the homecoming game, we carted along pillows to soften those bleacher benches, and carried a blanket in case the wind started up.

As we walked together towards the stands, holding hands, a few younger couples smiled indulgently at the silver-haired alumnus and his lady, officially part of the Old Guard now—the fifty-year-plus alumni.

How could they understand what our years marked by this annual autumn event had enclosed within them?

But clearly, on that brisk autumn day, we were now in a different universe. We were the very-very-married—still relishing the small rituals of wedded life that matter.

And as we gingerly took our seats, my husband leaned over and kissed my cheek. He told me that he remembered that plaid dress—and that first homecoming game as husband and wife.

I smiled all through the whole game.

It didn't matter a bit that Rutgers lost.

~Sally Friedman

73

R & R

Half of my heart is deployed.
~Author Unknown

oyfully, I watched the 707 slip out of the sky and touch down on the runway at the Honolulu International Airport. The terminal was filled with excited people eager to greet their loved ones. Eight long months of waiting, wanting, hoping and praying were over, at least for a while. My husband and I would have one glorious week of R&R before he went back into harm's way. Hawaii was the perfect place to meet since it was situated between the West Coast and Vietnam, not to mention that it sounded very romantic. I had purchased a new outfit for the occasion and invested in contact lenses so my black-rimmed glasses wouldn't get in the way of the long passionate kiss that I anticipated.

While waiting for the plane to turn around, I couldn't stop smiling as I thought of our whirlwind courtship. Two years earlier, with my teaching degree in hand, I had accepted a position in Laguna Beach. In 1966, young people from the Midwest were flocking to the West Coast, where there was a golden promise of plentiful jobs and higher salaries. Having grown up in South Dakota, the weather in California sounded heavenly and the opportunity was too exciting to pass up.

Camp Pendleton and other military bases in Southern California were teeming with soldiers preparing to go off to the "little" war. The teachers and officers gravitated toward the same parties and bars. My friend invited me to a beach party where I met Michael Reilly, a handsome lieutenant with a shy smile, and I was smitten. Days filled with teaching, beaching, playing darts at the Sandpiper pub, and moonlight walks led to his proposal of marriage and my heartfelt acceptance.

When school recessed for the year, Michael and I were married in the little chapel on base. The military ceremony with the archway of swords made me feel like Cinderella. We were settling down to live happily ever after when Michael received orders for Vietnam. Marines accepted the thirteen-month tour of duty with a week off for Rest and Relaxation as just part of their job. However, as a young bride, I was very apprehensive. The wait became excruciatingly long as the war news worsened. My friends told me "war changes people" and I began to wonder how and if Michael would change.

After taxiing up the runway, the plane stopped on the tarmac in front of the terminal, and the steel stairway was wheeled out. The doors opened and as the Marines began to disembark, I stared in disbelief! They were all dressed in khakis and looked "lean, mean and combat ready." From my vantage point, they all looked alike! Tears welled up behind my contact lenses and blurred my vision. I began to panic. In my mind I tried to conjure up an image of Michael's face, but I couldn't remember what he looked like. We had been apart for more months than we had been married.

The atmosphere inside the terminal began to resound with excited shouts, cries and celebrations as Marines and their loved ones found each other. Michael had told me that planes arrived at this airport every hour, bringing troops for R&R. What if his plane had been delayed? What if we had missed each other! By now, tears were dribbling down my cheeks and my vision was completely obscured. I had come so far, I didn't know a soul and I had nowhere to turn. Doubts and desperation overwhelmed me. I wanted to shout his name, but no one would hear. I suddenly felt completely alone and helpless.

"Hello, pretty lady," said a familiar voice at my elbow. I couldn't see him, but I felt Michael's presence, and I turned and melted into his arms.

~Cherie Brooks Reilly

74

Chicken Soup for the Soul

Hello?

*Home is where you can say anything you like
cause nobody listens to you anyway.*
~Author Unknown

I received a call from a boy with whom I went to high school. Of course, he's not a boy now. He's forty-something like I am but that's the great thing about childhood friends. When you run into them — after you get over the initial "I know I don't look THAT old" — it can be like looking at a hologram or one of those Magic Eye pictures.

You look at this rapidly-approaching-middle-aged businessman/father-of-four/saving-for-retirement individual but even as you do, that puckish, fresh-faced boy wavers into view... then out again... then back. But you definitely catch fleeting glimpses of him in there — somewhere — almost like he's waving at you from beneath the crow's feet and laugh lines.

Your own inner cheerleader stirs inside of you and you forget — for a second — that what he's seeing in you is a woman who forsook her grandmother's advice, "You have to suffer to be beautiful," and opted to be comfortable: a few extra pounds, a hairdo that was the height of fashion about ten years ago (but you know how to do it so you keep it) and a body where low-riding anything is out of the question.

So this hunky quarterback from twenty-something years ago called because he'd heard from another former classmate that I'm a writer now and wanted to know if I'd consider ghost writing a book for him.

I would.

I invited him to come to our house on a Saturday when I knew the kids would be gone but my husband would be home working. I figured if this was going to be an ongoing business relationship it was important for things to be on the up-and-up right from the start. Keep in mind that for the past fifteen years I've either a) stayed home with the kids, b) worked in the school system where my co-workers were 95% women, or c) worked at home by myself. I haven't had a male co-worker since 1995.

I put on coffee and he came to the house. I introduced him to my (handsome, successful) husband and we sat in the very next room where David could overhear our entire conversation if he cared to. We talked about the project for an hour. It sounded fabulous and I was dying to sign on. Then we spent an hour or more laughing over old times.

As soon as he was gone, I went into David's office and told him what we'd discussed — even though he could have heard every word. I was determined to do everything right to launch a platonic business relationship with a former really cute classmate — who, I should mention, has a wonderful spouse himself and four fabulous kids.

I was covering all my bases and then some.

I told David pointedly, "Look, I want to make sure you're comfortable with the idea before I even consider it. If you have a problem with it, I'll tell him 'No' right now."

"Whadda' you mean?" he asked.

"Well, neither Ben nor I have ever done this before and we have no idea how much time we'll be required to spend together. And I want to know that you're okay with that."

"Okay with what?"

"Okay with me spending large amounts of time with another man."

"What are you talking about?"

That's when I copped my attitude, "You do still remember that I'm a woman. Right?"

(Deer-in-the-headlights) "Huh?... What?... So do you... think this guy's good looking or something? Wait, am I... in... trouble here? Do you WANT me to be jealous of this guy? Do I have a reason to be worried?"

(Me, with one eyebrow raised, voice calm to the point of scary.) "Now what reason would you have to be jealous of ME—your annoying kid sister who no one would ever find even vaguely attractive?"

"So... you're telling me I have a REASON to be jealous?"

"AAAHHH!!!"

(To my back as I stomp out of the room.) "I'd think you'd be glad that I don't care how much time you spend with other guys. I trust you... Right?"

(Door slam.)

"Wait... can we start this over? I know I can do better."

Poor David is still trying to figure out what he did wrong.

Ben's still waiting for me to call him back and tell him whether I'll do the job for him. I'm making him wait because, frankly, he's a guy too and I'm basically mad at that entire sex right now.

~Mimi Greenwood Knight

75

All About Eve

O jealousy! thou magnifier of trifles.
~Johann Christoph Friedrich von Schiller

There, at the bottom of the bedroom closet, I found it—a small slip of paper with the hastily written phone number for a woman named Eve. There was no way to deny the soft bend of my husband Bill's "v" and the way he crossed his sevens, European-style. It was his handwriting, all right. My hand shook as I tried to imagine a logical explanation for why my husband would have another woman's phone number hidden in the inner recesses of our closet.

Only moments before, as I readied my suitcase for vacation, I had been thinking that I was the luckiest woman I knew. Bill and I had celebrated our twentieth wedding anniversary the previous week with a special dinner at a restaurant where we had one of our first dates. During the meal, he surprised me with the promise of a second honeymoon to take place later that month. Then, after we returned home that evening we watched our wedding video for the first time in years, laughing at how young we once looked and marveling at all we had been through together since then. Illness, family issues, monetary problems—throughout it all, Bill had always been my stabilizing presence. That night, as I laid my head on my pillow, I said a few words of gratitude for my husband and the comfortable rhythm our life had become. Perhaps that was what I had learned to appreciate most about my husband in our twenty years of marriage,

I recalled thinking—his ability to remain calm and focused in any crisis, unlike me.

In the early days of our marriage especially, I had more of a tendency toward impulse when faced with problems and it sometimes irritated me that Bill did not have a similar reaction. It took me a while to understand my husband's more cool and collected ways, as I initially misread his style for lack of concern. Eventually though, I came to value and even strove to emulate his more laidback personality. Yet, as I held the piece of paper upon which he had scrawled another woman's phone number, I struggled to maintain my composure.

As I looked more closely at the wrinkled slip of paper, I began to plot my plan of action. My first instinct was to call Bill at his office and confront him over the phone. No, that wouldn't work, I thought. He couldn't speak freely under those circumstances, and besides, that gave him a full afternoon to conjure up a believable excuse. No matter how painful the truth might be, I needed to know. I had to be logical about this, too, I decided. Further research on my part was imperative before any confrontations took place.

My husband may be cool and calm, but he can also be absentminded. I knew that chances were good that he had forgotten to take his cell phone to work with him. So I did what any suspicious wife might do under such circumstances, I found his phone and checked the recently dialed numbers. And there it was—Eve's phone number—dialed only once, yet dialed just the same. I marched over to my computer, signed onto the Internet and commenced a full-out search for her.

However, my search through various telephone company reverse directories brought up little of a definitive nature. The only information I could confirm was that the phone number was attached to a landline in Pennsylvania, one state over from our home in New York. Pennsylvania? When did Bill go to Pennsylvania? He did sometimes travel for business, yet those trips had taken him out west or to the south, not to Pennsylvania. I recalled all his stories about morning presentations and stuffy afternoon meetings with fellow engineers, the majority of whom were older men. Had there been one seductive woman in a conference group who had caught my husband's eye? Had they met after meetings for drinks, dinner or perhaps a dip in the hotel's Jacuzzi? Or worse? My head began to pound. I just didn't have the strength to imagine the "worse."

Back in my bedroom, I pushed my suitcase aside and tried to do the same with all the thoughts that kept spinning around my head. Still, they kept resurfacing. The irony of the whole situation seemed surreal: finding another woman's number while packing for a second honeymoon, and the woman being so aptly named after the Biblical temptress, Eve.

Yet determined to go about my day, I proceeded with my usual tasks—focusing on some work deadlines, running a few errands and finally returning home to cook dinner. When my husband walked through the front door that evening, he seemed so genuinely glad to see me, even complimenting my new hairstyle. The predicament I found myself in seemed impossible. Maybe I really had misread his collected manner, I thought. Maybe he had been nothing more than a big phony all along. As we sat across from each other at the kitchen table that evening, I barely lifted my gaze from my dinner plate.

"Something wrong?" he asked. "You seem so quiet."

"No," I mumbled. "Just eating."

True to my husband's nature, he made no further ado and after finishing his meal, Bill cleared his place and took his usual seat on the living room sofa to watch the evening news. A few moments later I followed him into the living room, carrying the slip of paper in my hand. Quietly, I sat down and laid it between us. "Would you like to tell me about this?" I asked.

Bill lifted the paper toward his eyes and squinted at the scratchy handwriting. "That's a Pennsylvania area code," he said.

I watched as the wheels turned in his head. Here it comes, I thought. Here comes one good story.

His eyes drew into little slits as he concentrated on the number. "Oh, now I know. Eve. That's the phone number for my cousin Evelyn in Easton. I called her from my cell phone to ask about her father when he was in the hospital." He handed me the piece of paper. "Don't you recognize the number? I copied it out of your phone book."

No, I didn't recognize it. Or did I? I slipped into the bedroom where I took my phone book from the nightstand and compared the numbers. It was Cousin Evelyn's.

Feigning nonchalance, I returned to my seat on the sofa. After a few minutes, Bill turned to me, "Did you think I had gotten another woman's phone number?"

"Well..." I started.

Bill gave a low chuckle and tickled my cheek. "Crazy."

Me, crazy? Maybe. But still the luckiest woman I know.

~Monica A. Andermann

76

Candy-Apple Sweet

The secret of a happy marriage remains a secret.
~Henny Youngman

"Great drive!" one of my girlfriends remarked.

"Your longest yet," said another.

"Thanks," I replied sheepishly, as I put the head cover on and gently placed the golf club in my bag.

"What did you use?" one of the girls asked.

"Oh, it's a club from the garage."

"Let's see it."

I pulled it out and tugged the cover off. The candy-apple red head glistened in the bright sun, the black shaft accentuated the brilliant color.

"But that's a seven wood."

"Yeah, you know I can't hit a driver. I lose control of the big head on the down swing."

"Well, you hit that club further than all of us off the tee. Good job."

Weeks went by and I hit the sweet spot on that seven wood each and every time. It felt great to finally get some good drives down the fairway. But I knew it wouldn't last.

"You're really hitting that club well. Where'd you get it?"

"Ummmm," I hedged, not wanting to reveal the truth.

"Well, where did you buy it?"

"I didn't. It's my husband's club. And he doesn't know I have it."

"You didn't ask him if you could borrow it?"

"Nope, and if he finds out, I'm dead. He made the mistake of letting me use it once when we were playing together. I'd flubbed a shot off the tee so he handed me the seven wood and said, 'Here, try this.' So I did, and fell in love."

"So why can't you tell him you're using it?"

"When I asked him if I could borrow it he said no, it's a man's club with a graphite extra stiff shaft or something." I smiled, then added, "He probably thinks I'd wreck it."

My girlfriend started to laugh, then said, "So what are you doing—sneaking it out of his bag?" She glanced at me sideways.

I looked at her. "He plays with the guys on Saturdays, and I play with you girls on Wednesdays. I pull it out of his bag after he leaves for work and I put it back as soon as I get home."

"And he can't tell that you've used it?"

"Not yet."

We finished that hole and went up to the next. I stuck the tee in the hard ground, placed my ball on top and adjusted my stance. Then I took careful aim with what I now called "my sneaky seven wood," then let the ball fly. It went quite a way, resting in the middle of the fairway with a great approach to the green. I began to walk back to the cart and flipped up the club to look at the bright red head. That's when I noticed a nick, probably from the wooden tee.

"Oh, man, look at that," I said to my girlfriend.

"You'd better polish that out," she replied.

Scrubbing the head and face of the club when I got home from a golf game became a weekly ritual. I tried different polishes to bring the luster back and to remove the scratches. I knew my husband only used it in the fairway, and scratches from a wooden tee would raise an eyebrow or two. He was sure to suspect something if it looked used.

Months later, even though I was keeping the club polished, guilt got the better of me. I wanted to tell him, but I didn't want to give up what was now my favorite club. "Honey," I said one afternoon, "remember when you let me use your seven wood off the tee? I want to get one of my own, just like it."

"That's a man's club, made for a man. It's not right for you."

Stiff shaft or not, it was perfect for me, but I couldn't tell him I'd been hitting with it for almost a year. "So where did you buy it?"

"I got it from a friend of mine who designed it specifically for me and my swing. It's one of a kind."

Later, I dug out the receipt and called his friend. He agreed to make a club for me, with the exact same specs as the one he made for my husband. And he agreed to keep it a secret.

A few weeks later, I picked it up. Candy-apple red head, black shaft—a gorgeous club, just like the other one. That Wednesday I met the girls at the course.

"Guess what? I got a seven wood of my very own!" I shouted.

"But will you hit it as well?" they said. "We think you liked that club just because it was forbidden."

"You might be right. Let's see how this new one works today." I pulled out my brand new club and approached the tee. Just like before, I hit the sweet spot and sent the ball sailing through the air. "Magic!" I shouted.

"Well, you've got the number with that club. No need for you to ever get a driver. You hit that thing farther than all of us."

Did I ever tell my husband I used his club for almost a year? Nope. Some things a woman just has to keep a secret. And that sweet, candy-apple red club is one of mine.

~B.J. Taylor

Honesty Will Kill a Relationship

It's always the badly dressed people who are the most interesting.
~Jean Paul Gaultier

As I watched the woman walk by our table I said to my husband, "Get a look at her outfit. It looks like an artist's palette blew up on it. I wonder what she was thinking when she bought it."

"Probably the same thing you thought when you bought it," he replied and popped a French fry in his mouth.

Puzzled, I asked, "What are you talking about?"

My French fry froze midway to my mouth when he replied, "You have the exact outfit at home."

I devoured my French fry in quick, angry bites as I realized he was right. I demanded he tell me why he didn't say anything when I bought it.

"I wasn't with you when you bought it."

"Well, when I got home and tried it on why didn't you tell me I looked awful in it?"

"I thought you knew. Besides, you seemed so happy."

"You thought I intentionally bought a hideous outfit?"

"Yes."

"Why would you think that?"

"Because you're always telling me I have no taste in clothes and that's why it's imperative you buy my clothes for me. Remember?"

"Oh. Shut up and eat your French fries. When I ask for your honest opinion I expect you to give it to me."

"No you don't."

"Why would you say that?"

"Remember when we first got married and went to the beach and you asked for my honest opinion of the bikini-clad girl who walked by?"

"Yes. What's that got to do with anything?"

"Well, thanks to your physical reaction I haven't walked upright since. And since I'm fond of all my bits-n-pieces I haven't given you my honest opinion in over twenty-five years. It works for us."

"Then it's time we turn over a new leaf and be totally honest with each other. I've matured. I'll be able to handle the truth. Ready?"

"Oh, this isn't going to end well."

"So, now that we're being honest… that orange and black striped blouse I…"

"Made you look like a bumblebee—a cute bumblebee, but a bumblebee nonetheless."

"What about the low-cut blouse?"

"I loved it. Honestly."

"What about the color?"

"Don't know. Don't care. Just loved how low-cut it was. Honestly."

"What about the earrings I wore with it?"

"Earrings? You wore earrings? Honestly, I never noticed. Did I tell you how much I loved the blouse?"

"Certainly you must have liked the plaid, button down shirt I bought you."

"Nope, I hated it. It's still in my closet, in the wrapper."

"Oh."

"I must say I had no idea honesty could be so refreshing and liberating. While we're at it, that purple and green dress you bought was a major mistake. And that Christmas sweater… I wonder what in the world you were thinking when you bought it."

"Before I separate you from your bits-n-pieces why don't you cram the honesty and the French fries in your mouth?"

"I told you this wouldn't end well."

Honesty—don't believe the hype.

~Cindy D'Ambroso Argiento

78

Hunky Magoo

My wife says I never listen to her. At least I think that's what she said.
~Author Unknown

Hunky Magoo is a fitting nickname for my husband. It's unusual and so is he. I call him "H.M." He likes to think it stands for "His Majesty." H.M. sometimes gives the impression of being unfriendly, but deep down in his heart, he's really anti-social.

Like all men, he has his little idiosyncrasies. For one thing, he's a packrat. I haven't been able to park my van in our three-car garage for ten years because it's overflowing with all the junk he's collected. He hangs onto everything he's ever owned, including the wingtip shoes he bought for our wedding over thirty years ago. I can't sneak them out of the house, because he routinely checks the garbage to see if I've thrown away any of his stuff. He thinks the groovy polyester leisure suit he wore in the seventies still has a few good years in it. I've even caught him wearing my cleaning rags.

Hunky's the most handsome, thoughtful, charming husband in the universe—in his opinion. He brags that he can do the work of three men; and it's true, if the three men are Larry, Moe, and Curly. He also brags about having a mind like a steel trap. I tell him he's right about that, because nothing can penetrate it. I also tell him the trap must be stuck in the open position, because he keeps forgetting who's the boss around here.

H.M.'s perspective is very different from mine. For instance, he doesn't feel as strongly as I do about things like empty toilet paper rolls. Then there's the issue of dirty underwear. He thinks it belongs on the bathroom floor.

He also has some odd ideas about home decorating. Once, we were to show our house to prospective buyers on a day I had to work. That left H.M. in charge of giving the tour. That morning, I ran through the house giving it a quick inspection. Everything looked good. I grabbed the dirty laundry from the bedroom, ran downstairs, and dropped it into the washer before going out the door.

When I came home that night, the couple was just leaving. I met them on the front porch, thanked them for coming, and went inside to ask how the showing went.

As I stepped through the door, I saw them. There, on the stairs leading up to our bedroom — on the third step to be exact — was my holey, white, cotton "Grandma" underwear.

At that moment, I can't be sure, but I think I had a stroke. I could almost hear those ragged old bloomers screaming, "Nya, Nya! We've been here all day, right out in the open for all the world to see, and there wasn't a darn thing you could do about it!"

I was mortified. After my stroke, I got up off the floor, turned to the husband, and groaned, "Please tell me these were not here when the couple walked through the house."

"Yeah, they were," he answered, with the same casual tone he would use to say, "Nice weather we're having, huh?"

I felt a second stroke coming on. An volcano of anger was erupting in the pit of my stomach and felt as if it would shoot out my ears. Yet, I made a valiant attempt to control myself. I spoke as calmly as I could. "Tell me," I said quietly. Then, a little louder, I asked, "Why would you leave them there?" Finally, I yelled, "Why didn't you pick them up?"

Looking at me as if I were Quasimodo's ugly cousin, he sighed and said, "I didn't want to call attention to them, that's why!"

~Marsha Mott Jordan

79

Welcome to Our World

Never feel remorse for what you have thought about your wife;
she has thought much worse things about you.
~Jean Rostand

I am a planner and executer of plans. I teach time management skills. My husband, on the other hand, is an absentminded professor type who does not like to make decisions and managing time is not a priority.

I have known for years that he is not talented when it comes to planning trips, moves, etc. so I have taken on that role and have not minded it at all. Sometimes though, I really get tired of my role as "Lead Dog." When he decided that he wanted to take a trip to visit his uncle in Alabama, I naively suggested that he be responsible for making the plans. He agreed to do that. Of course, I had to do a little nagging to get him to decide on a date, so I could arrange my plans accordingly, but he did decide. He announced that we would leave on Saturday, and would travel on I-85 to arrive on Sunday, which sounded like a good plan to me. I suggested that we could spend the night with relatives on our way and offered to make those calls, which I did. I also changed my appointments for the week we were to be gone.

About six days later, Fred announced that we might cancel our trip because Hurricane Bertha had formed and was projected to come our way. I did not tell you that he is a meteorologist, and a hurricane historian. In my warmest, wifeliest voice I said, "Fred, most people leave home when a hurricane is headed toward them."

His response was, "Well, not me."

"And why is it that we have to be here?"

"I have to be here to protect the house."

I took a deep breath and reminded myself that this was his trip, that he is a fine man who does not drink, smoke, or chase women and is very good to me. Then I said, "What can you do during the storm to protect the house that you can't do before we go?"

"Just never you mind, I am going to be here if it comes this way."

Three days later, the storm decided not to arrive at our doorstep so he announced that we could go. He also said that he did not want to go on I-85, but would rather go by way of I-95. So, after taking a deep breath, I reminded myself once again that this was his trip, that he is a fine man, does not drink, smoke or chase other women, and is very good to me. I called relatives to tell them that we would not be spending the night, but thanks anyway.

The evening before our trip I asked what time he wanted to leave. The answer was 10 a.m. At 10:15 I was ready to walk out the door. Fred, however, was stark naked, had not packed the car, had not changed the litter box, nor given instructions to our neighbor who was to be the cat's nanny while we were gone. I took a very deep breath, and thought to myself, "Okay, this is his trip, do not nag or complain about the time." I started cleaning the house, which it desperately needed, and said to myself, "This is not a bad thing and I am okay. I can keep my mouth shut." At 11:45 we rolled out of the driveway and turned right instead of left. I asked, "Where are we going?"

"To the bank. How much money do you think we will need?"

"This is your trip. You decide, but we pass two banks on our way to 95 so, why are you going this way?"

"I like the downtown bank. Sometimes those two banks run out of money on weekends."

I took a very deep breath and thought to myself, "I doubt very seriously that both of them would run out of money before lunch, but this is his trip and surely soon we will get on the road." We got to the bank and while getting money he realized that he did not have his sunglasses. He began to fret because he remembered that he had them in his hands and maybe he had put them on top of the car when he put his golf clubs in the trunk. There was nothing else for us to do but go back and check to see if they fell off in the driveway.

I began gritting my teeth, taking multiple deep breaths and reminding myself that this was his trip and it did not really matter when we left. I also reminded myself that he is a fine man, does not drink, smoke, or chase women and is very good to me. We drove back to the house; he looked for his sunglasses in the driveway, the garage, and in the house and did not find them. He finally gave up and we started out again.

On our way out of town we planned to drop off some leftover food to a friend. So on our way to her house I said, "It is lunch time. Should we stop and eat something before we leave town?"

"That is a good idea. Where would you like to stop?"

I looked up and said, "There's a Subway. We could stop there after we go to Linda's or we could go to the diner which is right next to the highway." He voted for the diner, so, being the planner I am, I began thinking about what I would order. I started looking forward to their toasted chicken salad and fries. We stopped at my friend's, dropped off the food, turned around, and as he passed the shopping center, he turned into it and parked the car in front of the Subway. He cut off the ignition and looked over at me. He immediately saw that I was about to blow a gasket, and innocently asked, "What is wrong with you?"

"You are about to get on my last nerve."

"What have I done?"

Repeating to myself what had now become my mantra — "He is a fine man, he does not drink, smoke or chase women and he is very good to me" — I took my deepest breath yet, held it for a second or two and said, "Absolutely nothing Fred, you are just being you, and I am just being me. Let's get something to eat."

The rest of our trip went wonderfully, and upon our arrival in

Foley, Alabama, Fred found his sunglasses in the trunk where he put them when he packed his golf clubs. All's well that ends well.

~Diane Henderson, LCSW

A Real Fixer-Upper

Women hope men will change after marriage but they don't;
men hope women won't change but they do.
~Bettina Arndt, Private Lives, 1986

Gather near, my children,
Sit close beside my knee.
I'll tell you just exactly
How your grandpa came to be.

If I remember rightly
'Twas his mane first caught my eye
With the part so way down low
And his hair heaped far too high.

But I knew that I could show him
How to fashion it just so.
I would mold him and remake him
To create the ideal beau.

The words he spoke so tritely,
"Don't I know you from somewhere?"
Could be re-taught, I quickly thought,
And then he'd speak with flair.

His clothes, a wee bit tacky,
Were not the least in style
But, with some gentle coaching,
I would fix that in a while.

He was tall and somewhat pimply;
He was slender, much too lean.
(But I notice as he ages
Some things self-correct it seems.)

So I began my mission
To save this sorry man
To prove how very lucky
That he fell into my hands.

I tutored. I instructed.
I advised and I designed.
But somewhere in the process
Our courtship redefined.

Time taught me a lesson
And opened my eyes wide:
Forget the perfect package;
Find the gift that waits inside!

~Carol McAdoo Rehme

Married *Life!*

I Will Always Love You

A man is not where he lives, but where he loves.

~Latin Proverb

Somewhere Over the Rainbow

While we try to teach our children all about life,
our children teach us what life is all about.
~Angela Schwindt

Our wedding day was an event to remember for my husband and me, our friends and family, and my first grade class of twenty-four six-year-olds. To my students, not only was it a big deal that my name was going to change in the middle of the year, but the fact that I was getting married also meant that I was in love (a word that cannot be spoken among a group of kids without giggles).

Throughout the year, my teacher's mailbox collected hundreds of crayon-sketched wedding pictures from my kids. Drawings of my future husband and me holding hands while frolicking under rainbows, beautifully adorned wedding gowns fit for a princess, and larger than life wedding rings were among the common themes. The kids loved hearing and talking about my plans to be wed to "Mr. Scott." In the final days leading up to the wedding, when my mind couldn't help but drift to thoughts of our big day, I came up with an impromptu creative writing assignment.

Wouldn't it be intriguing to find out what advice a group of first graders would give their teacher in regards to maintaining a happy marriage? Here is a list of tips brainstormed by my community of little people.

1. Be nice!
2. Go on picnics.
3. Give each other presents.
4. Sing to each other.
5. Have a baby.
6. Get a babysitter.
7. Go on a dream vacation.
8. Share your food.
9. Help each other.
10. Go on rides.
11. Dance!
12. Get dressed up and go to fancy restaurants.
13. Play sports together.
14. Find a pot of gold.
15. Say "I love you."

Aside from thinking this was completely endearing, I was stunned by the actual quality of responses that came from kids who had only been in this world for a handful of years. From watching the relationships of their loved ones, or the relationships of book or TV characters, or perhaps even from just thinking about the kinds of things that make them happy, they were able to come up with a list of valuable, albeit simple tips to maintaining a happy life with your spouse.

This list speaks very clearly to me. Mutual respect, showing appreciation for one another, and setting aside some time for fun are desires that are intrinsically in our hearts from a very early age. As my husband and I venture through the journey of marriage together, we will reflect on this list as a reminder to enjoy the simple pleasures in life, stay young at heart, and maybe if we're really lucky, find a pot of gold somewhere along the way.

~Bevin K. Reinen

Sock Fuzz

If you don't like something change it;
if you can't change it, change the way you think about it.
~Mary Engelbreit

My toes dug into the soft carpeting in our new home. Gone were the hard wooden floors of the apartment we'd rented the first two years of our marriage. I luxuriated a moment before I hurried off to feed our year-old twins their breakfast and send my husband Bob off to work.

After breakfast, while the boys were safely ensconced in the playroom, I returned to the master bedroom to run the vacuum over the new almond colored carpeting. The almond color was a wise choice. It complimented the dark cherry wood of our bedroom furniture. I hummed and smiled as I took pride in the look of a freshly vacuumed floor. When I rounded the bed to Bob's side, I gasped.

Little black bugs were scattered all over the carpet next to the bed. Yuck! There was an infestation of bugs in our perfect new home. I wanted to cry. I collapsed in the chair in the corner to plan my course of action. What should I do? Should I spray? Should I vacuum them up? How many more were there and where were they hiding?

While I pondered my choices, I noticed that the little black spots hadn't moved. Cautiously I got down on my hands and knees and approached the critters. Summoning up courage beyond my paranoia, I pushed at one with a fingernail. It didn't budge. I pushed again. It clung to the carpeting like a scrap of yarn. I straightened. They weren't bugs. They were little pieces of black fuzz!

Then I remembered. The last thing Bob did every night was sit on the bed, remove his black socks, and shake them straight out again with a snap. He was flinging black sock fuzz all over my new carpeting! Hands on my hips, I surveyed the blemishes before me. I knew they would vanish into the vacuum but tomorrow I would only face more. What could I do?

I refused to vacuum that area and disturb the evidence that would convict the perpetrator. "I'll nip this habit in the bud right away," I huffed as I pictured myself pointing out the flawed habits of male inconsideration.

While the twins napped, I sat at the kitchen table with a cup of coffee and my devotional book. I groaned when I found the scripture reading for the day in my Bible. It was Proverbs 31 and it was a long passage. I was never going to catch up on my reading at this rate. But as I read on, I was encouraged. The passage was about the perfect woman.

Bob was blessed to have me. I was virtuous. I worked with my hands. Certainly I was "like the merchant ships, bringing her food from afar." Grocery shopping with the boys was quite a trick — pushing one cart full of kids and pulling another full of food. I didn't sell garments but I was a stay-at-home mom by choice and I did not "eat the bread of idleness." I was sure my kids would call me "blessed" if they could say the word. Not flicking sock fuzz on the carpet was a minor concession Bob could make to such a wonderful wife. I closed my Bible, satisfied with my self-examination and my course of action.

Dinner was always at six and Bob was usually home by five-thirty. That night his arrival time passed with no cheery, "Honey, I'm home!"

Six o'clock arrived and I began putting things on hold, wondering where he could be. The hands of the clock inched forward. I paced by the phone. Why couldn't he call out of consideration for the woman who cooked him dinner every night? Just as I was about to begin feeding the twins, the phone rang. I grabbed it, expecting to hear Bob offer his excuses.

"Mrs. Robbins?" asked a strange male voice.

"Yes?" I was annoyed when I realized it wasn't Bob. I wanted to know what to do with dinner, not talk to some stranger.

"First," he said solemnly, "let me offer my condolences on the late Mr. Robbins."

Did he say the late Mr. Robbins? I clutched the kitchen counter and braced myself. Didn't the police come to your door for this sort of thing? Did they just call the next of kin now? Wasn't he at least going to tell me to sit down?

"We at Sacred Monuments have special prices on our granite if you are…"

I exhaled. It was a telemarketer. He must have been reading the obituaries and called the wrong Robbins family. I just prayed he wasn't psychic.

"Mr. Robbins is only late for dinner," I explained with a voice shaking from relief. The man apologized profusely.

I hung up the phone and took a deep breath. That was as close as I wanted to come to being the Widow Robbins. A few minutes later, Bob's "I'm home!" was a welcome sound. I hugged him tightly as he came in the door.

"I'm sorry I'm late," he said warily.

"It's okay. Everything is on the back burner." I smiled warmly at a man who looked especially good after his narrow brush with death.

All through dinner I wrestled with the sock fuzz that needed attention upstairs, measuring it against the impact of the monument salesman's phone call. What kind of wife would haggle over a little sock fuzz? Certainly not one who had come so close to being a widow.

After dinner, I snuck upstairs, vacuumed the infestation of fuzz from the carpet and thanked God for it. Gone too was the infestation of pride. It was sucked away and replaced with thanksgiving for a loving husband and the father of my children.

~Karen Robbins

My Other Half

Don't marry the person you think you can live with;
marry only the individual you think you can't live without.
~James C. Dobson

There's a scientific method to finding the perfect spouse—not that I'm scientific—but my husband is and therein lies the secret. When a right-brained person marries a left-brained person you get one whole brain and from then on anything and everything is possible.

Prospero is very math and science oriented. He likes things proven. He speaks several languages. He is a gifted and meticulous craftsman. And what amazes me the most is that he can do mental math.

I, on the other hand, am a literary soul. I love art, history, and have never needed anything as silly as facts to believe in the possibility of something. I'm a gourmet cook but can't bake because that would require measuring ingredients and I can't be bothered.

Together we make the perfect couple.

When I told Prospero that I wanted our new home to look like an old Italian villa, he laid black and white marble floors. I brought home grapevines and he not only planted them, but also planted a grove of fig trees. I dream up an idea; he executes it. We work in perfect harmony.

This is especially helpful when vacationing. I think up these fabulous vacations and by the time we get there I know everything there is to know about the history of the civilization, major works of art, sights to see and restaurants in which to dine. Prospero can speak the language, convert money in his head, figure out the shortest distance between cities, and—most importantly—drive a stick shift.

Occasionally there's some trouble in paradise, like the time I wanted to do a little shoe shopping in Rome.

"I love those shoes," I said, looking into the store window. "Come in and help me buy them."

"No." No? "You want the shoes, you go buy them," he decided. "I'll see you later." And with that he walked off in the direction of a café leaving me in a mild state of panic.

But I really wanted those shoes.

Shopping is a universal sport and the basic rules apply wherever you are. Besides, almost everyone in Italy speaks English. With that, I opened the door, took a seat, and was helped by probably the only salesman in Italy who only spoke Italian. But that didn't stop me. I dragged him out to the street and pointed to the shoes. After a few, "*troppo grande*" and "*troppo piccolo*" I, like Goldilocks, managed to find shoes that fit just right.

In fact, by the time Prospero came into the store to find me, I had done so well that there were seven shoeboxes stacked next to me. I wasn't even worrying about converting money since I decided to charge the whole thing and let the bank worry about the math.

That would teach him not to break up the team.

Prospero and I are two halves of the same whole. Our basic goals are the same but we're each able to tackle the challenge of getting there in our own way—and bring our partner along. It not only works but has the added bonus of creating a harmonious atmosphere in our lives. We can never be jealous or competitive because we can't even do the same things!

Yes, of course there was that initial spark of lust on our first blind date that ignited our romance. And there's still a mad passionate love between us that's lasted over thirty years. But when it comes to having a marriage that runs smoothly for over three decades, it's being two halves of the same whole that counts.

~Lynn Maddalena Menna

Proud

We look forward to the time when the Power of Love
will replace the Love of Power.
Then will our world know the blessings of peace.
~William Ewart Gladstone

t was a very early morning. I knew it was going to be gloomy. As a military wife, I knew this day would eventually come, but was I really ready for it? Would I ever be ready for it? Then, as I saw my husband walk into the living room in his light green, tan and brown uniform, I could not have been prouder. He gave me a yellow ribbon pin that had the deployment flag on it, to wear every day, along with a part of his dog tag.

"You ready, babe?" Chris asked as he smiled. As we were loading his bags in the truck, his mom, sisters, nephews and my brother arrived to join us. When everyone was ready, we were off to the airport. I sat in the passenger seat trying to keep my mind off the day ahead. I found myself very fidgety. Chris slowly placed his hand on my leg for a few seconds to calm my nerves. I quickly turned my head away to be sure Chris did not see the tears in my eyes.

When we arrived at O'Hare International Airport, I opened the passenger door and walked toward the back of the truck, standing a few feet away as I watched Chris and my brother take his bags out and put them on the ground. My mind was blank. I knew that soon I would be saying goodbye to my husband of only eight months, not knowing if he would come back to me.

As we all started heading to the entrance of the airport, I brushed my hand against his, just hoping I could hold it since he was in uniform. "I don't care what they say," he said as he grabbed my hand. I held his soft, yet rugged hand so tight, telling myself to remember the moment. Once again my eyes swelled up with tears.

When we arrived at the airline ticket counter, everyone began digging for their drivers' licenses. We needed them so we could get past security and go to the gate to see Chris off. It was chaos going through security with two children under the age of two and a whole ton of cargo. Who knew that taking off half of the clothing we were wearing would be such a chore! After conquering security, we waited for Chris's boarding time. We found a nice spot in the waiting area by a window so the boys could watch the planes land. I was sitting on the floor talking to Chris's sister when Chris sat down behind me and put his arms around me. I tried as hard as I could not to cry. I did not want him to see me so emotional. I felt like I had to be strong… for him. I felt guilty for getting so much attention from Chris; there were other people there too who wanted to say goodbye.

"We will now start boarding Flight 652." When I heard the announcement, my mind raced and the hugging procession began. Chris went around and hugged his family. As he stood hugging his mom, my heart melted. Her baby boy was leaving for war. That's a situation no mom wants to be in, but I have never seen a prouder mother in my life. Eventually it was my turn. I didn't know what I should do, but he just pulled me into his arms and hugged me tight. He held me in his arms so perfectly. My face was in his muscular chest and my arms were wrapped tightly around his waist. As I lifted my head, he kissed my forehead.

After we shared what I hoped was not our last kiss, they called three names to board. One name was his. "I better go," Chris said. "I love you." My chin was trembling as I mumbled, "I love you, too." As he let me go, the tears I was trying to hold in fell and my whole body went numb.

I stood there watching the man I love walk away. After he handed the lady his ticket, he and the other two soldiers being deployed turned around. I managed to give him a half smile. Chris smiled back, lifted his right arm and put his hand up to his lips and blew a kiss. No matter who else was there that day, I knew that kiss was for me. After he turned back around, I just closed my eyes and took a deep breath. My mind was empty. No thoughts.

We started the long walk back through the airport to the parking lot. As we stepped outside a plane flew overhead. I said a prayer to myself, praying harder than ever. While I drove his truck home, the image of him standing at the terminal, blowing me a kiss, stuck in my head. I know that image will stay with me forever.

~Melissa A. Lowery

85

As She Sleeps

In the night of death, hope sees a star,
and listening love can hear the rustle of a wing.
~Robert Ingersoll

I sit in a chair next to her. I watch as her chest rises and falls with each breath. I listen to the sound of her breathing, a soft comforting sound. I reach out and hold her hand; she stirs, but does not wake. Instinctively her hand closes around mine, like it has done so often before. I kiss her cheek gently. I whisper, "I love you." Still asleep, a smile spreads across her face. She has heard me. I sit back into the chair, still holding her hand and I think: Does she know how much I love her? Does she know how much I care? Does she know I am here?

I remember the days of our youth, two teenagers in love. How I loved to hug her and to hold her, to feel her arms wrapped around me. I remember how I asked her to be mine, for now and for all time. I see the tears in her eyes as she looks at me, not answering at first, then a smile and a soft yes. I see us fall into each other's arms; I remember the smell of the rose I gave her. I wonder if she dreams of this as she sleeps.

I see our wedding day—two young adults, not children anymore, too young some say, but we are in love and we know it is a true and deep love. I remember how nervous I was that day; my knees were weak, and I was holding her hand so tight. When she said, "I do," I saw her sweet gentle smile. I remember the kiss at the end of the ceremony and I remember the smell of the roses in her bouquet. I wonder if she dreams of this as she sleeps.

I remember the day our daughter was born. How I held her hand. This time she was scared; I held her hand, telling her I was there for her. I remember the look in her eyes as she saw our daughter for the first time. I remember her soft smile as she looked at me and mouthed, "I love you. I remember the smell of the roses I gave to her after our daughter was born. I wonder if she dreams of this as she sleeps.

I see the day our son was born; the day I nearly lost her and our son because of complications. I see how I fell to the floor, and on my knees I unashamedly cried and asked God to please let them survive. It was a long recovery, but I remember the smell of roses I had delivered to her room. I wonder if she dreams of this as she sleeps.

I remember our twentieth anniversary. I took a vacation that week and I remember cooking dinner for her that night. She came home; I had made steaks and baked a cake. We celebrated with our children. We exchanged gifts. After we finished eating I put "Color My World," our song, on the stereo, and we danced, we embraced and held each other tight. I remember the smell of the twenty roses I gave her that night. I wonder if she dreams of this as she sleeps.

I think about the Columbus Day Ball. I see her in her wheelchair, how embarrassed she was when I took her in the chair onto the dance floor and we danced; we danced to "The Dance." We were alone on the dance floor; no one wanted to intrude on us. After the dance I knelt in front of her and we hugged—we held each other tight. I remember the smell of roses from her corsage. I wonder if she dreams of this as she sleeps.

As she sleeps, she breathes her last; she was tired and needed to rest. I look at her and stroke her face, I run my fingers through her hair, I hold her hand tight, tighter than I ever did before. My tears fall from my eyes onto her cheeks as I kiss her again and say goodbye. As I rise, I smell the roses. There are no roses in the room. I ask the nurse where the aroma is coming from, and she answers that she doesn't smell them. I know now, as she sleeps, she dreams of all of this.

~Mark Anthony Rosolowski

86

Turning the Page

The language of friendship is not words but meanings.
~Henry David Thoreau

The book sale reminded me why I had fallen in love with my ex-husband Larry. My daughter Jessica borrowed my card tables for the occasion. On this sunny Saturday she hoped to earn a little money and sell some of the many books she had inherited when her father died.

Her driveway and yard brimmed with tables and boxes, evidence of Larry's great intellect and insatiable curiosity. When I met Larry in college, I was swept away by his ability to be poet, philosopher, historian or economist, depending on the occasion. Larry was a prodigious reader, delving into any subject that piqued his interest. As his interests grew, so did his bookshelves.

Even though Larry and I had turned out to be emotionally and spiritually incompatible, I always admired his intellect and humor and we had remained connected after our divorce. Now, I smiled as I saw the religious books, exploring Christianity, Judaism, and Islam. When I met Larry in college, he described himself as an agnostic. But when he learned I was Jewish, he revealed he was three-quarters Christian and one-quarter Jewish. When he was drafted during the Vietnam War, his religious preference imprinted on his dog tags read, "Pantheist." Perhaps it should have said, "Flexible." Later, he became a born-again Christian. Even then, he still read about Hinduism, Buddhism and Paganism.

I stopped by a stack of science fiction and thumbed through a battered copy of Robert Heinlein's *Starship Troopers*.

"You'll probably want to save this," I told Jessica. This was one of Larry's favorite childhood books. As a kid growing up with an alcoholic father, he had needed a world to escape to. Science fiction provided that and I tenderly touched his well-worn copies of *Dune, Stranger in a Strange Land, The Moon Is a Harsh Mistress* and *Dandelion Wine*.

One box held a hardback collection of Isaac Bashevis Singer books. Larry had introduced me to the famous Yiddish story, *Gimpel the Fool*, by Singer, on our second date and it became one of my favorites. During the next months, I avidly read all of Singer's works, transporting myself from our college town of Columbia, Missouri, into old world Poland, rich with tradition, superstition, humor, and faith.

I leafed through a thick book, *The 500 Top Poems*. On our first date, Larry recited poetry to me. He loved Ginsberg, T.S. Eliot, and Ferlinghetti. But his favorite was John Ciardi. I rescued the slim Ciardi book hidden behind a volume about the Boer War. Larry had this book when I met him, more than forty years ago. On the flyleaf, he'd scrawled "Love is all."

There was a certain irony in finding the flowered yellow Sarah Ban Breathnach work, *Something More: Excavating Your Authentic Self*, settled amongst the Michael Connellys and the James Lee Burke mysteries. Self-improvement was a definite mystery for Larry—he often mocked the concept, even while he searched for answers in history and poetry. Perhaps some hopeful woman bought him the book, wishing he would take the hint.

I looked for the book Larry had been reading when I last saw him—the story of America's upcoming economic collapse. Although divorced, Larry and I had arranged to sit together at a mutual friend's anniversary party. When I arrived, Larry was alone on a sofa, reading. As usual, he was passionate about his current obsession and cited several other books on economic upheaval.

"I'll lend them to you, if you want," he said. But I knew I'd never read past the first pages.

"I'm buying some property in the country," he added. "For when the world ends. I'll be off the grid. I'll grow my own food."

I thought of our vegetable garden, back in our Whole Earth days. We had planted the seeds together, but somehow Larry always ended up indoors, reading about gardening while I weeded, controlled the pests, harvested and cooked.

"Who's going to grow the food?" I asked.

"Oh, one of the kids will do it," he said, waving his hand. "Anyway, the property's about fifty miles from town. If things get bad, you can come if you want to."

I smiled as his words, some of the last he spoke to me, played back through my mind. If my friends browsed this eclectic collection, they would easily understand why I had fallen in love with this quirky, curious, brilliant young man. But one thing they wouldn't be able to read into our relationship was Larry's enduring generosity. Early on, he had promised to look out for me, and years later, he was still trying to do just that.

Carefully, I selected the books I wanted: the Ciardi, a Singer, a copy of the *Upanishads* with Larry's handwriting on the bookplate.

After I paid my daughter, I carried my modest armful of books to the car.

Though our marriage didn't survive, our friendship did. With this odd assortment of titles, I was keeping a part of Larry with me, allowing his legacy of reading and discovery to live on within my bookshelves.

~Deborah Shouse

Drive Fast, Take Chances

The greatest discovery of my generation is that
a human being can alter his life by altering his attitudes.
~William James

"You're not wearing that shirt, are you?" I asked Paul in a rather harsh tone. The shirt was a complete mismatch with his black cargo shorts. But I didn't want to get into yet another fight about his clothes sense, so I let it go.

Why did all the things that used to thrill me about this man now drive me crazy? He always looked great when we were dating. Now, his fashion faux pas drove me nuts. I used to find his favorite saying, "Drive Fast, Take Chances!" exciting. Now his driving scared me to death. I thought his idea of jumping around the dance floor, which he called dancing, cute; now it just annoyed me. I used to feel safe riding in his car all cuddled up next to him with the radio blasting. Now I detested his Eagles blaring on the radio. I used to lie in bed and watch him sleep, thinking how lucky I was to have him. Now I just poked him in the side to turn over when his snoring was too loud. His quirky little ways were driving me crazy.

Never mind that he did all the grocery shopping, cooking and put away the laundry. Those things didn't count. We each had chores. Those were his... I had mine.

Over the years I tried to change him. I suggested we take a

dance class together but he laughed, thinking I was joking. I told him he drove too fast. Now when we went anywhere, if I wanted to arrive without my nerves in a knot, I drove or lay my seat back and didn't look. The coffee slurping I put up with; after all, I love to dunk doughnuts myself. I labeled his closet with tags on the rod: clothes for when you go out with Sallie, clothes for grunge wear around the house, and clothes for work. Unfortunately he moved them all to the first category. As for the Eagles, I just burned a new CD and slipped in a blasting Lady Gaga whenever I could. I totally identified with her song, "Bad Romance."

Which, speaking of that, ours lasted forty-seven years. Forty-seven years! You'd think in that amount of time I could train this puppy. I achieved some success but only a modest amount. And yet I loved this man-child.

He provided a wonderful home for our children and me, worked hard all his life, was a good-natured intelligent companion, skillful lover and never cheated.

As Paul entered his Medicare years, he came home from a doc-tor's appointment one afternoon. I could tell from the look on his face, the news wasn't good.

"My kidneys are starting to deteriorate," he said solemnly. "Looks like dialysis is an option I may face soon. You know the prognosis after dialysis is a life span of two to five years."

"What? You must be wrong!" I said.

"Nope, once you start, the stats aren't good when you have other health challenges like I do: diabetes and high blood pressure."

I did my own research that night on the Internet after he went to bed. I was stunned. I found out I could be a widow in less than five years. This wasn't in our plan. What happened to the "Golden Years" of travel and entertainment? What happened to the side-by-side bathtubs on the beach? How many years did we have left together? I cried myself to sleep.

From that night on I knew the color of his shirt was irrelevant. When I wanted to complain about his coffee slurping, I was thankful I wasn't drinking mine by myself. When he snored, I knew I could be sleeping alone, so I wore earplugs. I learned I liked Foreigner, thanks to his choice of tunes. And well, the dancing, we did that in the privacy of our living room so who cared if he couldn't dance? I realized I would be so lucky to have the pleasure of Paul's quirks for many years to come.

~Sallie A. Rodman

For Better or Worse

No matter what else goes wrong around us,
with that one person we're safe in our own paradise.
~Richard Bach

"I'm sorry" was what I wanted to say. Too bad I lacked the nerve to say it. Two little words, that's all they were, but if I'd the courage to say them, they'd only open the door to more words—many more. An inevitable conversation would result if my thoughts were given a voice, and to be honest, talking about it was something I'd been trying to avoid.

And so we sat out on our deck in silence and watched the intermittent bursts of lightning in the distant nighttime skies. The muffled rumbles of thunder that followed gave fair warning of the coming storm—the symbolism suggested by its approach wasn't lost on me as I thought about all we'd been through lately—especially the infertility. I wondered if she thought about it as much as I did, and if so, what was she thinking? A part of me wanted to know, but fearing what she might say, or worse yet, how she might react, I was curious enough to wonder, but cautious enough not to ask.

In truth, my silence sustained my sense of security, but it was merely postponing the inevitable. I knew that sooner or later she was going to want to talk about it, and when she did, my fragile defenses would most certainly crumble—especially if she became emotional. Should that happen we were going to have another problem—perhaps a bigger one—I wasn't going to be able to comfort or console her. No reassuring words from me would be forthcoming.

Infertility was the sole obstacle to the idyllic life that we'd planned. After marriage, we saved money and bought a house. Renovations followed and so did a new puppy. When the work was done and our house had become our home, it was time to begin filling the freshly painted bedrooms with babies, but it didn't turn out that way. We did come close to achieving our goals though, but without children, living that 1950s sitcom life that I'd envisioned while growing up watching shows such as *The Adventures of Ozzie and Harriet* or *Father Knows Best* just wasn't happening. In the end, even our puppy wasn't enough to provide me with the sense of family that TV dad Ozzie Nelson must have felt when he came home at the end of the day to Harriett, David and Ricky.

As the storm approached, I knew we should talk, but my fears demanded otherwise. They did, however, provoke an unexpected memory. I was at camp, a young scout, standing on the edge of the dock, waiting for the signal to enter the cold, dark and frightening waters for my swimmer's test. Not being very good at camp aquatics, I knew that I'd have to push aside my fears, take a deep breath and jump in. So many years had passed since then, but once again I found myself standing on the edge, knowing what I had to do, knowing that it was almost time to jump back into the frightening waters.

A brilliant flash crossed the sky and was immediately followed by the sounds of rolling thunder, and then silence. The air became still—the calm before the storm—another fitting metaphor. I closed my eyes, gathered my thoughts, and then, finally, allowed them a voice. Choking back my fears, I took a deep breath and jumped in.

I began by saying how frustrated I'd become with everything having to do with infertility. I'd grown weary of living by the dictates of the calendar, thermometers and early morning temperature taking, of charts and graphs that predetermined the optimum time and date to make a baby—and then our failures to do so. I was sick of doctor visits and waiting rooms. I just wanted to be like any other dad playing catch with his son, or the proud pop walking his daughter down the aisle on her wedding day.

I'd had my fill of friends asking when we were going to start having kids, and family members wondering if a new niece or nephew, cousin or grandchild would be making an appearance anytime soon. I was tired of wanting children, waiting for it to happen, and knowing it might never. I mentioned medical alternatives, questioned God's wisdom, and then I went for broke: I asked her to tell me how she really felt about all this, without holding back, without sparing my feelings, without the sugarcoating. And then, I was done. I exhaled and shut up.

She didn't say a word. I prayed for a flash of lightning, a clap of thunder—anything to break the silence. I blew it and I knew it. I never should've said all that I had, and now I waited to suffer the consequences for being a horrible spouse. And then I remembered—the one thing that I'd wanted to say, but had forgotten to mention. This time it didn't require taking a deep breath or any courage to say the two little words that I'd been carrying around in my heart for far too long. "I'm sorry." And then, I added something that we both already knew, "It's all my fault."

And of course, it was. Whereas she was physically ready and able to become a participant in the adventures of parenting, apparently I wasn't, and therein was my dilemma. If our failures to conceive a child caused her sadness, how could I be the supportive husband, the comforting partner that she might need and certainly ought to have when after all, I was the cause of her unhappiness. I was the reason that she has never received a card on Mother's Day.

Her expression was disarming, comforting, reassuring. Her smile immediately told me what she was thinking, but I knew that she was going to tell me anyway. "Sometimes you can be so stupid," was what she said. "The problem," she added, "isn't 'yours,' and it isn't 'mine,' it's 'ours,' and no matter what happens, it happens to 'us,' for better or worse." I knew she meant it too. For better or worse, part of our wedding vows. Suddenly they took on a whole new meaning, providing the comfort that I'd worried I couldn't give, but now, I needed far more to receive. And that was it. I'd jumped into the frightening waters and survived—rescued by the person I most loved in the world, and nothing else, as it turned out, mattered more than that.

The storm that had been slow in arriving suddenly dissipated—becoming little more than a gentle summer night's rain. It was impossible to foresee the future; no way of knowing if we'd ever conceive a child. And yet, I felt a comforting reassurance in knowing that no matter what life held in store for us, we would face it together, as partners, as friends, and as husband and wife, for better or worse.

~Stephen Rusiniak

We Danced Through Life

Dancing is moving to the music without stepping on anyone's toes, pretty much the same as life.
~Robert Brault, www.robertbrault.com

I held Georgia close. We swayed to the music and slowly turned. Next to us, a couple twirled and spun in elegant circles. Their feet and bodies moved in harmony with the music as they floated over the dance floor. "Wouldn't it be wonderful to dance like that?" Georgia asked me.

"It sure would," I replied into her ear.

A few weeks later, my daughter, Vanessa, announced plans to attend her boyfriend's prom. Georgia decided to give them dance lessons as a Christmas gift.

She found a dance studio and called them. "Are you sure you and your husband don't want to take lessons with them?" the gentleman asked. "There's a discount for a second couple."

"Well…" my wife hesitated. "Why not?"

We stood with ten other couples in the center of the floor at Jimmy's Dance Studio. I listened to the conversations.

"I've always wanted to do this," one woman said.

"I hope I don't step on someone's feet," a man of about fifty said to his graying wife.

A dapper gentleman of about sixty stepped into the room and

We Danced Through Life: I Will Always Love You   303

faced us. He was five foot two inches—if that. "I'm Jimmy. You're here to learn to dance and you will. I promise you, by the time you finish your first six weeks, you'll make your friends jealous." His toupee, obviously fitted many years ago, was slightly off center and barely covered his spreading baldness.

We started with the basic box step, a simple waltz for those who know how to dance. We practiced the steps facing each other but standing several feet apart. The men stepped forward with their left feet; the women stepped back with their right. Our steps were mirror images of each other. "One! Two! Three!" Jimmy shouted.

It seemed easy.

"Okay!" Jimmy said. "Watch how it's done." He took one of his assistants in his arms. An Anne Murray song began to play. "Could I Have This Dance," she sang. Jimmy and his partner drifted elegantly around the room.

"We're going to start the music again. Take your partner in your arms. Now let's give it a try." Jimmy smiled at us. "It's easy. You'll see."

Anne Murray sang again. The song would haunt us for months. I held Georgia in my arms. My right hand held her waist; the left held her hand. Across the room, I saw our daughter and her boyfriend do the same. The music began. I moved my left foot forward and stepped on Georgia's toe. We stood, waited for the beat, and tried again. Halfway through the box, we faltered.

"Hold her firm!" One of the assistants came to our side. She grabbed my arm. "Here! Put your arm around her waist! Hold her hand with the other! Don't move it. Keep it firm! You have to guide her!"

Anne Murray wailed again. We got through the full box without stumbling or stepping on each other. Compared to the instructors, we looked like two kids dancing for the first time. We were awkward, but we learned.

Several weeks later, something happened. While Anne Murray asked for a dance, Georgia and I began to flow across the floor. Our awkwardness was gone. We were partners. We were one.

"Yes! Yes!" Jimmy yelled and smiled. "Look at them, class. They got it." He clapped his hands, which caused his toupee to slide to the left. "I told you it was easy." He smiled.

It took a lot of practice and time, but we did it. We became a team. We anticipated each other's moves and interpreted the slightest signal from the other. What seemed hard before became natural.

Once we learned how to dance, we looked at our relationship. We stumbled cooking together. We stepped on each other's toes when disciplining our children. I wanted to go right, she went left: When to mow the lawn, how much to spend on a car, where our vacations should be spent, and all things couples struggle with. But once we got the steps down, we danced through life.

~Michael T. Smith

90

From This Day Forward

I had rather be on my farm than be emperor of the world.
~George Washington

"From This Day Forward" read the message on our wedding invitation. It was 1969; I was twenty-one years old and life was exciting. After the wedding, I moved from Moncton, New Brunswick, to the big city of Toronto, Ontario, where we both pursued our careers. On weekends we drove to car races in our purple Challenger. We traveled across Canada, holidayed in resorts, bought a house in the suburbs and eventually our family grew to five.

One day my husband said, "I think I'd like to buy a farm." Not long after that, the farm next door to his parents in New Brunswick went up for sale. I loved looking at farms when we went for Sunday drives; the cows looked so peaceful in the fields. We would be close to our families and the ocean. We could go to the beach on hot summer afternoons instead of sweltering in the city!

"Yes, a farm would be nice," I said, "but what about my beautiful house?" The farmhouse was over 100 years old.

"I promise I'll build you a new house; building my own house is one of my goals in life."

"And my roses?"

To that, he replied, "There will be lots of room for a big garden." Decisions and plans were made, and after fourteen years of climbing the ladder at IBM Canada, my husband Ralph decided to become a farmer.

My brother-in-law Raymond came from New Brunswick to help us move. We packed our belongings into a truck, and with our children — Grant, age six, Andrew, age three, and Melanie, age one — we left the city behind. Three days later we arrived at the farm.

The boys excitedly picked out their new bedrooms and we tucked our baby girl into the smallest of the rooms. I remember thinking she would soon have a beautiful new, larger room.

When I stood in the farmhouse kitchen, I wondered why it was so big. And I wondered why Ralph had been gone so long with the cows.

Then reality hit. Those peaceful cows had to be milked twice a day, seven days a week, at 6 a.m. and 5 p.m. And the big kitchen? On hot summer days, I had from six to twelve extras at any given mealtime. It seemed like my stove and oven were never turned off.

One day my farmer stood at the edge of a field and said, "This can be your new garden!" It was 240 feet long! Roses were forgotten; I now had to produce food to feed the family. There was no time to visit the ocean.

The first winter in the old house, we "dressed" our baby for bed and cuddled under sleeping bags as we watched TV in the evenings, than ran to our rooms. One evening, I heard the boys calling excitedly from their bedrooms, "Mom, we can see our breath!" As the second fall approached my husband announced, "We need to expand the barn, and I think we should put a wood stove in the kitchen." The second winter at the farm was much better. We drank hot chocolate around the wood stove as we planned the location for our new house. Soon it was farming season again, and the new expansion was under construction. When fall arrived, I learned how to cord a pile of wood and had a root cellar with enough vegetables to make do until next planting season. During the third winter my husband designed and drew up the plans for our new house.

By this time getting up for 6 a.m. chores had become routine. The boys had grown strong enough to help with evening chores and before I knew it, my daughter Melanie was at my side, feeding baby calves. On our trips between the old farmhouse and the barn we surveyed the Big Dipper, the Northern Lights and even Rudolph's bright red nose. One moonlit evening when Melanie and Andrew were making snow angels close to the barn, they spotted Halley's Comet. City lights paled in comparison.

Soon the new expansion was complete and filled with more cows, but now we needed more crops. I remember the words clearly. "This old tractor will no longer do the job."

It wasn't long before a shiny, new green John Deere tractor rolled off the delivery truck into our yard. With the new tractor, the farming season certainly ran much smoother. We even made it to the ocean! It didn't seem to take any time until Ralph announced, "The crops are growing so well, and the cows are milking so well, it looks like we're going to need a bigger and better milk tank."

The milk tank was a good investment. It washed automatically and cooled the milk much quicker. It took pressure off meeting the 8 a.m. deadline for milk pick-up. It also freed up extra time in the evenings and we sat around the kitchen table a little longer, talking about our day.

Finally, we dug the basement for the new house. The same summer, we bought a new hay-drying system. Yes, the cows were milking so well we had to buy more milk quota just so we could stay in business.

By and by we framed the new house, picked out siding, roofing and windows. But then, Grant wanted to play hockey, Andrew wanted a new snowmobile, and Melanie wanted modeling classes. Way too soon there was high school, licenses and extra insurance premiums, and — maybe the old truck wasn't safe enough for them to drive. We bought a new truck. There were friends and more friends. Girlfriends and boyfriends. When I went to the barn at 6 a.m., I counted the shoes at the door to see how many extras there were. Cheez Whiz, Sloppy Joe mix, and purple Kool-Aid were staples. The old farmhouse became the gathering place.

There was a spell when everything went smoothly. The machinery didn't break. Good crops were in the barn. The cows were healthy and milking excellent. Teenage expenses leveled off. Ralph said, "This is it, this is the year I will finish the new house!"

Fifteen years have passed, and I am finally in my new house. Outside the wind blows another storm across our fields. I close my eyes and listen to the stillness. No creaking house. No whistling wind. No clinking sound of Kool-Aid mixing in my kitchen. I open my eyes, admiring my beautiful surroundings. A warm fire glows in our new fireplace. Grampie is sitting in his favorite chair, in his shirt-sleeves. An angel sleeps in my arms. We are sitting in our new house as grandparents. Is this a dream or is it real? Small fingers reach out and tighten on mine. Reality touches my heart. I brush back the soft curls that cover my granddaughter's face; I've never had time to plant many flowers—together we'll grow a rose garden.

~Darlene Lawson

Married Life!

Chapter 10

Circle of Love

Where there is love there is no darkness.

~Burundi Proverb

91

Lucky, Lucky

The highest happiness on earth is marriage.
~William Lyon Phelps

"Want to go to Strawbridge Lake?" my husband asks as he scoops up the last spoonful of his breakfast oatmeal.

"Sure," I say.

I can tell that this will be a serendipitous weekend day—busy but unplanned—the kind of day I love.

On the way to the car he reaches for my hand and says, "Lucky." I smile. It is our shorthand for expressing thankfulness when words are not adequate for the day, for our lives, for each other.

We are not gamblers but we know that any marriage is a gamble. Its success depends on a whole slew of factors, many of which we cannot foresee. Sometimes the marital hand we are dealt is not what we hoped for or expected and the best thing to do is to fold. More often, we choose the cards we play, like holding onto respect when disagreements arise and letting go of blame, or keeping a tight hold on caring and releasing competition because it doesn't serve a marriage well. We have our bad deal days, too; when you are married for over forty years, as we are, there are bound to be some. And then there is the wild card—luck.

We drive to the lake, which is more of a creek, and walk along the grassy edge. The mallards are peacefully floating mid-lake. A male dips his green head underwater looking for food. His wet feathers shine in the morning sunlight when he pops up again. We each take photos, my husband with his Nikon, me with my point-and-shoot; the images will be different not just because of the quality of our cameras but because of our different ways of seeing things. We complement each other.

Back in the car and traveling to a diner for lunch. He loves diners. Being vegetarian, I find their menu selections sometimes less appetizing but that doesn't matter when we are together enjoying the day. I am almost finished drinking my tea when my husband says, "There's an art show…"

He doesn't need to complete the sentence. "Let's go!" I say and we are off again.

We have attended many art shows. He prefers landscapes, I like people pictures. He laughs because sometimes I think the frames are more dramatic than the paintings. We both like ceramics, glass, and wooden bowls. This is a juried photography exhibit. Some of the photos are intriguing; others make us wonder why they were chosen. We talk in hushed tones about what pleases us and what doesn't. We often agree but not always.

After the show, we stop off at the market for some last-minute dinner ingredients. The store is crowded and my husband is not fond of shopping so we make it a quick visit, though long enough to purchase necessities plus my favorite cheese and his favorite cookies.

I am cutting the vegetables for a stir-fry supper when I notice a male cardinal on the feeder outside the kitchen window. His brilliant red is breathtaking. I call my husband over to see. He stands next to me with his arm around my waist. We stay like that for a while, until I feel our special word rising within me. I turn around and hug him.

"Lucky, lucky," I say, my face pressed against his chest.

He wraps his arms around me and we breathe one long, deep sigh together. I think of our relationship, how much can be said with so little, how a simple word can be packed full of gratitude and love. It has been a sweet, busy day but now it is time to return to our normal routines. I find myself humming as I slice the carrots, green peppers, and other vegetables that will fill our plates tonight.

~Ferida Wolff

92

Free Baseball

The beginning of love is to let those we love be perfectly themselves...
~Thomas Merton

"Way to go, Cardinals!" shouted my husband, Jeff, jumping up from his seat at Busch Stadium, home of his beloved St. Louis Cardinals baseball team. We were celebrating our first anniversary, a truly hot Saturday afternoon in June, with all of the humidity typical of summer in Missouri. In spite of the excitement I'd previously felt about this, our only vacation since our short honeymoon the year before, I was now tired and more than ready to go. Add in that my sunburned shoulders rivaled the color of the players' red hats and that I didn't understand baseball all that much (neither its rules nor my husband's over-the-top obsession with it) and you have a game plan for grumpiness.

Not that Jeff appeared to notice.

No, he merely grinned at me, the awful heat not even fazing him. His eyes shone as he gave me a high-five. "How about that, hon?" he said. "Looks like we're going into extra innings. It's not every day we get free baseball."

"Whoa," I replied. "What do you mean, free baseball?"

"Well, you know, the Cards just tied it up in the bottom of the ninth. Hello? A baseball game has nine innings? Okay, so we've paid to watch nine innings, right? Well, if the teams are tied coming out of the ninth, the game will keep going until one team out-scores the other. Anything after the ninth? Bonus baseball, baby. How lucky are we?"

"Oh, boy," I said.

Now I knew I shouldn't complain. The weekend had been a total joint endeavor. We had traveled the four hours to St. Louis from our hometown of Springfield on Thursday, shared a romantic dinner that night, spent Friday at the zoo (my pick), Saturday at the ballpark (his pick), and planned to take in a museum on Sunday before heading home. He had promised I'd love my first Major League ballgame. He'd only been to a few games himself, attending with his parents, and I could well imagine him as a little boy, all wide eyes and fascination. And he was right—the game did fascinate me too. I loved the frenzy of the crowd, the hot dogs and sunshine, the sounds of the ball smacking against the catcher's mitt, and Jeff yelling, "Sit down!" when a batter on the opposing team struck out.

But that fascination, and even my pride at our ability to so effortlessly compromise, had worn thin. We'd been within minutes of exiting the stadium, of retreating to our air-conditioned hotel room, and with one swing of the bat, here I sat, elbow-deep in sweat, while Jeff tugged on his well-worn ball glove, heartily anticipating "free baseball."

Little did I know how familiar those two tiny words would become in the ensuing years.

On that day, though, I coped by doing what I'd always done when stuck somewhere with too much time on my hands: I pulled a book out of my purse and began reading.

"Wait, wait, wait," sputtered Jeff, glancing around to see if other fans noticed. "What's this, honey? You can't read at a ballgame."

Little did he know that in my mind books and baseball were already wed.

"He's obsessed!" I confided to my best girlfriend Kathy after that weekend. "I guess I never realized we were so different."

"So?" Kathy only shrugged. "You love each other, right?"

Yes, I decided, we surely do. Still, I'd never before considered what brings two people together. Whether "opposites attract" or "like minds draw like minds," I suppose I always felt that if you were lucky enough to find someone to love, let alone marry, you also just magically knew how to make married life click. But after that ballgame, I worried. Though Jeff and I had met at work and shared many of the same friends, though we enjoyed an easy partnership and a heart-stopping love, our differences suddenly glared at me like a neon sign flashing WARNING. I ticked those differences off in my head: he was a rightie, I was a leftie; he had played varsity baseball, I'd performed in musicals and wrote short stories in bed; he'd excelled at calculus, I'd stuffed *Great Expectations* inside my algebra book and read my way through math. How could two people be so different and still navigate marriage and love?

Flash forward thirty-three years and four children later and I'm still not sure I know the answer. But I do know I've discovered a few things. I know that a player has to commit fully in baseball, just as you have to love your spouse completely and give the marriage all you've got. I know that baseball is as much about the strikeout or the disabled list as it is about the grand slam or the walk-off home run, and I realize that a lot of hard work goes into each play, yet sometimes you have to sacrifice an out to move your runner along. Mostly, I know that, yes, there is just a bit of magic to baseball, but that if you stick with your teammate, if you communicate well and celebrate strengths while complementing weaknesses, that magic can last a lifetime.

It's a hot night in September as Jeff and I sit in the bleachers at Pittsburgh's lovely PNC Park. The humidity is oppressive, but we've embarked on this little baseball road trip to see our beloved St. Louis Cardinals play. We've just had some excitement in the top of the ninth as the Cards tie the score, and now, in the bottom of the inning, our relieving pitcher must bear down and do his job. Watching intently, Jeff balances his well-worn ball glove atop his knee as I keep my book reassuringly close at hand. Suddenly, our reliever delivers a wicked curve ball and the opposing batter strikes out, taking us into extra innings. "Sit down!" I cry, as Jeff and I leap out of our seats to jump into each other's arms.

Just then, my phone trills with a text from my older son's fiancé. Reading the text, I laugh out loud. Clearly, she and my son are watching the game at home on TV. My boy has grown up on baseball, following in his father's footsteps with an over-the-top Cardinals obsession that continues to amaze. I've always known it would take a special girl to finally win his heart, and the message she's sent confirms that now for me.

"Free baseball!" is all it says, but those two tiny words tell me everything I need to know. They assure me that my son and his girl are well on their way to fashioning their own love story, and I can't help but smile as I text her back with my usual response: a resounding, though just a wee bit cynical, "Oh, boy!"

~Theresa Sanders

93

The Softer Side

Grow old along with me! The best is yet to be.
~Robert Browning

When we got married we were very young. That was the trend then. We were still in college and we were both working. We started with nothing. Nothing. I finished my degree and started teaching. And then came the babies—three of them. Three boys in less than six years. I stayed home to take care of them and my husband continued to work. He worked two jobs and also continued with school to finish his degree. A few more classes were all he needed. We had very little time to spend together. But that was okay. It was not unusual for the times. Most of our friends were doing the same thing. And we were all working towards a goal.

Frank worked long, hard hours. He would finish at one job and go on to the other one. And when he wasn't working, he was studying. He didn't have much time to be with our kids but I was home and that was my job. He did play with them... when he had time. He did read to them... when he had time. He did teach them how to help around the house and fix things... when he had time. It's just that he didn't have much time. But that was okay. It was not unusual for the times.

Graduation came, and with it, the hope of a new and promising career. Starting that career meant long, hard hours of work with not much time left for anything else. We wanted a good life for our family.

We knew we had to make sacrifices to make our dreams come true. This was important to both of us. And the hard work and long hours paid off. Promotions came, one after another, and with those came even more responsibilities and longer hours at work. Many times the boys were already asleep when Frank got home from work. Not to say that we didn't have fun and do things as a family. We did. The boys were very close to Frank when he was home but those times were not as plentiful as we both would have liked them to be. But that was okay. It was not unusual for the times.

Married life was good. Frank had a wonderful career; I was delighted to be a stay-at-home mom and the boys were all happy and doing well in school. All of our years of hard work and sacrifice had started to pay off. The boys graduated from college, left home and started successful careers of their own. We were proud parents. Time passed… quickly. And then—we became grandparents… for the first time. They say you can't understand what it feels like to be a grandparent until you actually become a grandparent. And you know, whoever "they" are… they're right!

Suddenly I was married to a grandfather. (And we all know what that makes me!) This guy I had been with since high school was a grandfather. At first he didn't exactly know what to do with this new position in life. Our son and daughter-in-law, Mike and Crescent, would bring baby Eli over for us to babysit. And I would be the one to take care of him; Frank was more of… an observer. Oh, he would also make helpful suggestions on what to do or how to do it but I didn't listen. I'd smile at him and then I would do what I wanted. That's what long-time married people do. I would feed the baby. I would change him. I would sing to him. Frank would stand by and… watch. Although he had been around all three of his own babies, he never really had the opportunity to spend a lot of time caring for them. He was working so hard to make ends meet and give us a good life he didn't have too much time with them on a day-to-day basis.

But, having more time on his hands these days, things gradually changed with his grandchild. It started one day when we had Eli and it was time for his feeding. I got the bottle ready while Frank watched.

But as I got ready to feed the baby, Frank said, "I'll do that." I stopped, wondering if I had heard correctly. Was this the man I had married? Telling me he'd feed the baby? Without being asked? I handed him the bottle, the blanket, the burp cloth and… the baby and watched as he sat in the big comfortable chair in our kitchen, feeding his grandson. He held him close, gently snuggled him, and gave him his bottle. How beautiful! About halfway through the bottle, Frank stopped and put Eli on his shoulder to burp him. He talked quietly and lovingly to this tiny baby, supporting his head while patting him gently and rubbing his back. I just watched… in awe. After a while, we both heard it. Burp! Frank looked up at me and smiled sweetly, and told Eli what a nice burp he had done for Grandpa. The man I married was changing right before my eyes.

As Eli grew, so did Grandpa's participation in the baby's activities. Soon he was the one who was feeding him, changing him, taking him for walks. I was only around to assist. "Would you please get a diaper and the wipes?" "Would you please get a bottle ready for Eli and give it to me so I can feed him?" Grandpa was the one playing on the floor with him, eating his toes, making silly noises and faces at him to make him laugh, and walking him for hours when his colic made him cranky. We were all so frustrated when Eli was cranky. But not Grandpa. He was so patient. He just took over: carrying Eli around the back yard in his arms, showing him the birds, showing him the flowers and the fruit trees and by his gentle voice and gentle touch, soothing his upset tummy. Grandpa's softer side was really emerging. I liked it. And when Eli would come over, he would only want to go to Grandpa. There is such a bond that has developed between these two guys.

Now Eli is a year old and the bond between grandfather and grandson strengthens every day. The man who, so many years ago was working so hard to provide for his family that his softer side didn't have an opportunity to develop, now has the time to show his true colors. And that softer side has spilled over to his everyday behavior and is not just limited to Eli. He is much more patient with everyone. He smiles more and compliments more. He is sillier. He is... well, the best way to describe him is just to say that... he is softer. I don't know how else to say it. This hard-working man who I married years and years ago has turned into a soft, gentle man. It is his soft side that is so beautiful to watch. It is so attractive and sexy, and I am so proud to be his wife. I love him even more today than I did when I married him so very many years ago.

~Barbara LoMonaco

Marriage Is Like a Fireplace

*Coming together is a beginning. Keeping together is progress.
Working together is success.*
~Henry Ford

In my single days, I was a television field producer for Montreal's CTV affiliate. I had one of the best gigs in town. I wrote and directed stories about all kinds of fascinating people for a consumer affairs program that helped viewers in need. I got to tell stories that mattered to my community, and worked with talented professionals who made me laugh. By far the best perk, however, was the unsolicited advice about love and marriage that I received from Boris Bouchard, a veteran cameraman who was also about to be ordained as a minister.

Happily married for more than thirty years, "Born-Again Boris," as I called him, couldn't have known then the profound effect his words would continue to have upon me even today. I was always delighted when he was assigned to shoot one of my stories, because it meant that he, our sound recordist, our reporter and I could travel together in the company van to our shooting location, and be treated to one of Boris's fascinating takes on relationships.

"Marriage is like a fireplace," he began one day, as he calmly navigated rush-hour traffic and Quebec's famous potholes while en route to shoot a story about mothers against pesticides. The others looked at each other and rolled their eyes, but I leaned forward in anticipation.

"Everyone loves the idea of having a fireplace," he continued. "People make fireplaces the center of their homes, building whole rooms around them because they bring warmth and comfort. Fireplaces encourage people to gather around together."

"Boris, I think you missed the exit," the reporter interrupted impatiently.

Boris smiled patiently at her in the rearview mirror and made a U-turn. "But let's remember what having a fireplace really means," he continued. "You have to chop wood, stack it, bring it inside, lay the logs inside in a specific way, create a spark, and keep the flames burning by constantly feeding and stoking the fire."

Boris paused for effect. "If you don't do all of those things, all of the time, a fireplace is nothing but a dark, empty, cold hole," he concluded.

We all sat in silence, reflecting on the cameraman's words. The sound recordist and reporter were both divorced. Perhaps they were thinking about how they had allowed their fireplaces to grow cold.

"And you know what else? A couple in love is like a pair of scissors," Boris said brightly. "Two useless pieces of metal, until they are inextricably connected at the core so that they can move together as one and accomplish great things."

I briefly thought about taking out my notebook and jotting down some notes so that when I met the person I wanted to spend the rest of my life with, I could heed Boris's worthy advice. But I thought my sound guy would laugh at me, so I didn't.

As it turned out, I didn't need to take notes. I never forgot a word he said.

When I started dating my husband several years after leaving CTV to pursue a freelance career, I told him about Born-Again Boris's words of wisdom one night over dinner. "I've always lived in apartments," he told me, "but I always wanted a fireplace."

When we first visited the house that we would eventually buy together and start our family in, the first thing we noticed was the beautiful brick fireplace in the family room. We looked at each other and smiled, knowing it would be ours. "Fireplaces are a lot of work," I said to my soon-to-be husband. "Yes, they are," he replied. "But can you think of anything better to work on?"

And today, I think Boris would be proud; our fireplace is continuously aglow, just as he told me it should be.

~Wendy Helfenbaum

Secret to a Long Marriage

Chains do not hold a marriage together. It is threads, hundreds of tiny threads which sew people together through the years.
~Simone Signoret

I woke up this morning and realized that I have been married for twenty-three years to the same man. I KNOW. Who would have thought? I mean, first of all, I got married when I was… um… ten or so. Yes, I believe I was ten. And no, I don't care if you believe me. That's my story and I'm sticking to it, no matter what my mother or the DMV has to say about it. As long as I have that wedding picture in the attic, I will never age. And yes, I do live in a lovely place called denial.

Anyway, that aside, I realized that twenty-three years of marriage is a total anomaly. Actually, I didn't realize it was an anomaly; I just always wanted to use that word in a story. What I really realized is that I am one heck of a patient person. Or maybe Harry is. Or maybe we both are so stubborn neither of us will admit that one of us has been more patient through the years, I don't know.

What I do know is that through all the years it never once occurred to me that my marriage wouldn't last forever. Oh yes, there have been days—and I'm sure there will be more—when I searched the back yard for a place to hide Harry's body.

The thing about marriage is that it changes frequently. Just when

Secret to a Long Marriage: **Circle of Love** 327

you think you've got this whole relationship thing down, something shifts. Take the last few weeks for example. For reasons unknown to me, Harry's cell has been calling me without Harry's knowledge. That means that I have spent the last month answering the phone only to get to hear the lovely sound of his radio blasting as he drives to work, his voice in a meeting, or my personal favorite—the toilet flushing.

While that's annoying, I will admit that Harry's had to put up with a lot for the past twenty-three years. Unless he's cooked or gone out, the man has spent far too long eating my food. I don't know what his stomach is lined with, but they should use it on the space shuttle. The shuttle would be safe from the heat of the atmosphere on re-entry or even an attack by alien boogers—which is exactly what some of my creations resemble, by the way.

And I know he deals with a lot more than just burnt dinners or recipes that sounded good when I was making them up in my head—although I do maintain that brown rice with raisins and melted cheese would taste really good if I'd just tweaked the recipe a bit. But I've been known to cause kitchen fires—sometimes even when I'm not cooking (a long story that is frankly too humiliating to share). I've been known to keep writing checks when the account is empty on the theory that if the bank gives me lots of checks, they must want me to use them.

I've been known to purchase way too many shoes. I've been known to have several sizes of jeans in my closet so that no matter what weight I am, my jeans fit. I've been known to become obsessed with strange things like belly dancing. Poor Harry's had to watch me practice. I've been known to eat dessert first because the main course is often burnt or tastes yucky and my fat jeans are fitting just fine. I've been known to yell really loud and ask for explanations later.

But after twenty-three years, I think we both may be doing something right. I just wish I could figure out what it was, because if I bottled it, I could make a fortune.

~Laurie Sontag

96

Running Through Sprinklers

March on, and fear not the thorns, or the sharp stones on life's path.
~Kahlil Gibran

It is almost midnight and the parking lot of the library is empty except for a few scattered cars. It's finals time and I have just finished a marathon study session with Mike, my new husband and a fellow history major. The football practice field that stands adjacent to the library is illuminating the parking lot with its stadium lights. Sprinklers throw water across the lawn and under the bright lights the droplets appear to dance. I suddenly feel the urge to join them.

"Feel like running through some sprinklers?" I ask Mike.

"Of course," Mike says with a smile.

We run to his car and put our textbook-laden backpacks in the trunk, excited about the prospect of doing something other than studying.

"Shoes?" he asks, pointing to his feet.

"Leave 'em," I say, already out of one of my sandals. I wiggle my toes in anticipation as I wait for him to finish taking off his shoes.

We run towards the field and I can feel the weight of finals falling off my shoulders.

"I've needed to do something like this," I say breathlessly, trying to keep up with Mike's 6'3" frame.

"You better hurry or I'm going to leave you behind," he says as he rushes past me.

With two leaps he is over the empty drainage ditch that surrounds the field and into the sprinklers. I know my short legs won't be able to cover the same distance so I cautiously begin to make my way across the ditch.

"Ouch!" I suddenly cry out. My bare feet have been anticipating the refreshing feel of wet grass, but are stinging with pain instead. I quickly hop away in an attempt to get away from the pain, but to no avail. The pain follows.

"Ow!" I yell again. I look at my foot and immediately feel sick. Instead of being the color of skin, my foot is the brownish gray color of goat head thorns. They are stuck in the bottom of my foot, covering my toes and my heel. I check my other foot. It is the same.

I start to panic, not only from the pain, but because the idea of my thorn-filled feet is disturbing. I look around and quickly realize that the ditch surrounding the field is filled with thorns. We are trapped.

"Mike!" I yell, trying to make my way to where he is obliviously frolicking.

"What?" he yells, straining to hear me over the sprinklers.

"I stepped in a bunch of thorns! They're everywhere!"

"What?" he asks running towards me.

"Stop!" I yell, frantically waving my arms in an effort to stop him.

Mike's smile and happy gait instantly disappear as he frantically backtracks onto the grass and sits down with a thump.

"I'm sorry. I tried to warn you. My feet are full of them," I say as I make my way to a patch of green grass. I fall down and immediately set about trying to pick thorns out of my feet. The thorns are long and each one leaves a pool of blood in its wake. It sends shivers down my spine. Mike crawls to me and silently starts pulling thorns out of his feet. They look like a thousand tiny swords have stabbed them.

"How did I miss them on my way over here?" he asks me.

"Because your legs are so long, you just sailed right over them,"

I answer, inwardly cursing my lack of height. "How are we going to get back to the car?"

"We'll just walk up the field until we find a place where there aren't any thorns and cross there."

"But the field is surrounded by the ditch. I'm pretty sure they're everywhere."

We sit there for a few minutes, staring at the promised land of the parking lot, the sound of the sprinklers mocking us in the background.

"Well, there's nothing left to do, but live out the rest of our lives here on this field," I say, falling onto my back in a sign of surrender. Living the rest of my days on a sprinkler filled football field seems like a much better option than attempting to get back to the car. Plus, I won't have to take any finals.

"You stay here," says Mike with a laugh. "I'll go get your shoes and bring them back to you. Hang tight."

I watch as he walks up and down the field looking for the best path across the ditch, but the thorns are everywhere. He looks at me and shrugs and I know that he is going for it. His takes a tentative first step and then begins to walk as quickly as he can across the thorns. He looks like a man walking on coals and even from my distant perch I can hear him yelping in pain.

"Thank you," I call out, hoping that the sound of my voice will keep him motivated. He raises his hand to acknowledge my words, but keeps his eyes on his feet.

True to his word, Mike reaches the car and then brings my shoes to me, even going as far as to carry me back to the car because my feet hurt too much to walk. We drive back to our apartment in silence where we proceed to care for our wounds. Side by side on the edge of the bathtub, our pant legs still rolled up, we soak our throbbing feet. The bottom of the tub turns a pretty shade of pink as the blood of our feet mixes with the running bath water. Although we had tried out best to rid our feet of the thorns, many had broken off in our feet, giving them a freckled appearance.

"Well, that was an interesting experience," Mike says with a chuckle, finally breaking the silence. "I think we bonded."

"Definitely a memory," I agree.

"Let's never do that again."

"Never!"

For weeks after, we will have tender spots on the bottoms of our feet where we hadn't quite been able to get the thorns out. They hurt, but they also remind us of our shared misadventure.

• • •

It is four years later and Mike and I have returned to the practice field to reminisce. Our botched attempt to run through the sprinklers that night taught us that shared pain can bring you closer together, a lesson that has repeated itself time and time again over the span of our married life. Although never so funny as our romp through the thorns, the pain that we have shared since college has been just as memorable and has succeeded at bringing us closer together every time.

As we hold hands and walk around the field I realize that I don't know many people who would have wanted to run through the sprinklers with me that night, let alone someone who would have walked through thorns for me. I'm lucky enough to have married a man who was willing to do both.

~Jessie M. Santala

97

You Gotta Laugh

Laughter is the shortest distance between two people.
~Victor Borge

Every evening my husband Neal and I spend an hour or so talking over our day. We like to call it downloading. During this time we solve the world's problems, work on our own, plan and dream. However the best times during our downloading are when we laugh together.

Over the years I've come to believe the glue that holds relationships together is communication liberally sprinkled with laughter. Just the other day we enjoyed one of those moments.

To begin with, Neal and I are proof that opposites attract. He is rational, logical, orderly, and loves lists. Me? I'm creative, messy, and forgetful. One Saturday he decided to run errands. Thirty minutes after he left he called me to say he'd forgotten to get the address of one of the businesses he had on his list and asked me to find it and get back to him asap! Did I mention he is also extremely time conscious?

I did as he asked and called him right back. No answer. That was odd. I called back. This time he answered in a rather brusque tone, "Hey, I can't talk now, I'll call you back."

Miffed, I hung up the phone. How rude. After all, I did exactly as he asked. A few minutes later he called back and in a more patient voice apologized before getting the information he needed.

That evening on the front porch, he looked at me with a sheepish expression. "I have a confession to make about this afternoon."

"What?"

"You know when you called the first time?"

"Yeah?"

"I had stopped at a fast food place and gotten an ice cream cone. Well, while pulling out of the parking lot onto the road I held the cone in my left hand while trying to steer, and with my right hand I held my phone while trying to shift gears."

"Yeah?" He never was a good multitasker.

"So when the phone rang, I answered the cone."

"You what?"

"I stuck my ice cream cone in my ear!" He grinned.

Images of my near perfect husband with an ear full of ice cream made me erupt in a fit of laughter. He caught my mirth and started laughing just as hard. Tears ran down our faces as we gulped enough air to accommodate the next burst of guffaws. Finally we were able to control ourselves. Exhausted we leaned back in our chairs and smiled at each other.

There is a Yiddish proverb that says, "What soap is to the body, laughter is to the soul." If that is the case, our souls were sparkling clean. Before we went back into the house, Neal said, "I suppose you are going to tell everyone about this."

I smiled. "Only a few million of my closest friends."

There's another proverb that claims a merry heart is like a medicine. I can attest to its truth. Laughter is the prescription that keeps our marriage healthy and has for over thirty-four years!

~Linda Apple

Heroine

Let your love be like the misty rains, coming softly, but flooding the river.
~Malagasy Proverb

She is so short, less than five feet now as more than eight decades of life have shrunken her. She moves slowly, the arthritis of course, but mostly her breathing, her lungs damaged and diseased. The various medications, the pills and inhalers help somewhat when she takes them.

Her appearance belies the truth. She is a heroine, strong, determined, relentless.

She is my mom.

"He's never coming home, is he?" she asks me, her son the doctor, a few weeks after my dad has been admitted to the nursing home.

"No, Mom, he isn't." I answer as gently as I can.

And of course he is not. Parkinson's disease has made getting about difficult, and he is so very frail. But it is the theft of his mind by the continued progression of dementia that has made continued living at home impossible and, after a brief hospitalization, led to his admission to the nursing home's dementia unit.

Nobody ever comes home from the dementia unit.

It is a wonderful nursing home. The rooms and corridors are sparkling clean; it is brightly lit and cheery, and the care is provided by a staff that is skilled, caring, kind and patient. It is literally just down the hill and across the street less than half a mile from their home.

A few months later she tells me, "I'm bringing him home."

And she does. She has live-in assistance for a few months, but thereafter cares for him herself. He lives in his own home, with his wife, for another three years. He is the only person ever discharged from the dementia unit.

Six decades of marriage, of love, of loyalty and commitment.

She is a heroine.

She is my mom.

~Harvey Silverman

Dreams Can Come True

Dreams are today's answers to tomorrow's questions.
~Edgar Cayce

A s I entered the hospital to visit my husband, a Lay Eucharistic Minister from my church approached me. "I came to give Jim communion, but something's amiss," he said. "They won't let me see him."

When Jim's doctor recommended hernia surgery, we were confident of the surgeon's expertise and were relieved when it was successful. Jim's recovery went without complications and on the Sunday before he was to come home, I went to church full of gratitude and thanksgiving.

Afterwards, I drove to the hospital, relieved and excited that the ordeal was over and he would soon be able to travel again.

Puzzled, we went to Jim's room and found a "NO ADMITTANCE" sign on the door. When we inquired why, a nurse took us aside and said Jim's doctor wanted to talk to me. We didn't wait long, and as the doctor approached us, the sad look on his face warned me that that something was indeed amiss.

He sat down beside us and said, "After Jim took his shower and shaved this morning, a nurse took his vitals and asked how he felt. Jim said he felt great and then collapsed. She called code blue. Doctors tried to revive him, but Jim had suffered a fatal heart attack."

I listened in disbelief. Jim and I had never been aware of any heart problems. Although stunned, I heard myself say, "Jim wanted to donate any useable organs and I know there are time limitations. Can you take care of it?"

The doctor nodded and said he could. He would contact me later on details and arrangements for the body. Earlier, Jim and I had agreed to organ donations and cremation so we had bought a plot in our church columbarium.

While the doctor and I talked, my Eucharistic Minister had called the church. Before I left the hospital, church friends arrived, drove me home, and stayed with me while I contacted our daughters.

Within an hour, my Denver daughter and her husband were with me, and my Seattle daughter made airline reservations to fly to Colorado that afternoon. Their love and support was of great comfort to me over the following days.

Of course, they had jobs and their own responsibilities and when they resumed their daily lives, I pondered my future without Jim. Throughout our idyllic fifty-one-year marriage, Jim and I shared a fascination with dreams. We often discussed them, and when we interpreted them correctly, benefited from them.

Years earlier, through dreams and meditations, I learned my purpose in this life was to seek, share and spread love. Jim had made it so easy. Now he was gone. How could I fulfill my mission without him?

After prayers one night, I fell asleep and began dreaming. Jim's face appeared. Although he didn't say anything, he flashed his magnetic smile and looked as he had in his prime.

Upon awaking, I interpreted Jim's appearance to mean he was happy on the other side. While comforted that he was at peace, it didn't relieve my loneliness. Oh, I went through the routine of daily life and spent more time with my children and grandchildren, which gave me many happy hours, but my lust for life was gone.

Months later, in desperation, I prayed one night for God to send me a message about what I was supposed to do with the rest of my life.

I fell asleep and soon Jim reappeared in another dream. This time, he spoke. "I love you, Sally, but it's time for me to ascend to a higher plane. Your grieving is hampering my transition. I'll always love you and care for you, but I must move on with my life just as you must start a new life for yourself."

I knew I was dreaming, but it was so real I felt his presence. Then, two angels materialized, one on each side of Jim, and led him out the front door.

After hearing the door close, I heard a hammering sound coming from my kitchen. Still dreaming, I went there to find an older, unfamiliar man replacing my back door. "Don't be afraid and don't worry," he said in a soothing voice. "I'm going to keep you safe and take care of you for the rest of your life."

I awakened with the dream etched clearly in my mind and wrote it down in my dream diary before I forgot it. I knew this would be Jim's way to contact me and I wanted to make sure I understood his message.

The first part about Jim ascending to a higher plane was understandable, but the second part about the stranger replacing my back door baffled me.

My back door didn't need replacing. Furthermore, I didn't recognize the man's voice and couldn't see his face because a mist obscured it. Even more puzzling was the word ME printed on the man's shirt. Mystified, I prayed that Jim would return and clarify the meaning in another dream.

He didn't.

Days passed into weeks, and weeks into months, but Jim didn't reappear. I consoled myself that he had made the transition to a higher plane and the stranger fixing my back door wasn't important.

Almost a year later, a church friend introduced me to her widowed cousin, an intelligent, attractive man with a delightful sense of humor. A few years older than me, he was, like Jim, a retired insurance vice president and seemed to enjoy the same things Jim did. We quickly became friends.

He and I communicated easily. We went to dinners and plays, and he even took ballroom dance lessons to please me.

Although we agreed that companionship was all we desired, we

surprised each other by falling in love. During our months of courtship, I remembered my dream about the stranger who fixed my back
door, wearing a shirt with the word ME imprinted on it.

Shortly after we married, Jim visited me in another dream.
Although, he didn't speak, his twinkling eyes and engaging smile
told me that he and God had sent Mel Engeman into my life and
approved of our marriage.

~Sally Kelly-Engeman

Always

For you see, each day I love you more today more than yesterday and less than tomorrow.
~Rosemonde Gérard

he gentle, old man met me on the footpath. Mesmerized by the swaying treetops and the multitude of birds at his feeders, I stood motionless, admiring the view.

Pleased, he watched me glancing toward the silvery creek beckoning from below. "This property was our dream," he said. "Planned many years ago. There are even mushrooms down there by the creek," he offered.

"We'll go for a walk later."

His wife had been referred by her family doctor and I was to coordinate the services the couple would need for the next little while. As a visiting nurse, I'd grown accustomed to being thrust unexpectedly into people's suffering. I'd even developed a shield, a protective mechanism to do my job. But, I wasn't prepared for the effect this visit would have on me personally.

The tall, dignified man in his eighties politely invited me into his home. Hearing voices, I learned that his wife and her spiritual advisor were talking and praying in the next room. This gave us time to get acquainted.

Looking about the comfortable home, I imagined what it must have been like in days gone by: lively conversations, noisy games, and lots of laughter. The furniture, the rugs all showed years of family use. So much character. I felt like an intruder, yet he seemed pleased to have me there. He wanted to talk. He needed to talk.

He told me he and his wife had been married for sixty-two years and as a young couple had come to Canada to raise their family. Their children, who now lived in different provinces, were expected home in the next few days. And then he talked to me about his wife. The love of his life.

"When we first moved here, she became very melancholy," he said. "So I took her back to the old country. Within a few years she was ready to return to our new home." He pointed out photos of his wife and his sons and daughter. "There were lots of trials and tribulations for sure, but oh so much love," he reflected. "And now she's ready to leave again."

When the priest left, he escorted me into her sickroom. Obviously very ill, the frail little lady in the big bed was alert and responding, trying bravely to resist the urgency to sleep. She looked lovingly at her husband; however, she wasn't so sure about me.

"I'm not afraid to die," she whispered. "But, I don't want to go to the hospital."

Only when I reassured her that the purpose of my visit was to help her stay at home did she relax. Every breath, however, was laboured. When I finished my assessment, I proposed a care plan and asked for their input—allowing them time to think about the changes it would make in their daily lives: a visiting nurse to help alleviate pain and to monitor vital signs; a homemaker to provide personal care and assistance with meals until their family arrived.

As I sat quietly writing my notes, I sensed the love and compassion in the room. Then something beautiful happened. The old man confidently picked up his delicate wife and carried her across the room. This gesture probably occurred many times in the past; however, as a bystander watching such devotion, I was awestruck. He carefully placed her in a soft chair beside the bay window overlooking her flowerbeds and their creek. What struck me was his tenderness. As if he was carrying all his worldly possessions to the altar of our

Lord. He took her tiny hand in his and, lost in thought (forgetting I was in the room), his easy voice lifted in song.

"I'll be loving you, always. Not for just an hour, not for just a day, not for just a year, but always. Always."

"She's my world," he said when he finished. "Whatever you can do will be appreciated." Poignant moments.

Love indeed shows you whole new rooms in your heart. Life suddenly becomes all the more precious. He wasn't afraid. She wasn't afraid. There was no anxiety. They simply wanted to spend their last days together. I felt my heart lurch. I knew I was witnessing something close to God. Absolute love between two people. The scene touched me deeply and reminded me to cherish the love and the close bond I have with my own husband.

Later, the gentle old man and I did take our walk down to the creek. With the stillness that comes with the end of day, he stood beside me, gazing intently, a profound calmness about him. Through the mist building behind my eyes, I too saw and felt the splendor—as if God had left a portrait of Himself on the mantle of earth.

"Are you going to be okay?" I asked.

"Oh, I think so," he said. "I know it will take courage to honour this pain I carry, to trust the unfolding. But I truly believe we'll be together one day. Together, always."

~Phyllis Jardine

My Coffee Cup Epiphany

Could we change our attitude, we should not only see life differently,
but life itself would come to be different.
~Katherine Mansfield

I had a huge epiphany the other morning. Maybe my experience will give you some food for thought.

I had gotten together with some women friends who enjoy sharing thoughts on life. We spent part of the evening discussing a book with such a funny title it makes most people smile: *Why Men Don't Listen and Women Can't Read Road Maps.*

Yes, men and women come into this world wired so differently it's a wonder that relationships last as long as they do. I personally think if this book were given as a wedding gift there would be far fewer divorces.

Speaking of books, I gave a copy of *Chicken Soup for the Soul: Runners* to a male friend who is a runner. Since my story of taking part in the Newport (Oregon) Marathon was published in that book, I took pains to autograph it for my friend. A few days later he sent an e-mail thanking me "for the loan of the book." Loan? I e-mailed back that it was a gift and did he not see that I autographed it on the first page? He e-mailed back a very nice "thank you" and added that maybe it was a "guy thing" to not look at the first page. Whatever. So it was a guy thing. So what? No big deal. But men and women are definitely different in dozens of ways.

If you are a woman reading this, maybe you are thinking, "Oh yeah, and how come they leave the toilet seat up?" If you are a guy reading this, you might be thinking, "Sure I don't listen—because she never shuts up, that's why!"

During the discussion with my women's group of the book, *Why Men Don't Listen and Women Can't Read Maps*, I decided to share one of my major pet peeves that my husband does—or doesn't—which is never carrying his darn coffee cup to the kitchen even though he is going right past the kitchen on his way to somewhere else. This has bugged me for over forty years and no amount of nagging makes a bit of difference. I did not feel one bit disloyal sharing this with my women friends. Some of them chuckled as if they deal with the same thing at home.

The very next morning my weekly radio program was on the air and it was one in which my husband helped me do a funny comedy routine that sounds best with two people. An hour later the telephone rang. It isn't unusual to get e-mails and phone calls regarding my *Chicken Soup for the Soul* stories, my column in the local newspaper or my weekly human-interest program on the radio.

But this call was from a dear lady I've known for over twenty years. She lost her husband not long ago (a sixty-year marriage) and this is what she said on the phone: "Bobbie, I loved the show you and Burt did together this morning. Don't ever stop appreciating him and what a blessing it is that you have each other!"

Her words smacked me between the eyes. I hung up the phone and sat there staring at our two empty coffee cups. As usual, my husband had wandered off and, as usual, the only way those cups would make it to the kitchen was if I carried them. But instead of feeling irritated, I started thinking, "What if there was only ONE coffee cup to carry? Mine." It was a major epiphany and a total turnaround in my perspective over a dumb coffee cup (and a few of the other irritating things he does).

Indeed, how blessed I am to have TWO cups to carry to the

kitchen—and not just one. None of us know how long we will be here and that life can change in a heartbeat.

So what if men don't listen and so what if women (well, not all women) can't read road maps?

Vive la différence.

May I never complain again about that coffee cup!

~Bobbie Jensen Lippman

Married Life!

Meet Our Contributors
Meet Our Authors
Thank You
About Chicken Soup for the Soul

Meet Our Contributors

Eric Allen has been enjoying life with his wife now that their newspaper surplus has dwindled... although his inbox is another story. E-mail him at ericthered1980@hotmail.com.

Monica A. Andermann lives on Long Island with her husband Bill and their cat Charley. In addition to several credits in the *Chicken Soup for the Soul* collections, her writing has appeared in such publications as *Skirt!*, *Sasee*, *The Secret Place*, and *Woman's World*.

Linda Apple is the author of *Inspire! Writing from the Soul* and *Connect! A Simple Guide to Public Speaking for Writers*. Her stories have appeared in many editions of the *Chicken Soup for the Soul* series. Linda and Neal have been loving and laughing together for thirty-four years. Visit her at www.lindaapple.com.

Cindy D'Ambroso Argiento lives in North Carolina with her family. She is a freelance writer and has published a book entitled *Deal With Life's Stress With "A Little Humor"*. To purchase a copy and read her work, check out her website at www.cindyargiento.com or e-mail her at cargiento@aol.com.

Pam Bailes earned her degree in math from Trinity University in San Antonio. She has been a teacher, real estate agent, and small business owner, but her true passions revolve around animals and writing, with the occasional golf round thrown in to keep her humble. E-mail her at pbailes@aol.com.

Lisa Beringer is a piano teacher who likes to write inspirational stories. She lives with Dale, her husband of thirty-three years, in Ontario, Canada, where they enjoy acting in their church drama troupe, spending time with their four kids, now grown, and spoiling their precious first granddaughter, Quinn.

Karla Brown has had a varied career, but writing is her first love. She lives in Philadelphia, PA, and kisses her husband when he asks "Are you happy?" Her family also makes her happy. E-mail her at karlab612@yahoo.com.

Kristine Byron worked as a trainer for Tupperware and in later years as an interior designer. She loves to cook and entertain. Kristine also loves to travel with her husband and spend quality time with her five grandchildren.

Robert Campbell turns seventy-eight this year. He wrote about his childhood, captaining charter and private vessels for fifteen years, family life, living with the love of his life (Judith), and his children and grandchildren for the fun of it. They all make him laugh, thus all are fair game. E-mail him at camppear@gmail.com.

Elynne Chaplik-Aleskow, founding general manager of WYCC-TV/PBS and Distinguished Professor Emeritus of Wright College in Chicago, is a Pushcart Prize nominated author and award-winning educator and broadcaster. Her nonfiction stories and essays have been published in numerous anthologies and magazines. Her husband Richard is her muse. Visit her at http://LookAroundMe.blogspot.com.

Kristen Clark is a speaker, writer, and gratitude expert. Her articles on marriage and relationships have appeared in numerous journals, magazines, and compilation books. Along with her husband, Lawrence, she also writes for and manages Hiswitness.org and NewBeginningsMarriage. org. E-mail Kristen at kristens@hiswitness.org.

D'ette Corona is the Assistant Publisher of Chicken Soup for the Soul Publishing, LLC. She received her Bachelor of Science in business management. D'ette has been happily married for nineteen years and has a fifteen-year-old son whom she adores.

A journalist living in Waltham, MA, **John Crawford** has written for various newspapers, magazines, and websites through the years.

Billie Criswell is a freelance writer and columnist. Billie enjoys cooking, playing with her dogs, Zumba, and a great Bloody Mary. She also maintains her blog, Bossy Italian Wife. E-mail Billie at Billie36313@yahoo.com.

Priscilla Dann-Courtney is a writer and clinical psychologist living in Boulder with her husband and three children. She recently published her first book, *Room to Grow: Stories of Life and Family*, which is a collection of all her essays. Her passions include family, friends, writing, yoga, running and baking.

Laura J. Davis is the author of the award-winning book *Come to Me*, a novel about the life of Christ through the eyes of his mother. When not writing, Laura is reviewing books on a professional basis. She loves historical fiction. You can contact her through her website at www.laurajdavis.com.

Shawnelle Eliasen and her husband Lonny raise their five sons in Illinois. She home teaches her youngest boys. Her stories have been published in *Guideposts*, *MomSense*, *Marriage Partnership*, *A Cup of Comfort*, numerous *Chicken Soup for the Soul* books and other anthologies.

Melissa Face teaches special education and devotes her free time to writing. Melissa's stories and essays have appeared in numerous magazines and anthologies. She lives in Virginia with her husband, son, and boxer, Tyson. E-mail Melissa at writermsface@yahoo.com.

Andrea Farrier is a very happy wife and homeschooling mother of three girls. She graduated from The University of Iowa with degrees in English and Speech Communication/Theater Arts and teaching certifications in both areas. These days she keeps her writing skills sharp by blogging at www.andreafarrier.blogspot.com.

John Forrest is a retired educator who writes about the exceptional events and people that have enriched his life. He lives with his wife Carol in Orillia, Ontario, Canada. E-mail him at johnforrest@rogers.com.

Sally Friedman graduated from the University of Pennsylvania and has been writing about family life for over four decades. Inspiration comes from her own clan: one husband, three daughters, and seven astounding grandchildren. Sally is a frequent contributor to the *Chicken Soup for the Soul* series. E-mail her at pinegander@aol.com.

Marilyn Haight has authored four how-to books and one book of poetry. She lives in Peoria, AZ, with her husband, Arnold, and Cameo, their Italian Greyhound, who decides when it's time to turn off the computer and play catch. Visit her website at www.marilynhaight.com.

Cathy C. Hall is a writer from the sunny South where she lives with her husband and any junior Halls passing through. She writes for children and adults, so check out her blog at cathychall.wordpress.com to find her latest byline!

Patrick Hardin is a freelance cartoonist whose work appears in a variety of books and periodicals around the world. He lives and works in his hometown of Flint, MI. E-mail Patrick at phardin357@aol.com.

In her twenty-three years as a writer and television producer, Montreal-based **Wendy Helfenbaum** has explored the elite world of Olympic diving, the intricate make-up design for the Twilight films, traveling Springsteen groupies and the fine art of renovating your home with young children underfoot. Visit her at www.taketwoproductions.ca.

Diane Henderson, MSW, LCSW received her master's degree in Social Work from the University of North Carolina. She is a speaker, life coach, and has a private psychotherapy practice in North Carolina. She conducts Reboot Your Life personal growth groups on the phone and in person. E-mail her at diane@dianehenderson.net.

Carolyn Hiler is an artist living in the mountains outside Los Angeles. When not drawing, painting, or hiking with her two adorable mutts, she works in private practice as a psychotherapist in Claremont, CA. Carolyn posts cartoons almost every day at www.azilliondollarscomics.com, and she sells funny things on Etsy at www.etsy.com/shop/AZillionDollars.

Gretchen Houser delights in observing the human condition and putting pen to paper to prove it. She is a long-time editor and freelance writer living in the Pacific Northwest. She is busy at work on a young adult novel and a short story collection.

Gina Farella Howley taught for fifteen years in Illinois schools. The past six, she's been pursuing her love of writing, freelancing, and relishing being published. For now, she enjoys her life's calling: her husband John and boys Martin (six), Joe (four), and Tim (two) as her full-time work.

Phyllis Jardine is a retired nurse living in the Annapolis Valley of Nova Scotia with her husband, Bud, and black Lab, Morgan. Her stories have been aired on national radio and have been published in *Chicken Soup for the Soul* books and numerous other magazines and anthologies. E-mail her at phyl.jardine@gmail.com.

Kara Johnson is a freelance writer living in Eagle, ID, with her husband Jim and their dog Barkley. She enjoys traveling, scuba diving, camping and mentoring high school and college girls. E-mail her at karajohnsonprose@gmail.com.

Marsha Jordan, a self-proclaimed jelly doughnut addict, is a ten-year-old masquerading as an adult. She's dropped out of enough exercise classes to make the *Guinness World Records* book. Her hobbies include ignoring dirty dishes, mailing complaint letters, and writing about her rocket scientist husband. E-mail her at jordans@newnorth.net or visit www.hugsandhope.org/queenie.htm.

Sally Kelly-Engeman is a freelance writer who has had dozens of short stories and articles published. In addition to writing, she enjoys reading and researching. She also enjoys ballroom dancing and traveling the world with her husband. E-mail her at sallyfk@juno.com.

Mimi Greenwood Knight is a mama of four living in South Louisiana with her husband, David. She enjoys gardening, baking, martial arts, Bible study, and the lost art of letter writing. Mimi is blessed to have over 500 essays and articles in print including over twenty in *Chicken Soup for the Soul* books.

Lynn Worley Kuntz is an award-winning writer whose credits include five books for children, magazine and newspaper articles for a variety of publications, and essays and stories in a number of anthologies. She has co-written five films for children and one feature family film. Contact her via e-mail at saralynnk@hotmail.com.

Cathi LaMarche resides with her husband, two children, and three spoiled dogs in Missouri. Cathi has numerous essays published in various anthologies as well as a novel titled *While the Daffodils Danced*. She has a master's degree and teaches eighth grade composition and literature. She is working on her second novel.

Darlene Lawson is a freelance writer. She writes for a local newspaper, magazines and anthologies. She and her husband live on a farm in Atlantic Canada where she receives inspiration for her stories.

A former substance abuse therapist, **Lisa Leshaw** now spends her time loving her grandkids (Mush and Gab) and hanging with her husband Stu. At the proverbial crossroad she dreams that one day someone somewhere (anywhere) will discover her children's story, "How Do You Do Your Royal Highney" and publish it to rave reviews.

Bobbie Jensen Lippman is a prolific professional writer who lives in Seal Rock, OR, with her husband Burt, their dog Charley and a cat named "Lap Sitter." Bobbie's work has been published nationally and internationally. She writes a weekly human-interest column called "Bobbie's Beat" for the *Newport* (Oregon) *News-Times*. E-mail her at bobbisbeat@aol.com.

Barbara LoMonaco has worked for Chicken Soup for the Soul as an editor and webmaster since 1998. She has co-authored two *Chicken Soup for the Soul* book titles and has had stories published in various other titles. Barbara is a graduate of the University of Southern California and has a teaching credential.

Patricia Lorenz is the author of thirteen books including *The 5 Things We Need to Be Happy*. She also has contributed to nearly sixty *Chicken Soup for the Soul* books. She's a professional speaker who travels the country, often speaking about one of her favorite topics: "Humor for the Health of it." Contact her at www.PatriciaLorenz.com.

Melissa Lowery is currently a student at a community college and works as a customer service representative. Melissa and her husband Chris have been married for five years. His deployment has shown them different ways to communicate. They enjoy watching movies, camping, riding the Harley and just being together.

Rita Lussier's column, "For the Moment", has been a popular weekly feature in *The Providence Journal* for twelve years. She was awarded first place in the 2010 Erma Bombeck International Writing Competition, an honor she also won in 2006. Her writing has been featured in *The Boston Globe* and on NPR.

Gloria Hander Lyons has channeled thirty years of training and hands-on experience in the areas of art, interior decorating, crafting and event planning into writing creative how-to books, fun cookbooks and humorous slice-of-life stories. Visit her website to read about them all at www.BlueSagePress.com.

Dana Martin is a writer/editor living in Bakersfield, CA. She has her B.A. in English, is President of Writers of Kern (a branch of the California Writers Club), and adores Halloween because she works happily in the haunted attraction industry. Dana loves to encourage new writers, so please e-mail her at Dana@DanaMartinWriting.com.

David Martin's humor and political satire have appeared in many publications including *The New York Times*, the *Chicago Tribune* and *Smithsonian* magazine. His latest humor collection, *Dare to be Average*, was published in 2010 by Lulu.com. David lives in Ottawa, Canada, with his wife Cheryl and their daughter Sarah.

Tim Martin is an author/screenwriter living in Northern California. He has two novels due out in 2012: *Scout's Oaf* (Cedar Grove Books) and *Third Rate Romance* (Whispers Publishing). Tim is a proud contributing author to numerous *Chicken Soup for the Soul* books. E-mail him at tmartin@northcoast.com.

Kathleen Swartz McQuaig shares stories from the heart shaped by her deep faith. As a writer, speaker, teacher, wife and mother, she lives to encourage others. After earning a master's degree in education and living in military communities around the world, Kathleen settled, with her family, in South-Central Pennsylvania.

Lynn Maddalena Menna is a freelance writer and former educator. She is a columnist for *Main Street Magazine*, writes for *NJ Education Now*, and frequently contributes to the *Chicken Soup for the Soul* series—it beats therapy! Lynn lives in Hawthorne, NJ, with her husband Prospero.

Christine Mikalson is a Reiki Master, writer and eternal student. Her articles have been published in Chicken Soup for the Soul, *Woman's World*, and *Grandparents Day Magazine*. Visit www.heal-the-healer.com, www.selfgrowth.com. She can be found at http://labyrinthdancer.blogspot.com.

Katherine Ladny Mitchell married her best friend, Jason, in 2005 and graduated with a B.A. in Sociology in 2007. Katherine and Jason share the rest of their romance in a book, *Don't Settle for a Fairy Tale: A True Love Story*. Katherine and Jason have three children. Learn more at www.dontsettleforafairytale.com.

Carine Nadel worked as a radio newscaster until she literally fell in love at first sight with her husband of over thirty years. After a short (twenty-two year) break from writing, she re-discovered her passion and has been a full-time feature writer since 2003. E-mail her at 4thenadels@cox.net.

Marc Tyler Nobleman is the author of more than seventy books, including *Boys of Steel: The Creators of Superman* and *Bill the Boy Wonder: The Secret Co-Creator of Batman*. His cartoons have appeared in more than 100 international publications. At noblemania.blogspot.com, he reveals the behind-the-scenes stories of his work.

Linda O'Connell, from St. Louis, MO, is a frequent contributor to the *Chicken Soup for the Soul* anthologies and many other publications. Laughter and compromise are keys to her happy marriage to her best friend and funny honey, Bill. Linda blogs at http://lindaoconnell.blogspot.com.

Mark Parisi's "off the mark" cartoons appear in newspapers worldwide. You can also find his cartoons on calendars, cards, books, T-shirts, and more. Mark resides in Massachusetts with his wife and business partner, Lynn, along with their daughter, Jen, three cats, and a dog. Visit www.offthemark.com to view 7,000 cartoons.

Andrea Peebles lives with her husband of thirty-four years in Rockmart, GA. She is a frequent contributor to the *Chicken Soup for the Soul* anthologies and enjoys reading, writing, travel, photography and spending time with family. E-mail her at aanddpeebles@aol.com.

Lisa Peters lives in the New England area and is a writer, wife and mother of two children diagnosed with special needs. She shares her humorous and heartwarming life experiences on her family blog at www.onalifelessperfect.blogspot.com.

Patt Hollinger Pickett, Ph.D., a licensed therapist and certified life coach, writes with humor from a warm, no nonsense perspective. Dr. Pickett draws from her personal life blended with over twenty years in practice as a relationship expert. She has a book ready for publication. Contact Patt through www.DrCoachLove.com.

Stephanie Piro is a cartoonist, illustrator, and designer. She is one of King Features' team of women cartoonists, "Six Chix" (she is the Saturday chick). She also does the cartoon panel *Fair Game*. Her work appears all over, from books to greeting cards. In addition, she designs gift items for her company Strip T's and her CafePress shop. Learn more at www.stephaniepiro.com.

Brenda Redmond is blessed with two children and a wonderful husband. She is thankful to have a husband who encourages her in her dreams and ambitions. She knows that love like theirs is rare, and she falls deeper in love with him every day. E-mail her at bredmond3@hotmail.com.

After thirty-nine years, **Carol McAdoo Rehme** has stopped searching for marital bliss, settling, instead, on deep contentment and sporadic, breathtaking joy. Carol, an award-winning author and editor, spends two or three nights each week in husband Norm's arms—ballroom dancing.

Cherie Brooks Reilly (B.A. M Ed.) taught elementary school until she married Michael Reilly (USMC). After twenty years as a marine officer's wife, she and her family of six, moved to Pittsburgh, PA. Lt. Col. Reilly started a pumpkin patch and greenhouse operation, and they are living happily ever after.

Bevin K. Reinen holds a B.A. in English from Mary Washington College, an M.S. Ed. in Early Childhood Education from Old Dominion University, and was voted the Top Teacher of 2011 for *Hampton Roads Magazine*. She enjoys athletics, spending time with friends and family, and helping children grow both socially and academically.

Karen Robbins is a columnist for PositivelyFeminine.org. She has been published in regional, national, and online publications including Yahoo.com. Karen coauthored *A Scrapbook of Christmas Firsts* and *A Scrapbook of Motherhood Firsts*. Her first e-novel is *Murder Among The Orchids*. An award-winning speaker, Karen and her family live in Ohio.

Sallie A. Rodman has a certificate in professional writing from Cal State Long Beach and is an award-winning author. She is published in many *Chicken Soup for the Soul* anthologies. Her hobbies are writing true-life stories and mixed art media projects. Catch her at sa.rodman@verizon.net.

Mark Rosolowski served in the U.S. Navy after graduating high school. He was married for twenty-eight years to his wife Donna.

After her death he started to write inspirational stories. He is currently planning to put those stories together for publication.

Gary Rubinstein is a teacher from New York City. He has written two books about teaching, *Reluctant Disciplinarian* (1999) and *Beyond Survival* (2010). He also co-wrote a picture book, *The Girl Who Never Made Mistakes* (2011). This is his fourth story in the *Chicken Soup for the Soul* series. E-mail him at garymrubinstein@gmail.com.

Marcia Rudoff, author of *We Have Stories—A handbook for writing your memoirs*, has been teaching memoir writing classes and workshops for over a decade. A freelance writer, her columns and personal essays have been published in various newspapers and anthologies. Marcia lives and writes in Bainbridge Island, WA.

Stephen Rusiniak is a husband and father from Wayne, NJ. He's a former police detective who specialized in juvenile/family matters, and now shares his thoughts through his writings. His work has appeared in various publications and *Chicken Soup for the Soul* books. E-mail him at stephenrusiniak@yahoo.com or visit him on Facebook.

Theresa Sanders is honored to be a frequent contributor to the *Chicken Soup for the Soul* series. An award-winning technical writer and a Springfield, MO, native, she now lives in suburban St. Louis, where she and her husband have four grown children, a precious new grandson, and are passionate about their St. Louis Cardinals!

Jessie Santala is a teacher, photographer, and volleyball coach who spends what little free time she has writing and going on dates with her husband. She has started work on a book and hopes to finish it in the near future.

Dayle Shockley is an award-winning writer, the author of three books and a contributor to many other works, including the *Chicken Soup for the Soul* series. She and her husband can often be found traveling around the country, enjoying God's handiwork. Visit Dayle's website for more information at www.dayleshockley.com.

Deborah Shouse is a writer, speaker, editor and creativity catalyst. Deborah is donating all proceeds from her book, *Love in the Land of Dementia: Finding Hope in the Caregiver's Journey*, to Alzheimer's programs and research. So far, she has raised more than $80,000.00. Visit her website at www.TheCreativityConnection.com.

Harvey Silverman is a retired physician living in Manchester, NH, who writes mostly for his own amusement. E-mail him at HMSilverm@yahoo.com.

Michael Smith lives with his loving wife Ginny in Idaho and works in the computer industry. In his spare time, Michael writes stories from his heart. To sign up for Michael's stories go to visitor.constantcontact.com/d.jsp?m=1101828445578&p=oi and to read more of Michael's stories, go to ourecho.com/biography-353-Michael-Timothy-Smith.shtml#stories.

A Master Gardener and former Wall Street editor, **Darlene Sneden**, done with her daily heavy lifting Mom job, is writing again… when she's not working on a public school beautification project or in her own garden! Visit her website at www.darlenesneden.com or read her blog at adventuresofamiddleagemom.com.

Laurie Sontag is a writer whose humor column appears weekly in California newspapers and has been published in seven other *Chicken Soup for the Soul* books. She is a parenting guru at Yahoo! Shine and the author of the popular blog, Manic Motherhood, which can be found at http://lauriesontag.com or http://manicmotherhood.com.

W. Bradford Swift is one of the foremost experts on the subject of personal life purpose, having co-founded Life On Purpose Institute in 1996 with his wife Ann. He's the author of numerous books including *Life On Purpose: Six Passages to an Inspired Life*. Visit him at www.lifeonpurpose.com and www.wbradfordswift.com.

Annmarie B. Tait and her husband Joe Beck live in Conshohocken, PA, where she enjoys cooking and many other crafts. Annmarie has contributed to several volumes of the *Chicken Soup for the Soul* series and many other anthologies. She is also a recent nominee for the annual Pushcart Prize literary award. E-mail her at irishbloom@aol.com.

Tsgoyna Tanzman is a get-started later-in-life wife and mother. A former fitness trainer and speech pathologist, she now credits writing as the ultimate therapy for raising an adolescent. Her stories and poems can be read in *Chicken Soup for the Soul* books, *The Orange County Register* and online at More.com. E-mail her at tnzmn@cox.net.

B.J. Taylor found a beautiful driver discarded in the garage rafters. When she asked, her husband said she could have it. She's an award-winning author with work appearing in *Guideposts*, *Chicken Soup for the Soul* books, and numerous magazines. Reach B.J. at www. bjtayloronline.com and check out her dog blog www.bjtaylorblog. wordpress.com.

Jayne Thurber-Smith is an award-winning writer for various publications including *Faith & Friends*, *Floral Business* magazine and *The Buffalo News*, and is a sports contributor for cbn.com. She and her husband's favorite activity is being included in whatever their four kids have going on. E-mail her at jthurbersmith@cox.net.

Becky Tidberg is on a first-name basis with many of the customer service/return desk clerks in Northern Illinois. She is a popular women's group speaker and freelance writer. You can connect with her at www.BeckyTidberg.com or e-mail her at campfireministries@ yahoo.com.

Terrie Todd is an administrative assistant for the City of Portage la Prairie in Manitoba, Canada. She blogs, acts, and writes a weekly column called "Out of My Mind." She and her husband Jon have been married since 1977 and have three grown kids and three grandsons. E-mail her at jltodd@mymts.net.

Stefanie Wass's stories have been published in the *Los Angeles Times*, *The Seattle Times*, *The Christian Science Monitor*, *Akron Beacon Journal*, *Akron Life & Leisure*, *Cleveland Magazine*, *The Writer*, *A Cup of Comfort* and *Chicken Soup for the Soul* books. She is currently seeking representation for her middle-grade novel. Visit www.stefaniewass. com.

Zoanne Wilkie lives with her husband David, who she has been married to for fifty-three years, and their Great Dane, Gracie. She is a retreat and conference speaker. Zoanne ministers with stories and songs, sprinkled with a generous amount of humor. Her recent book, *Treasures From The Attic*, features a collection of her inspirational writings.

Alan Williamson is a nationally published humor writer whose work explores the small dilemmas of everyday life. Shunning the complex issues and thorny global conundrums of the day, he chronicles the flaws, follies and convoluted capers that unite people in their humanity. Alan can be reached via e-mail at alwilly@bellsouth.net.

Diane Wilson would like to thank the publishers of the *Chicken Soup for the Soul* anthology for their faith in her writing. This story is dedicated to Diane's wonderful family, for remaining by her side during her illness. E-mail her at doe@cogeco.ca.

Ernie Witham writes the humor column "Ernie's World" for the *Montecito Journal* in Montecito, CA. He is the author of two humor books: *Ernie's World: The Book* and *A Year in the Life of a "Working" Writer*. He has been published in many anthologies including more than a dozen *Chicken Soup for the Soul* books. Visit him at erniesworld. com.

Ferida Wolff is the author of books for children and adults. Her work appears in newspapers and magazines and she writes a weekly nature blog www.feridasbackyard.blogspot.com. Visit her at www. feridawolff.com or e-mail her at feridawolff@msn.com.

Theresa Woltanski started writing young adult and adult fiction after a stint in the scientific world writing reports and journal articles. She is the author of several novels. She lives on a farmette in Michigan with her husband, children, a too-big garden, and a number of obsessive-compulsive animals.

Barbra Yardley is married, mother of three delightful daughters, and grandmother to two active boys! She works as a legal secretary in Utah, and enjoys the outdoors, photography, quilting, writing, reading, and spending time with family. She is also published in *Chicken Soup for the Soul: Christmas Magic*.

Phyllis W. Zeno has stories in eight *Chicken Soup for the Soul* books. She was the founding editor of *AAA Going Places* for twenty years and editor/publisher of *Beach Talk Magazine* until she met Harvey Meltzer on Match.com. They were married in 2009. Now eighty-six years old, they are on a perpetual honeymoon.

Meet Our Authors

Jack Canfield is the co-creator of the *Chicken Soup for the Soul* series, which *Time* magazine has called "the publishing phenomenon of the decade." Jack is also the co-author of many other bestselling books.

Jack is the CEO of the Canfield Training Group in Santa Barbara, California, and founder of the Foundation for Self-Esteem in Culver City, California. He has conducted intensive personal and professional development seminars on the principles of success for more than a million people in twenty-three countries, has spoken to hundreds of thousands of people at more than 1,000 corporations, universities, professional conferences and conventions, and has been seen by millions more on national television shows.

Jack has received many awards and honors, including three honorary doctorates and a Guinness World Records Certificate for having seven books from the *Chicken Soup for the Soul* series appearing on the New York Times bestseller list on May 24, 1998.

You can reach Jack at www.jackcanfield.com.

Mark Victor Hansen is the co-founder of Chicken Soup for the Soul, along with Jack Canfield. He is a sought-after keynote speaker, bestselling author, and marketing maven. Mark's powerful messages of possibility, opportunity, and action have created powerful change in thousands of organizations and millions of individuals worldwide.

Mark is a prolific writer with many bestselling books in addition to the *Chicken Soup for the Soul* series. Mark has had a profound influence in the field of human potential through his library of audios, videos, and articles in the areas of big thinking, sales achievement, wealth building, publishing success, and personal and professional development. He is also the founder of the MEGA Seminar Series.

Mark has received numerous awards that honor his entrepreneurial spirit, philanthropic heart, and business acumen. He is a lifetime member of the Horatio Alger Association of Distinguished Americans.

You can reach Mark at www.markvictorhansen.com.

Amy Newmark is Chicken Soup for the Soul's publisher and editor-in-chief, after a 30-year career as a writer, speaker, financial analyst, and business executive in the worlds of finance and telecommunications. Amy is a *magna cum laude* graduate of Harvard College, where she majored in Portuguese, minored in French, and traveled extensively. She and her husband have four grown children.

After a long career writing books on telecommunications, voluminous financial reports, business plans, and corporate press releases, Chicken Soup for the Soul is a breath of fresh air for Amy. She has fallen in love with Chicken Soup for the Soul and its life-changing books, and really enjoys putting these books together for Chicken Soup's wonderful readers. She has co-authored more than four dozen *Chicken Soup for the Soul* books and has edited another three dozen.

You can reach Amy with any questions or comments through webmaster@chickensoupforthesoul.com and you can follow her on Twitter @amynewmark.

Thank You

We owe huge thanks to all of our contributors. We know that you poured your hearts and souls into the thousands of stories that you shared with us, and ultimately with each other. As we read and edited these stories, we were truly inspired, and we shared many of our own stories about our marriages.

We could only publish a small percentage of the stories that were submitted, but we read every single one and even the ones that do not appear in the book had an influence on us and on the final manuscript. We owe special thanks to our editors Barbara LoMonaco and D'ette Corona, who in addition to their other duties as webmaster and assistant publisher, respectively, took on the task of reading every submission to this book and narrowing the list down to the finalists, shaping the chapters, and finding the wonderful quotations that add richness to each story. Our editor Kristiana Glavin performed her normal masterful job of proofreading the manuscript and coordinating our production process for this book.

We also owe a special thanks to our creative director and book producer, Brian Taylor at Pneuma Books, for his brilliant vision for our covers and interiors.

~Amy Newmark

Chicken Soup for the Soul

Improving Your Life Every Day

Real people sharing real stories—for nineteen years. Now, Chicken Soup for the Soul has gone beyond the bookstore to become a world leader in life improvement. Through books, movies, DVDs, online resources and other partnerships, we bring hope, courage, inspiration and love to hundreds of millions of people around the world. Chicken Soup for the Soul's writers and readers belong to a one-of-a-kind global community, sharing advice, support, guidance, comfort, and knowledge.

Chicken Soup for the Soul stories have been translated into more than forty languages and can be found in more than one hundred countries. Every day, millions of people experience a Chicken Soup for the Soul story in a book, magazine, newspaper or online. As we share our life experiences through these stories, we offer hope, comfort and inspiration to one another. The stories travel from person to person, and from country to country, helping to improve lives everywhere.

Share with Us

We all have had Chicken Soup for the Soul moments in our lives. If you would like to share your story or poem with millions of people around the world, go to chickensoup.com and click on "Submit Your Story." You may be able to help another reader, and become a published author at the same time. Some of our past contributors have launched writing and speaking careers from the publication of their stories in our books!

Our submission volume has been increasing steadily—the quality and quantity of your submissions has been fabulous. We only accept story submissions via our website. They are no longer accepted via mail or fax.

To contact us regarding other matters, please send us an e-mail through webmaster@chickensoupforthesoul.com, or fax or write us at:

Chicken Soup for the Soul
P.O. Box 700
Cos Cob, CT 06807-0700
Fax: 203-861-7194

One more note from your friends at Chicken Soup for the Soul: Occasionally, we receive an unsolicited book manuscript from one of our readers, and we would like to respectfully inform you that we do not accept unsolicited manuscripts and we must discard the ones that appear.